THE POLITICS OF THE ITALIAN ARMY 1861-1918

THE POLITICS OF THE ITALIAN ARMY 1861-1918

JOHN WHITTAM

CROOM HELM LONDON

ARCHON BOOKS, HAMDEN, CONNECTICUT

First published 1977

Croom Helm Ltd
2-10 St John's Road, London SW11

ISBN 0-85664-317-3

First published in the United States of America 1977
as an ARCHON BOOK, an imprint of
The Shoe String Press, Inc., Hamden, Ct.

Library of Congress Cataloging in Publication Data

Whittam, John
Politics of the Italian Army.

Bibliography: p.210
Includes index.
1. Italy. Esercito – History. 2. Italy – History – 1815-1870. 3. Italy – History – 1870-1915. I. Title.
UA742.W44 1977 945'.08 76-27702

ISBN 0-208-01597-3

Printed in Great Britain by Biddles of Guildford

CONTENTS

PREFACE

This is neither a monograph nor a source book for comedians with a penchant for military anecdotes. It contains no startling revelations like those to be found in Norman Stone's *Eastern Front*, no subtle exploration of unspoken assumptions as in Theodore Zeldin's *France 1848-1945*, and no historiographical jousting. It is simply a survey which attempts to do three things: to observe some of the familiar sights of nineteenth and early twentieth century Italian history from a slightly different viewpoint; to enquire into why one of the least militaristic of societies has been plunged periodically into aggressive wars by the deliberate action of its government; and finally, to provide an account of civil-military relations in Italy for use in comparative studies. Such accounts already exist for the other major European powers and even for countries like Spain. Perhaps the title, stolen from Gordon Craig helps to draw attention to this aspect.

I must begin by expressing my gratitude to Alistair Horne for his interest, his patience, and his generosity in establishing a Fellowship which I shared with Norman Davies in 1970-1. This was administered by St Antony's College and I am grateful to the Warden and Fellows for their unfailing hospitality. I am greatly indebted to the following for their financial assistance: the Italian Institute, the British Academy and the University of Bristol. For their help in this and other related pieces of research, I would like to thank the staff of the Archivio Centrale dello Stato and the Ufficio Storico dello Stato Maggiore Esercito, both at Rome, of the Istituto per la Storia della Resistenza in Toscana and the Biblioteca Centrale Communale in Florence, and of the Public Record Office. For longer than I care to remember I have sought and received advice from Professors Harry Hearder, Stuart Woolf and Michael Howard, and also from Denis Mack Smith and Brian Bond. In addition, my thanks to all the participants in the annual conferences of the British Inter-University Seminar on Armed Forces and Society for their stimulating papers and the discussions which followed. Finally, I thank Mrs Liliane Stunt and Mrs Dorothy Bjørnerud for working unsocial hours over a hot typewriter, and, of course, David Croom for giving me two bites of the apple.

Part One: Towards a National Army

1 'ITALIANS DON'T FIGHT'

On 4 May 1861 there was a terse announcement in the *Giornale Militare* in which the Minister of War, General Fanti, explained that the *Regio Esercito* had become the *Esercito Italiano* in the previous March, the month in which Victor Emmanuel II had assumed the title of King of Italy.[1] Behind this apparently straightforward change in nomenclature there lay a whole series of events which can be termed the the military Risorgimento. This was a development which did so much to shape the more celebrated politico-diplomatic Risorgimento and to determine the course of the new nation state, that to ignore it or relegate it to a subordinate position is to distort the history of the Italian peninsula in the nineteenth century.

The latest dramatic episode in this military Risorgimento had taken place just three weeks prior to Fanti's official announcement in the military journal. Garibaldi, Italy's most famous soldier, bitterly attacked Cavour and Fanti for their deplorable treatment of his Southern Army which had swept away the Bourbon regime in Sicily and Naples.[2] This was more than the public manifestation of a personal vendetta which had been brewing for some time: it was a clash of principles. Cavour and his War Minister stood as the exponents of the *Regio Esercito,* the royal army which in the spring of 1859 consisted of the five regular divisions of the Sardinian army but which, by late 1860, had been virtually quadrupled in size by the incorporation of military contingents from Lombardy, Central Italy and the South. Care had been taken to impose Piedmontese military discipline and to maintain the professionalism of the officer corps. The aim was the creation of a regular army, modelled on that of Sardinia, loyal to Victor Emmanuel and obedient to the political élite which ruled in Turin. Garibaldi, on the other hand, was the successful guerrilla fighter, champion of popular initiative and wars of insurrection, and a convinced adherent of the doctrine of the Nation in Arms. Only by fully utilising what his sympathisers called *'le forze vive della nazione'*, could a just and democratic society emerge. But Garibaldi's attempt to implement this programme in 1860 had met with two serious, almost symbolic, reverses, one at Bronte and the other at Teano. On 6 August 1860, Nino Bixio, one of Garibaldi's best known lieutenants, felt constrained to fire on the peasantry of the Nelson estates near Bronte.[3] The 'vital forces of the nation' evidently did not see eye to eye with the liberating army of Garibaldian volunteers. This sort of incident was not unknown to Piedmontese officers: in 1848 they had pushed into the Lombard plain expecting to be greeted as saviours by the Italian subjects of the Habsburg Emperor, but found the peasants busily engaged in flooding them out by opening the dykes. The tragic failure of the Bandiera brothers and Carlo Pisacane also indicated that, outside the cultured classes of the larger towns, *italianità* scarcely existed. The Bronte shootings were not the last of such disillusioning episodes. Garibaldi's historic interview with Victor Emmanuel at Teano on 26 October 1860 was his second and, as it proved, most fateful reverse. Even before the war with Austria had broken out in 1859, Garibaldi had abandoned his intransigent republicanism and shown his willingness to collaborate with the House of Savoy if it agreed to lead the national crusade for Italian independence. During the war, despite mutual suspicion, he had led his volunteers in the Alps as a major general of the Piedmontese army. It was only after the sailing of The Thousand, that his Mazzinian friends saw a real chance of driving a wedge between him and Victor Emmanuel. In Sicily and on the mainland they begged him to maintain his independence or at least to use his conquests as bargaining counters in his negotiations with Turin. When the royal army swept down through Central Italy to block his route into Lazio, the threat of a war between the Garibaldini and the regulars seemed very real, and the Volturno, where the Bourbon army was making its last stand, could well have become the first battlefield of yet another fratricidal war. But the moment passed and the King came down to effect a bloodless transfer of power. Believing that his army would be honourably treated, Garibaldi slipped away to Caprera, leaving the whole of liberated Italy in the hands of the *Regio Esercito.* It was a triumph for all those who had worked for a regular, traditional army led by an orthodox, professional officer corps. It was not a verdict, however, which passed unchallenged. In April 1861, Garibaldi accused the Turin government of bad faith and at Aspromonte and Mentana showed his willingness to take the argument outside the walls of the chamber of deputies. Nor did the argument cease with his death. Many of the ideas of Garibaldi and other exponents of popular initiative and *'guerre per bande'* lived on in various political and irredentist groups, and were not unfamiliar to the D'Annunzians, the squadristi or the Resistance fighters of 1944-5. But, like Garibaldi before them, although they were sometimes spectacularly successful, they were swiftly superseded by the regular forces or absorbed into their ranks.

The interplay of these two theories on the nature of military force must be briefly examined against the background of actual events in the peninsula between 1815 and 1860, not only because it helps to explain why it was General Fanti and not Garibaldi who became the father of the Italian army, but because it raises fundamental questions about the relationship between civilians and the military, about the political, social and economic implications of adopting any given type of military establishment, and the role of the army in peacetime as well as in war. As it was the Piedmontese army which played the leading part in the final stages of the Risorgimento, the various options, theoretical and practical, open to the Turin government need some assessment. It will be seen that the government was uncertain whether the *Armata Sarda* should be modelled on the army of Prussia or the army of France, and that for some decades they opted for an unsatisfactory compromise. General La Marmora, who was Minister of War during most of the Cavourian decade, decided in favour of the French system, and this was in force until the Franco-Prussian War. The obvious superiority of Prussian techniques led another great War Minister, General Ricotti-Magnani, to reconstruct the Italian army along German lines, a fitting prelude to the Triple Alliance of 1882. La Marmora, who reformed the Piedmontese army in the 1850s, Fanti, who amalgamated the various contingents in 1860 to form an Italian army, and Ricotti-Magnani, who tried to modernise it, deserve an honourable place among the founders of the Italian state.

I

The unflattering assertion that *'gl'italiani non si battono'* had for many people almost assumed the validity of a natural law by the beginning of the nineteenth century.[4] It was a view not wholly confined to contemptuous foreigners. Apart from generals on the brink of defeat, an Italian of the stature of Massimo D'Azeglio could describe his compatriots as a 'spineless people of little character with small hope of internal cohesion',[5] For those who wished to prove to the world that Italians could fight, Italian involvement in the revolutionary and Napoleonic wars gave sufficient scope for them to talk about a *'risveglio militare'.* To prove the military prowess of their countrymen they no longer had to refer back to Renaissance sieges or the Sicilian Vespers, together with a compulsory quotation from Montecuccoli. It was true the Sardinian and Neapolitan armies – the only indigenous armies that really counted – had been less than inspiring, and that the French had been able to occupy the whole peninsula, but Italian soldiers were soon in action from Spain to the Russian steppes. Napoleon had removed the old rulers and the old boundaries. A large part of Italy, including Piedmont, was directly annexed and became an integral part of the French Empire, another portion became the Regno Italico, and Naples was ruled first by Joseph and then by Murat. All had to provide conscripts for Napoleon's insatiable war machine and several individuals rose high in the French service, while many Italian units achieved distinction. After Napoleon's abdication, the Italian troops in the imperial service returned home, and the Austrians disbanded the armed forces of the Regno Italico, absorbing some of these troops into the Habsburg army. That left only the army of Murat in the south, a perplexing situation for all concerned until he decided to throw in his lot with Napoleon during the Hundred Days. After the drawn battle of Tolentino in May 1815, Murat's army melted away. It was the last of a series of battles which had, for a generation, brought home to the Italians the realities of large-scale warfare. Even those outside the immediate battle zone had felt the strain of being forced to comply with incessant demands for conscripts and supplies. It was not an experience likely to imbue most Italians with martial zeal, but for a significant minority it was a turning point in their lives, and, so they hoped, for the Italian nation too.

Although the numbers must not be exaggerated, perhaps never in modern times had so many Italians been trained in arms, taught to think in less parochial terms, or presented with prospects of promotion which would have been unthinkable under the old, privileged order. For these Napoleonic veterans, the Restoration brought many unwelcome changes. As the exiles returned, in comfortable proximity to Austrian bayonets, tension grew between adherents of the old order and the new, and disquieting charges of collaborationism with the French invader began to be levelled by a provincial gentry galvanised into unwonted activity by the new turn of events. It was the reluctance of most of the restored regimes to dispense with certain aspects of French rule likely to be of assistance to them that saved many of the veterans from persecution. On 14 June 1814, for instance, only three weeks after his return to Turin, Victor Emmanuel I issued a proclamation calling upon all Piedmontese formerly in the French army or in the army of the Regno Italico to serve under the House of Savoy.[6] Saved from the rigours of civilian life, these officers and men were able to continue their military career but they were always subject to various forms of harassment. Jealous colleagues and a suspicious government were prompt to put them in their place if they imagined military competence to be more important than political orthodoxy. A similar process was also taking place in the south, where Murattiani joined the Neapolitan army but could never become an integral part of the Bourbon establishment. Massimo D'Azeglio remembered this period, and although he is referring to his own experiences in Turin, the same scene was being enacted in garrison towns up and down Italy.

> The way they filled administrative and military posts is notorious. They consulted the Court Almanac and Palmaverde for the year of the King's departure. Everyone was to occupy the post he held at that time, except those who had died meanwhile. . . But the old, quite apart from the dead, weren't enough, and they had to call in the young. I was one of these and had my epaulettes, all in a flash. . . Those who had returned from the French army were accepted, but they all lost a rank; corporals became rankers, sergeants, corporals, and so on up to the captains and colonels. This is a topsy-turvey state of affairs! We stripling cavaliers had a free gift without deserving it; those who had deserved their ranks, owing to their valour and the blood they had shed, were demoted.[7]

The governments were, of course, taking a calculated risk in keeping these Napoleonic veterans under arms. They would be needed, to act as auxiliaries of the Austrians, should war again threaten the peninsula, but the primary function of these newly constituted armies was to repress any subversive elements within the state. In addition to the unrepentant revolutionary and the ubiquitous brigand, each state seemed to possess a distinctive area of disaffection which it found difficult to assimilate. Piedmont had problems in the recently acquired Genoese territory, the papal government – and the Austrians – found the Romagna almost ungovernable, the Neapolitans had to contend with Sicilian hostility, and even the smaller states of central Italy were plagued by inter-city rivalries. Unless the restored rulers won the unswerving loyalty of their heterogenous troops or took ruthless action at the first hint of mutiny, there was always a possibility that disgruntled elements in the army might assist or even become the spokesmen of those discontented subjects they were being paid to control. Failure to adopt a consistent policy toward the military, combined with their dilatory approach to domestic and foreign issues, confronted the rulers of Turin and Naples with that very situation which had been their recurrent nightmare since 1815.

The revolutionary events of 1820 and 1821 in Naples and Piedmont are an important landmark in the history of civilian-military relations in Italy. Each so-called revolution was essentially an attempted military putsch. Never again, in fact, were Italian troops to play such a dominant role in politics, to participate in what later generations called 'Spanish charades'.[8] As in many other countries, post-war discontent had led to the proliferation of secret societies in Italy. Societies like the Carbonari in Naples or the Adelfi in the north became virtually the preserve of officers and NCOs. At their meetings they discussed their grievances and, as their memories of the past became increasingly selective, they contrasted the unheroic present with the grandeur of the Napoleonic years. Most of them had been disillusioned by the course of events since the Restoration, particularly those who had imbibed political and nationalist ideas which they had hoped to see implemented. But as the events of 1820-1 clearly showed, most of these ideas had been imperfectly understood and formulated. Equally unfortunate, little had been done to correlate a bewildering variety of political programmes. Questions of pay and conditions of service, supremely important for the rank and file, were not divisive issues. What did split the leadership were arguments about the political reforms they wished to introduce and the methods to be employed. Some aimed at transforming the entire peninsula, while others were content to concentrate on their own individual state. Some were liberal, seeking constitutional reform along the line of the French Charter of 1814 or the moderate Sicilian constitution of 1812 or a republic. Again, there were divergent opinions about the permitted degree of civilian participation, whether popular appeals for a mass uprising were indispensable or merely self-defeating.

Another fundamental weakness of both conspiracies was the failure to win over the entire army. Suspicion of the motives of the mutineers, loyalty to the monarch, and fear of the Austrian response, led to the active hostility or watchful neutrality of the majority of officers and men. In Naples, the startlingly rapid successes of the revolutionaries did indeed produce the semblance of unity in the early stages. Encouraged by Riego's achievement in Cadiz, Carbonarist elements among the NCOs and the provincial militia managed to win over the Murattiani in the army. They also enlisted the invaluable support of General Guglielmo Pepe. On 6 July 1820, only six days after the revolt had begun, King Ferdinand granted a constitution. Ironically, this easy triumph helped to bring about the downfall of the conspirators. Having met with such little opposition, they felt that they could afford to disagree among themselves. This euphoria began to evaporate when news came through in the middle of July that the Sicilians, or at least the Palermitans, had risen to assert their independent status. Pepe's elder brother, also a veteran of the Napoleonic wars, was sent to restore order, but Palermo resisted fiercely, only surrendering in early October. The island absorbed over a quarter of the best Neapolitan troops, men who would be sorely needed when the Austrian invasion came. As a result of the King's double-dealing and Metternich's nervousness, this invasion came in the new year, five Austrian divisions pitted against four Neapolitan. The disparity in numbers may not have been great, but as a result of interminable quarrels, military, political and diplomatic, Neapolitan morale had slumped. The 40,000 men led by Pepe and the reluctant Carascosa proved to be little better than an armed rabble, more prone to fire on each other than on the Austrians. In March 1821, the military revolt which had seemed so irresistible in the previous July came to an ignominious end.

Hopefully imagining that Austria was being sucked into an exhausting war in the south, a group of aristocratic officers in Piedmont, nearly all of them members of the entourage of Charles Albert, the heir to the throne, launched a revolt in the garrison town of Alessandria on 10 March. The conspirators had been urgently conferring with Charles Albert and, sensing the growing reluctance of this young prince to implicate himself, at least one of their leaders, artillery major Count Santorre di Santarosa, had decided to call off the whole operation. But during the evening of 9 March, Colonel Ansaldi and the Carbonari of Alessandria went ahead and declared themselves for Charles Albert and the Spanish constitution.[9] Unwilling to desert them now that the movement had begun, the young officers galloped off to enlist aid for Alessandria. Santarosa went to Pinerolo where he was modestly successful, inducing 300 men to accompany him, but his associates were not so fortunate, the Marquis di San Marzano, a colonel in the cavalry, coming away from Vercelli empty handed. These manoeuvres, however, thoroughly unnerved King Victor Emmanuel I, not a pillar of strength at the best of times. He first proclaimed a constitution – modelled on the French or the Sicilian but not the Spanish – and then rescinded it. The occupation of the Turin citadel by rebel troops the following day forced the King to a decision. Unwilling to offend the Holy Alliance powers assembled at Laibach or his loyal supporters, but unprepared to initiate a civil war in order to crush the constitutionalists, he decided to abdicate that same day, 12 March. Charles Felix was to succeed him and until the new monarch returned from his travels,

Charles Albert was designated regent. Events seemed to have played into the hands of the rebels. Charles Albert proclaimed the Spanish constitution on 14 March and this was accompanied by rumours that Piedmontese troops intended to cross the Ticino into Austrian Lombardy. The Neapolitan revolutionaries may have been at their last gasp, but the northern conspirators seemed to be on the threshold of a war for liberty and independence. Like the July days in Naples, this proved to be an illusion. Charles Felix peremptorily ordered the regent to loyalist Novara and Charles Albert, who was already attempting to organise a counter-revolution, obeyed. Santarosa, as the new Minister of War, took over Turin and continued his rather forlorn efforts to launch a war of independence, forlorn because he could only assemble 4,000 troops for this vast undertaking. The clash of arms between this small force and the 23,000 loyal Piedmontese and Austrian troops concentrated around Novara was not seriously pressed home. In early April both Turin and Alessandria were in the hands of the royalists and their Austrian allies. Whereas the military revolt in Naples could be measured in months, the Piedmontese mutineers had been crushed in a matter of weeks.

Although only a handful of soldiers were killed, the failure of these military mutinies had important consequences, both immediate and long-term. The fact that they had been a failure tended to discredit the whole concept of the putsch and made any similar attempts in the future unlikely. Looking back on these events, Italians, civilian and military, were thankful that there were no significant repeat performances. Had Pepe and Santarosa been successful, they might have inaugurated a pattern of military intervention which would have retarded future development.

> The military revolution of 1821 was something unique in our army. . . Piedmont, and now the whole of Italy will therefore escape the unhappy fate of some countries, which have been enslaved and rent by military risings, then torn to bits to become the prey of ambitious vulgarians.[10]

For different reasons, the revolutionaries tended to subscribe to this view of d'Azeglio's. Young guards officers or even grizzled veterans were not competent to run a revolution. They might become useful auxiliaries in a revolutionary movement if properly controlled and indoctrinated. The officer corps, even those who participated and went into exile, saw the deleterious effects of military *coups.* They wrecked the cohesion of armies, undermined discipline, and devalued the military profession by involving its members in politico-diplomatic affairs for which they showed no particular aptitude. Officers implicated in the risings of 1820-1 and 1831, who fought in Greece or Spain, often returned to Italy as conservative advocates of traditional military virtues and organisation, so appalled were they by the military anarchy which they had witnessed.

For monarchs and governments already suspicious of their military establishment, the lessons to be learnt from the events of 1820-1 had to be closely scrutinised. Politically aware officers and men were obviously dangerous, so intellectuals in uniform must be rigorously discouraged. As intellectualism was primarily associated with the urban bourgeoisie, middle-class officers or even gentry with literary inclinations must be excluded as far as possible. This, of course, merely reinforced the widely prevalent view that the best armies were those composed of healthy rustics officered by aristocratic gentlemen whose creed was 'a hard gallop, a gallant fight and a full jug', and whose academic pretensions were not significantly greater than those of the men serving under them.[11] Unfortunately for rulers like Charles Albert, who never forgot his traumatic experiences in 1821, this was a view which became increasingly anachronistic as nineteenth century warfare and the organisation of armies became more and more complex and scientific. To exclude those talented members of the middle classes – never numerically impressive – who were prepared to exchange 'the ring of coin for the roar of cannon', and to discourage the formation of a cultured officer corps, was to impair the effectiveness of any modern army. Charles Albert, especially after his discovery of Mazzinian influences in the army in 1833, was determined to take this risk, an important reason why his military reforms in the 1840s were unproductive and why his name is forever linked with the military disasters of Custoza and Novara.

Like Charles Albert, Mazzini was profoundly influenced by the military revolt of 1821, or so he claims in that well-known passage where he describes his encounter with Captain Nini at Genoa. Nini was collecting money for the defeated revolutionaries who were going into exile.

> That day was the first in which a confused idea presented itself to my mind – I will not say of country or of liberty – but an idea that we Italians *could* and therefore *ought* to struggle for the liberty of our country. . . The remembrance of those refugees, many of whom

> became my friends in after life, pursued me wherever I went by day, and mingled with my dreams at night. I would have given I know not what to follow them. I began collecting names and facts, and studied as best I might the records of that heroic struggle, seeking to fathom the causes of its failure.[12]

Perhaps few had this Wordsworthian approach, but there were many who shared his urge to examine the causes of the failures of 1821 and who, like Mazzini, went on to explore the whole field of military history looking for clues which would help them to solve the Italian question. The Austrian army's swift response to any revolutionary threat to the *status quo,* political or territorial, had shown that any solution which ignored military factors was totally unrealistic.

By demonstrating the inadequacies of the Neapolitan and Piedmontese armies during the crisis of 1820-1, it would be possible to ridicule the claim that a *'risveglio guerresco'* was taking place in Italy. It would not be possible to deny that the decades after the close of the Napoleonic wars witnessed a most remarkable awakening of interest in military questions. The revolutionary and Napoleonic wars had lasted for a generation and provided a seemingly inexhaustible supply of raw material out of which military theories could be constructed, strategic concepts tested and organisational development evaluated. There had been dynastic wars and guerrilla wars; the Jacobin *levée en masse* and the Prussian Krümper system had been inaugurated; rockets had been fired in anger and Lieutenant Shrapnel's 'spherical case' adopted by the British army; lightning campaigns, relying on speed and precision, had been fought, and huge armies of up to half a million had been set in motion to create as much consternation along their supply lines as in the ranks of the enemy. Jomini was engaged in taking notes which were to develop into 'the greatest military text-book of the 19th century',[13] and Clausewitz was evolving principles later incorporated in his famous philosophical treatise. In the midst of it all was the towering figure of Napoleon himself, whose personality had the power to attract and repel millions of people who had never even seen him.

Italy produced no Napoleon,[14] but thousands of Italians had been present on battlefields from Spain to Russia. Italy produced no Jomini or Clausewitz, but dozens of talented writers contributed their theories to a great military debate which did not confine itself to the world of books, but infiltrated legislative chambers, revolutionary societies, railway companies, army barracks and guerrilla strongholds. This was a debate about the regeneration of Italy which was certainly not restricted to old combatants or men with specialised knowledge about military affairs. All those who were dissatisfied with the existing state of affairs, of whatever party, region, class or profession, had to focus their attention on military factors, particularly after the abortive *coups* in Naples and Turin. It became part of the competition to capture the minds of the rising generation in which speeches, histories of Italy, novels, music and political programmes all had a part to play. For a country which had acquired the reputation of being unwilling to fight, this intense preoccupation with military questions seemed a remarkable phenomenon.

The overwhelming military preponderance of Austria was incontrovertible. It had received the backing of the great powers at Vienna who realised that Habsburg control over Lombardy and Venetia implied control over the whole peninsula, but even so, additional safeguards had been taken to ensure that Austria's role as the gendarme of Italy should be as undisturbed as possible. Members of the Habsburg family were entrusted with Modena and Tuscany and the right to garrison Ferrara gave Austria a military presence in the papal Romagna. A treaty relationship with the Neapolitan kingdom and close ties with the House of Savoy, completed the more noticeable aspects of this security system, while Metternich's police and spies operated less conspicuously, and perhaps less effectively. But as Mazzini had pointed out, the revolts of 1820-1 did at least prove that his system, as well as the absolutist princes, could be temporarily shaken. Santarosa argued that treachery and misunderstandings weakened the position of the Italian patriots before the Austrians intervened but he was proud to assert that this 'was the first revolution for centuries which was attempted in Italy without foreign help', and that although it had been a failure, 'let the Austrians beware; Italy is conquered, but not subdued'.[15]

The emphasis during the next three decades, despite the military and diplomatic strength of Austria, was on the possibility of Italy achieving her liberty and independence 'without foreign help', and it was by the light of this flickering *ignis fatuus* that many of the military theorists set down their conclusions. The two major armies of the Italian peninsula were in such a state of disarray in the years following 1821 that it is hardly surprising that some of these writers underrated the importance of regular troops, and sought to prove that Italians could emulate the achievements of the Spanish guerrillas in their war against the French after 1808. Carlo Bianco's work, for instance, was influenced by events in Spain. In 1817, after studying law at Turin

University, he became a lieutenant in the Piedmontese army and was one of those who supported the rebel cause in Alessandria in 1821.[16] He left the country shortly afterwards to fight in Spain for the liberal regime. The Bourbon intervention of 1823, meeting a very different reception from that accorded to the Napoleonic troops after 1808, forced him to continue his travels, to Malta and western Europe. Drawing on his experiences and his personal contact with Spaniards who had fought against Napoleon, he wrote a book which was published in France in 1830 with the instructive title, *Della guerra nazionale d'insurrezione per bande applicate all'Italia.* Keen to prove that the Italians were as warlike as the Spaniards, he argued that Italy was ideal for guerrilla tactics. To prevent various groups operating in isolation he advocated control by a secret society network. But this sort of war required popular support, so the attitude of the peasantry would be vital. Bianco tended to take this support for granted and so, unfortunately for themselves, did men like the Bandiera brothers when they tried to implement similar policies.

Giacomo Durando, who by the 1860s had become a kind of elder statesman comparable in stature to La Marmora, had much the same experiences as Bianco in his early years. He too was implicated in military plotting, being one of the *'Cavalieri della libertà'* of 1831. He also went to fight for the constitutional forces in Spain. The situation confronting him – and others like Fanti, Cialdini and Arduino – was, however, very different from that of the early 1820s. As a colonel in the Spanish army, he was fighting for the Queen against reactionary bands of Carlists. Most Italians seemed to form a low opinion of the Carlists and this tended to make them stress the deficiencies of partisan warfare. In 1846 he published what he subtitled a politico-military essay, *Della nazionalità italiana,* in which he refuted the concept of a people's war as suggested by men like Bianco or Mazzini. He did see the need, however, for employing the *'forze vive della nazione',* but in the form of organised reserves on the Prussian model. In addition, he also hoped that the regular army would be assisted by a co-operative National Guard. It was along these lines, in fact, that the Italian army developed after 1870.

General Pepe had the same low estimate of partisan bands, effectively arguing in 1833 that it was useless to draw a parallel between contemporary Italy and the Spain of 1808.[17] In Spain, the peasants and the priests had been fanatically anti-French for religious as well as political reasons and they had, moreover, the support of the British army and fleet. Pepe, at least in the 1840s, believed that the Italian war for independence should begin in the kingdom of Naples. Like Durando, he wanted fully to utilise all available manpower resources, and proposed the formation of a mobile National Guard of around 100,000 men. From Naples, these forces would advance to Bologna to link up with the Piedmontese and present a united front to the Austrians. If this failed, there was always the possibility of retreating to Calabria or even Sicily, where a war of attrition could be fought. This scheme depended on a patriotic response by the state governments.

A rather diverse group of writers, among whom were Carlo Cattaneo, the famous federalist, Professor Zambelli of Pavia, Luigi Blanch, a retired member of the Neapolitan general staff, and Carlo Pisacane, one of Italy's best remembered martyrs, looked more closely at those socio-economic factors which Bianco had touched upon in his advocacy of a popular war. To expect the masses to rise up and fight without redressing their grievances or to be enthusiastic patriots without first convincing them that they were an integral part of the Italian nation, were dangerous illusions. The implications of this – a political democracy and social justice – were sometimes too daunting for Mazzinian zealots.[18] It was tempting to drop the whole ambitious scheme and, like Cesare Balbo or Carlo de Cristoforis, a Milanese considered by Pieri to be the major Italian military theorist of the nineteenth century,[19] to rely on a regular army backed by trained conscripts.

Most advocates of the *guerra regia* and of the *guerra di popolo* saw that some combination of the two concepts was possible and even indispensable. As the debates in the Piedmontese parliament and elsewhere were to show, it was over the nature of this fusion that they had bitter disagreements. It was also hard to convince frightened rulers and conservative officers of the need for any radical transformation, and equally hard to convince the republicans and a sullen populace that they must actively support the regular army. Both concepts were tested in the revolutions of 1848-9 but as both were found wanting, the arguments continued throughout the 1850s. The eventual triumph of those supporting a *guerra regia* was not a foregone conclusion. How this somewhat pyrrhic victory was achieved is a complicated story because the formation of a united Italy out of various disparate elements was a complicated story. The strain and conflict involved in constructing a national army, whatever the principle adopted, reflected the tensions within Italian society for 'an army is always a social organisation, the expression of the entire collectivity'.[20]

Notes

1. L. Mondini, 'L'unificazione delle forze armate', *Atti del XL Congresso del Risorgimento Italiano* (Rome, 1963), p.333.
2. Section IX, *Il Parlamento dell'Unità d'Italia 1859-61,* vol.II (Rome, 1961).
3. An incident which is supposed to have inspired Verga's *La Libertà* (Nino Bixio, *Dizionario biografico degli italiani*) (Rome, 1968).
4. The fighting qualities of the Italian soldier have been very severely judged in the twentieth century. But Caporetto, Greece and North Africa have to be examined in relation to a defective high command, inadequate economic resources and a sometimes inept political leadership. The battles of the Isonzo and the exploits of the Resistance should prove that there is nothing inherently wrong with the Italian soldier.
5. M. D'Azeglio, *Things I remember* (trans. E. Vincent, Oxford, 1966), p.9.
6. P. Pieri, *Storia militare del Risorgimento* (Turin, 1960), p.38.
7. D'Azeglio. pp.82-3.
8. The appointment of generals in time of stress, like La Marmora in 1864 or Pelloux in 1898, or even Badoglio in 1943, was a disturbing tendency but was not the result of unsolicited intervention. The Fiume affair and the pro-Fascist sympathies of many officers in 1922 are much more significant.
9. 'Once the Neapolitan parliament had adopted the Spanish type of constitution', wrote Santarosa, 'Piedmontese liberals could not have accepted any other without bringing discord to Italy' (*De la révolution piémontaise* (Paris, 1822), quoted D. Mack Smith, *The Making of Italy, 1796-1870* (New York, 1968), p.39).
10. D'Azeglio, pp.172-3.
11. The phrase is Correlli Barnett's in 'The education of military elites', *Journal of Contemporary History,* vol. II, no.3 (1967).
12. *Life and writings of Joseph Mazzini,* vol.I (London, 1864), p.1.
13. *Précis de l'art de la guerre* (1837). See M. Howard, 'Jomini and the classical tradition in military thought', *The theory and practice of war,* ed. M. Howard (London, 1965), p.14.
14. 'Mirabeau . . . and Bonaparte were not true Frenchmen', wrote Gioberti in his *Il Primato*; 'two gifted men of Italian stock, transplanted onto Gallic soil, had their characters vitiated by such an unhappy adoption.' This is part of the passage reproduced in Mack Smith, pp.74-84.
15. Ibid., p.39.
16. Information about these writers can be found scattered in the authoritative works of Piero Pieri, particularly his *Storia militare del Risorgimento* (Turin, 1962) and *Guerra e politica negli scrittori italiani* (Milan/Naples, 1955).
17. *Memoria su i mezzi che menano all'italiana indipendenza* (Paris, 1833).
18. Mazzini himself was criticised by Pisacane for failing to emphasise these implications and, ironically, for undue reliance on a *tour de force* by dedicated bands of partisans.
19. Pieri, *Storia militare,* p.585.
20. R. Aron, *Peace and war* (London, 1966), p.56.

2 'ITALIANS DO FIGHT': THE FIRST WAR OF INDEPENDENCE 1848-9

By the third week in March 1848 it looked as if Mazzini's wildest prophecies were coming true. The People in Arms – and these arms ranged from sophisticated weapons like the Dreyse and Minié rifles to Milanese chamberpots – were everywhere dethroning monarchs, expelling unpopular ministers and forcing regular armies into a hasty retreat. For those Italians who resented Austrian domination the excitement which they felt over the birth of the Second Republic in France was virtually eclipsed by the exhilarating news from the Habsburg Empire. Revolution had broken out in Vienna and Metternich had fled. In Milan, that other important outpost of the empire, Marshal Radetzky was at first confident that he could control the situation, but was proved disastrously wrong. Milan rose on 18 March and five days later he was forced to withdraw his 12,000 troops from the city. Similarly stirring events took place in Venice where Manin succeeded in reviving the republic which had been extinguished fifty years before.

Everything seemed to be conspiring to overthrow the old order in Europe which had been so painfully reconstructed in 1815. The advance of new industrial techniques and the tenacious survival of the principles of '89, often insidiously disguised as 'liberalism', 'socialism' or 'nationalism', steadily eroded the foundations of European society. As blight, famine and credit crises converted the 1840s into the Hungry Forties, peasants, artisans and the professional middle classes bitterly challenged the validity of the existing system. Those in authority were failing to rise to this challenge or were responding in such a grotesque fashion, as in Ireland and Galicia, that they raised more problems than they solved. Powerful ministers like Metternich and Guizot were still convinced of their indispensability but were adopting a more and more fatalistic approach. In Berlin, the usually stable Hohenzollern dynasty had produced the quixotic Frederick William IV while the Habsburg line was represented by Poor Ferdy, a feeble-minded Emperor who had to be removed in December 1848, ten years before the Prussians were forced to take similar measures against their own rapidly deteriorating monarch. Nor was the House of Savoy or the Throne of St Peter immune from these strange maladies. Charles Albert, the *'re amletico'*, was a melancholic who was capable of the most disconcerting actions, and the conclave of 1846 had elected an epileptic pope, which was unremarkable, but Pius IX was also reputedly liberal, and this did cause astonishment.

In 1846, like Mazzini two years later, Gioberti saw the possibility of implementing an ambitious programme, but he advocated an Italian confederation under the presidency of the pope. Indeed, in the first months of his pontificate Pius IX succeeded in arousing an enthusiasm which rapidly spread from Trastevere to all parts of Italy, giving Gioberti's scheme the appearance of mass support. Pius IX's protests over Austrian provocation in Ferrara led to an outburst of patriotism which other Italian rulers had to acknowledge. They were also forced to emulate the reforms which were being instituted in the Papal State, and in the matter of amnesties, a civic guard, freedom from arbitrary arrest and a more liberal press regime there began a frenetic attempt to keep pace with the pope who was finally overtaken in January 1848 by Ferdinand of Naples. Spurred on by a rising in Palermo he granted a constitution. Reforms had therefore already generated a revolutionary situation in Italy before the news of the flight of Louis Philippe and Metternich, and from Palermo to Turin the piazza was threatening to wrest control from the palace. As commanders in chief, the princes had to decide whether to champion the popular cause or use their troops to thwart it.

I

For more than a decade after his accession in 1831, Charles Albert seemed content to allow his kingdom to remain a political and economic satellite of the Habsburgs, and this was after all the role assigned to the House of Savoy by the statesmen at Vienna. The Piedmontese army was seen as the auxiliary of the Austrian, its duty being to hold the passes against the French and only to move over to the offensive, as in the brief campaign of 1815, when the Habsburg troops were in a position to bear the brunt of the fighting. Its main function, however, was to protect the dynasty and maintain public order, *'difendere la Corona e mantenere illesa la dignità e la tranquillità dello Stato'*, as Victor Emmanuel I himself had ordered.[1] Unlike his immediate predecessors, Charles Albert had military pretensions. He was proud of the warlike traditions of his house and of his own performance in Spain in 1823. In his secret military alliance with Austria in 1831 he had demanded to be put in command of the joint army and this caused apprehension among his allies because they were unconvinced both of his political reliability and his technical competence.[2] Although ideologically he was a sincere adherent of Metternich, despite or perhaps because of his deplorable performance in 1821, it was the power of Austria which prevented the realisation of that centuries-old ambition of the Savoyard rulers, territorial aggrandisement in the Po valley. There was an old proverb which said that *'Casa Savoia cammina con il tempo e con il Po'* and in the mid-1840s there were indications that the time was right for a move in this direction. Influential figures like Cesare Balbo and Massimo D'Azeglio began to think so but the formation of a party of 'Albertisti' was constantly frustrated by the King's enigmatic personality. In an interview with Charles Albert, D'Azeglio had learnt that the King was prepared to sacrifice his life, his children's lives, his treasure and his army 'in the cause of Italy' when 'the opportunity arises'.[3] In later decades historians spoke of 'the king's secret', a clever and patient policy whereby he successfully fooled everyone into believing that he was indifferent to the national cause. While his compatriots were cursing him and lamenting the backwardness of Piedmont, he was in reality secretly preparing for his rendezvous with destiny and at the opportune moment, in March 1848, he cast aside his disguise and stood forth as the champion of Italy.[4] By their very nature such secrets cannot be proved or disproved in any conclusive manner. When he spoke with D'Azeglio in 1845 Charles Albert was almost certainly sincere; the vagueness, the emotionalism and, above all, the tendency to procrastinate, are all in character. In the next few months, the pope's anti-Austrian stance, his own economic disputes with Vienna, pressure from the increasingly articulate liberal elements within his country and dynastic ambitions with those old ancestral voices prophecying war, undoubtedly helped to prepare him psychologically for a change of front, but there is no evidence that he took any practical steps to implement a distinct anti-Austrian programme. The fact is that when he went to his rendezvous with destiny he was characteristically late, he had to be pushed, and he had no clear idea of what to do when he arrived.

There was a possibility that the parochial ambitions of the House of Savoy could be made to serve the loftier cause of an independent Italy. The military presence of Austria was the chief obstacle to the realisation of both projects. Unaided, the Piedmontese army stood little chance, but, as many of the military theorists had pointed out, with the support of Italians throughout the peninsula the task was not hopeless. This, however, presupposed a degree of understanding between Charles Albert and the exponents of the national cause which simply did not exist and would have to be created. No significant attempt was in fact made; the granting of the *Statuto* and the Piedmontese declaration of war were not the climax of long years of secret preparation but the reluctant concessions of a frightened King.[5] If he hoped to silence his critics his military intervention had to be decisive. It was soon discovered however that he was not only the wrong sort of leader for such an enterprise but that he had the wrong sort of army.

As befitted the ruler of one of Europe's oldest 'military monarchies', Charles Albert was preoccupied with the efficiency and welfare of his army. General Pes di Villamarina was his War Secretary from 1832 until the autumn of 1847 and together they created an army which the King described as the '*sistema prussiano perfezionato*'.[6] This was an inaccurate description because the Piedmontese army was in reality an unsatisfactory compromise between the Prussian and French systems. An interesting theme of nineteenth century history is the way in which attempts were made by the other powers to copy and adapt one or other of these two systems. The response of the Prussian military reformers to the humiliations of 1806-7 had been the Krümper system. Of necessity, this had stressed the rapid training of conscripts from all classes who then went into reserve after their period of service. These trained reserves, together with the Landwehr, provided what was commonly referred to as 'the army of quantity', and its debt to the French revolutionary concept of the 'nation in arms' is obvious. After Waterloo the French continued to pay lip service to the doctrines of the early 1790s but in practice they reverted to the more venerable 'army of quality', based essentially on long-term professionals.

As in both the Prussian and French armies, the kernel of the Piedmontese army was the professional soldier who voluntarily signed on for a number of years and usually remained in the army until death, disease or disgrace removed him from the ranks. Charles Albert's reforms doubled the size of these regular troops from 8,000 to 16,000. They enlisted for eight years and most of them were expected to renew their contract. Each year they were joined by 8,000 *provinciali* chosen by lot from those who were not exempt or too poor to buy exemption. They served for about a year and then spent seven in the mobile militia and eight in the reserve. The peacetime strength was therefore 24,000 men which, in time of crisis, could be raised to 80,000 by calling in the seven classes of militia, and to about 120,000 by bringing in the reserve.[7] There were, however, some serious defects in this Piedmontese version of the Prussian system. Whereas the Prussian reservist had spent three years with the colours, the Piedmontese had spent only one, and was therefore insufficiently trained. There was also a grave shortage of officers, particularly serious in an army which would have to cope with a massive influx of scarcely trained reserves in time of war. Charles Albert's suspicion of bourgeois elements and those members of the aristocracy who had shown themselves to be unreliable in the crisis of 1821 meant almost total dependence on a restricted number of 'safe' noble families and on career officers. This tended to produce an officer corps in which there were a disproportionate number of conservative Savoyards and in which any progressive tendencies or signs of initiative and independent thinking were frowned upon. The experience of the young Raffaele Cadorna, who later led the Italian army into Rome, was typical of all officers who displayed any learned tendencies. 'So you want to become a savant', said his commanding officer. 'But just think, I have never opened a book and yet I have become a general just the same!'[8] Charles Albert's unadventurous officer corps was perhaps adequate for the sort of conflict which he envisaged, a dynastic war fought alongside other dynastic armies, but it was unlikely to prove adaptable enough to fight a war of independence where quick decisions and constant improvisations would be necessary.

The war secretary Villamarina had stated that his aim was *'addestramento adeguato, elasticità dell'Armata, pace pronte alla guerra'.*[9] The army of 55,000 men which took the field in 1848 was neither badly equipped nor unprepared for war, but the reforms of the 1830s and 1840s had not adequately equipped or prepared it for the type of war it was now called upon to wage, and whatever Villamarina had meant exactly by 'elasticity' he had signally failed to produce this. There were five cumbrous divisions, including one held in reserve, grouped into two army corps, and this unwieldiness was reproduced lower down where the battalion, made up of four companies, comprised over 1,000 men. This inflexibility was further emphasised by the heaviness both of the artillery with its big 8 lb and 16 lb guns, and of the cavalry with its 36 heavy squadrons. The Piedmontese staff was desparately short of maps but must have been aware that the Lombard plain was dissected by innumerable watercourses and that it was over this broken terrain that their heavy divisions would have to move. Their difficulties would also be increased by the fact that there were only five companies of engineers to serve the entire army, and that supply problems and sanitary and medical requirements had received insufficient attention. But few armies can bear too close a scrutiny and despite its deficiencies the Armata Sarda was far from being contemptible. Its officers, if unimaginative and often lacking in technical expertise, were brave and loyal. The infantry was tough and disciplined and the Bersaglieri, created by General Alessandro La Marmora in 1836, were excellent but in short supply. Major Cavalli's experiments in 1845 with a breech-loading rifled gun were symptomatic of the increasingly intellectual and scientific approach to be found among young artillery officers where Charles Albert's prejudices had to be ignored in order to achieve greater efficiency.

Progressive officers, however, found it extremely difficult to make any impact on the entrenched conservatism of the military establishment. By being appointed an aide-de-camp to one of the royal princes or by securing the patronage of someone influential at court it was sometimes possible to implement reforms here and there, but this procedure was slow and uncertain. In this absolutist state, where the King was supreme commander of the armed forces, the impetus for any rapid overhaul of the army would have to come from him, but Charles Albert was as incapable of firm leadership in the military sphere as in the civilian.

It was certainly the time for firm leadership. Already, in Florence and Rome, the initiative lay with popular leaders like Ciceruacchio whose skilful manipulation of mobs was forcing the governments to concede reform after reform. In September 1847 there was bloodshed in Milan and attempted risings in Reggio and Messina, clear indications that the reformist drive was developing revolutionary tendencies. The need to grant reforms before it was too late was emphasised by two distinguished visitors to Italy, Richard Cobden in the spring and Lord Minto in the autumn, and Massimo D'Azeglio had written a pamphlet in which he warned the sovereigns that failure to collaborate with the *liberali moderati* would convert them into *liberali esaltati.*[10] It was said that Charles Albert had not smiled since his sister's last visit to Turin in 1845,[11] and the disquieting events of the latter part of 1847 were certainly not calculated to cure his melancholia. His two outstanding ministers, Villamarina and Solaro della Margarita, gave him conflicting advice, the War Minister urging him to make concessions and the Foreign Minister urging him to stand fast.

The pressure of events beyond his frontiers and within Piedmont was inexorably forcing him to make a crucial decision. He would have to become a reforming monarch or use his army against the progressive forces in his country. Early in October he rid himself of both Villamarina and Solaro della Margarita and later on in the month promulgated various reforms. Not only was this too little and too late, but the reforms he offered were largely irrelevant. He was attempting to improve the efficiency of his absolutist state when his critics were demanding its abolition. They only had the effect of stimulating more demands and making it decidedly less dangerous to voice them. A new political press sprang up in Turin, the attitude of Genoa became more menacing, and even a right-wing liberal like Cavour, the son of a former police chief, began to speak of the need for a constitution. Della Rocca was exaggerating when he wrote, many decades later, that 'nearly the whole army and the men of middle age about the court were as keen for Liberal institutions as the younger generation',[12] but Charles Albert was clearly unwilling to risk an appeal to the sword in order to crush the reformers. He still vividly remembered the events of 1821 and 1833 and many of his staunchest supporters in the army made it clear that they regarded the Austrians, and not their compatriots, as the enemy which must be fought.

II

The way in which the Statuto was granted, the outbreak of war with Austria a few days later, and the military collapse which followed, had a profound influence on the future political development of Piedmont and Italy and on the relationship between the army and the state. Charles Albert announced his decision to become a constitutional monarch on 8 February 1848 because of the success of the 'people in arms' in far away Palermo. That the timing of this decision had been dependent on the triumph of popular insurrection over a regular army was an apparent vindication of those military theorists who had advocated such a course over the past decades.

An amazing manifesto had been distributed through the streets of Palermo on 9 January calling upon the people to arm themselves and make a revolution three days hence. The announcement declared that *'la forza dei popoli è onnipossente'*, and events after 12 January seemed to confirm the truth of this, because although forewarned the Bourbon authorities were forced to retire from the island, with the formidable exception of their stronghold at Messina. News of this led to an uprising in the province of Salerno and this proved too much for Ferdinand II who decided to grant a constitution rather than wage a civil war. The Neapolitan constitution of 29 January forced the hand of Charles Albert, Leopold II of Tuscany and Pius IX. Hurried consultations were held in Turin, and the King's determination 'to fight to the last' to avoid the awful fate of a Ferdinand II or become a constitutional monarch like the despised Louis Philippe, began to waver perceptibly. His advisers pointed out that it was better to concede before rather than after an armed insurrection and that in this way he would be able to preserve his monarchical power. The wording of the Statuto which he signed on 4 March and published the following day seemed to justify the wisdom of this advice.

In the words of one of the royal advisers, they had sought 'a constitutional system which would take least power from the king'.[13] The French Charter of 1814 and the Belgian constitution were the basic models and the document was so drafted that no reference was made to the crucial problem of ministerial responsibility. Article 5 revealed its monarchical character, stipulating that 'to the king alone belongs the executive power. He is the supreme head of the state; commands all land and naval forces; declares war; makes treaties of peace, alliance, commerce and other treaties. . .' It was, in fact, virtually identical to the Prussian constitution of 1850 which came to be regarded by nineteenth century liberals as starkly reactionary.[14] Why Piedmont began to evolve into a parliamentary state almost before the ink was dry on this conservative document was largely the result of the outbreak of war on 23 March 1848 and the politico-military developments of the next twelve months. It was, in fact, exactly twelve months because it was on 23 March 1849 that the Piedmontese army fought and lost the battle of Novara which induced Charles Albert to abdicate that same day in favour of his son Victor Emmanuel.

Just as the successful rising in Palermo had led to the granting of the Statuto, so the successful insurrection of Milan on 18 March prompted Charles Albert's declaration of war against Austria. The urban guerrillas of these two cities had not only expelled their garrisons, they had provided that final impetus which produced the transmogrification of a conservative dynast into a constitutional nationalist. This was a remarkable feat which many of them bitterly regretted later, and Charles Albert himself could never adapt himself to this new role. The February Revolution in Paris, the March Revolution in Vienna and the *Cinque Giornate* in Milan made it increasingly difficult for him to turn back. Initially, there were no technical restraints to underline his loss of absolutist power. Parliamentary elections would not take place until April, Balbo and the new ministers which he had appointed seemed unlikely to menace his prerogatives, and article 5 gave him supreme command over the army and the unquestioned right to declare war on his own initiative. He also intended, despite the qualms of some officers, to lead his army in person. He was constitutionally entitled to do this and to refer to it as 'his' army because it was not until later that the oath to the King 'and constitution and laws' was introduced.[15] General Franzini, whom he had appointed as Minister of War, became his quartermaster general, and was thus both a member of the ministerial team which would sooner or later have to have dealings with parliament and an officer under the direct orders of the King. But these political niceties would have to be tackled later. For the moment, the major problem was the mobilisation of the Armata Sarda and the prosecution of the war.

Despite the crusading fervour of the patriots, Charles Albert was understandably apprehensive. He had just reluctantly launched a new régime in his kingdom, there was the possible military and ideological threat from revolutionary France – and Savoy and Nice were on the wrong side of the Alps – but equally disconcerting was the inauspicious way in which he was entering the war, as a kind of auxiliary to the triumphant Milanese. There were also, of course, the technical problems connected with moving his heavy divisions into Lombardy, the shortage of good officers, and the fear that the performance of the reserves would be unsatisfactory because of their lack of training. Further complications resulted from the fact that so many Italians were convinced that this was a war of liberation in which they must participate. The attitude of the King and his generals to this volunteer movement was a clear indication that they were intent upon a *'guerra regia'*. Although Charles Albert's proclamation of 24 March addressed to the 'people of Lombardy and Venetia' had spoken of Italy being in a position *'di fare da sè'*, of 'the liberation of glorious Milan', and of his decision to superimpose the Savoyard emblem on to the Italian tricolor, his fundamental reaction to any popular initiative was one of fear and distrust. It was not this lofty proclamation but the explanations given to foreign representatives in Turin which are a more reliable guide to his conduct. He was intervening, said his Foreign Minister, to prevent the triumph of republicanism.[16] Properly used, the volunteers could have been a source of great strength, but the King saw them as a threat to the stability of his throne and most of his officers regarded them with distaste either because they would prove a military liability or because they would challenge their traditional monopoly of arms. As the war progressed it became increasingly obvious that various attempts were being made to neutralise the volunteers, and despite the desperate shortage of officers the high command was extremely reluctant to employ students or any members from the professional middle classes. Hardened veterans of the Spanish civil wars received a cool welcome because of their dubious political past,[17] and so did Garibaldi, already becoming a legendary figure, when he presented himself at royal headquarters.[18] This unwillingness to utilise the *'forze vive'* of the nation hampered the war effort in northern Italy, accentuated the differences between the two schools of thought and produced one of the most bitter controversies of the next two decades.

In the last days of March 1848 the Piedmontese troops could have dealt a decisive blow against the Austrians and perhaps even have expelled them from the soil of Italy. In the columns of the newly founded *Risorgimento* Cavour was calling for audacity with the fervour of a Carnot, but in the columns of General Pes there was little sense of urgency. With the vanguard of the army, he crossed the Ticino on 25 March and reached Milan the following day.[19] Although he only had 3,000 troops, General Trotti was in Pavia with another 4,000 and the Lombard and Venetian volunteers were eager to fight. The main body of the Piedmontese army could be expected within days and contingents from Naples, Rome and Florence were moving northwards. When Charles Albert arrived at Pavia with the bulk of his army both he and his chief of staff Salasco seemed more intent upon consolidating their hold over an already liberated Lombardy than any vigorous pursuit of the Austrians. By the time they resumed their march on 31 March, Radetzky had already begun to stabilise his position around Verona and the Quadrilateral, and reopen his communications with the Tirol and Friuli. Each day lost made it more difficult for the Italians either to catch them unprepared or to cut them off from their home bases. The first small encounters took place on 5 April and culminated in the Piedmontese success at Pastrengo at the end of the month. But these minor successes were illusory. They came too late, and, equally significant, they were not fought within the context of an overall strategic plan.

The commander of II Corps, General De Sonnaz, had presented a workable plan for an offensive into Venetia which would enable the Piedmontese to link up with the papal troops and the Venetian volunteers, to threaten the weakest of the Quadrilateral fortresses, Legnago, and to cut Radetzky's supply lines to Friuli. Much to his disgust, the King and his other generals had turned this down. Salasco, who was incapable of imposing any sort of unity of command, perhaps preferred to avoid a specific commitment he would be incapable of implementing.[20] Franzini, De Sonnaz and Bava, the commander of I Corps, were only likely to work together as a team if Charles Albert asserted himself as commander in chief. Unfortunately, he was too hesitant to be a decisive leader but too stubborn to delegate his powers.

As long as his army was successful he could afford to ignore attempts to remove him from the supreme command. Cavour, Roberto D'Azeglio and others had, in fact, drawn up a memorandum before parliament met in May suggesting that a constitutional monarch should not be in personal command of the troops. But Balbo, who believed that any interference in the military sphere was inadmissible, was not prepared to support this. When the deputies assembled in Turin, news of victories like Goito and Peschiera at first prevented any serious attempt to criticise the King's conduct of the war.[21] Far more serious from the King's point of view was Pius IX's refusal to champion the national cause, and his recall of Durando's army. The Neapolitan contingent was also withdrawn so that Ferdinand could dedicate himself to the restoration of Bourbon power in Sicily and the destruction of liberalism in Naples. Although Pepe, Durando and some of their followers refused to retire from the war against Austria, these defections came at a bad time. The decision to incorporate Lombardy and possibly Venetia into a Piedmontese-dominated Kingdom of Upper Italy induced many patriots to consider the war virtually won when in fact it was about to be lost. The political, personal and regional problems involved were dangerously distracting just as the military basis for such a scheme was being rapidly eroded. A series of plebiscites in Lombardy, a large part of Venetia, and even down in the duchies of Parma and Modena, revealed an apparently overwhelming support for the House of Savoy and for incorporation into an enlarged Piedmont. The basic reason for this widespread unanimity among those who had voted was that the moderates who had seized power after the Austrian withdrawal needed Piedmontese troops to protect them against their possible return and, equally compelling, to prevent the triumph of democrats, Mazzinians or federalists. Charles Albert's insistence on immediate annexation in the midst of a war confirmed the worst suspicions of other Italian princes, but this emphasis on political rather than military objectives resulted, in the short term, in his achievement of neither, and in the long term in the intensification of party conflicts and regional feuds.

Dynastic preoccupations played their part in the Piedmontese defeat at Custoza on 25 July. Not for the first time, General Bava's sensible precautions were ruined by royal intervention. Venetia was being steadily reconquered by the Austrians, and in order to protect as much of his Lombard possessions as possible Charles Albert ordered his troops to be spread out on too wide a front. Radetzky hastened to take advantage of this strategic weakness and as the pressure mounted De Sonnaz, the commander of the Piedmontese II Corps, began to lose control of the situation. In the crucial days between 22 and 27 July the morale of the Italian troops was lowered by the tactical errors and confusion of their leaders and by the almost complete breakdown of the supply system. Many of the units in action had spent days without adequate rest or food and, although they fought better than might have been expected in such disadvantageous conditions, they were forced back in a series of isolated encounters. The Austrians, however, made no attempt to finish them off and the Piedmontese and their allies retreated unmolested. At a council of war on 27 July Charles Albert decided to ask for an armistice but Radetzky's conditions were rejected as too harsh, and the army continued its retreat across the Oglio.

Because of the euphoria of the past two months the news of this military reverse produced a dangerous mood of frustration and vindictiveness,[22] and as Charles Albert had refused to delegate his powers as commander in chief he was held fully responsible for the disaster. His failure to defend Milan and the Salasco armistice in August, both personal decisions, provided further ammunition both for those who had always been suspicious of the *guerra regia* and parliamentarians whose complacency in the successful phase of the war now turned to apprehension. The earlier attempt to impose constitutional controls was now renewed with a greater chance of success. Balbo, who had never been a keen supporter of such moves, had resigned on 6 July although he had been induced to carry on the government until 27 July when the leader of the Milanese moderates, Casati, succeeded in forming an 'Italian' ministry.[23] Two days later the renowned Gioberti joined it but even so it only survived a few days. Casati and the majority of the deputies were in favour of continuing the war and mobilising the resources of the country. Five classes of reservists were to be called up, Gioberti was allowed to pursue his plans for an Italian league, and the national guard was summoned. By a vote of 95 to 48 the King was granted full powers to carry out this patriotic programme. Casati, like Cattaneo in Milan, was convinced that French aid should be requested to supplement the other defensive measures which were being taken. Charles Albert, however, refused to consider any suggestion of French military assistance, and he was similarly opposed to the *guerre à outrance* advocated by the new ministry. Such a war could only succeed by calling upon the support of democratic and nationalistic forces which would be a direct threat to his dynasty. Indeed, his major preoccupation at this time seemed to be the prevention of any repetition of the *Cinque Giornate.* If the Milanese, who had already organised a committee of public safety, were again successful, or even if they were an heroic failure, the prestige of the King and his army would sink even lower. Bava had wanted to retreat to Piacenza but on 1 August Charles Albert decided to move to Milan. Historians have argued about his motives for giving this order for more than a century, but it does seem that the primary motive was not to defend Milan but to ensure that it was not defended. After a brief show of resistance by the Piedmontese on 4 August, Charles Albert arranged for the capitulation of Milan on the following day. The enraged Milanese besieged him in the Palazzo Greppi for a time but they were now virtually powerless to prevent the re-entry of the Austrians. Charles Albert managed to slip away and his chief of staff Salasco signed an armistice with Hess, his Austrian counterpart, on 9 August. It was hardly surprising that the Casati ministry, its programme shattered, angrily resigned.

The new conservative ministry under the presidency of Sostegno took office to protect the King from the consequences of his defeat but, ironically enough, this could only be done by removing the King from the effective command of the army. Count Revel, the dominant personality among the right-wing politicians, put this bluntly to the King and added that there would have to be an inquest on some of his generals to satisfy an outraged public opinion. While Colonel La Marmora was despatched to Paris to find a French general willing to command the Piedmontese army,[24] the new War Minister Dabormida instructed all officers to submit written reports on the part they had played in the last campaign. So damaging were these reports that they were not in fact published until 1910, but General Bava made his views known to the press. He had never revealed a conspicuous talent for tact or diplomacy and , predictably, he was harshly critical of the King. Equally predictably, these revelations virtually ruined his military career.[25]

When parliament reassembled in the autumn both government supporters and opposition deputies were determined to secure the territories which had voted for union with Piedmont. Their aims may have been identical but their methods were not. Revel and his following hoped that Anglo-French mediation would reverse the verdict of the Salasco armistice, whereas the opposition advocated a resumption of the war, only this time a democratic war. But in the debates which followed, both sides tacitly assumed that the great questions of war and peace, the reorganisation of the army, and the command of the troops, were too important to be decided by the King. The Statuto had ceased to be a royal fortress and was becoming something of a royal prison. Charles Albert, who bitterly resented the humiliations which the conservatives had forced him to undergo, took malicious delight in their failure to activate the scheme for Anglo-French mediation, and their consistent failure to acquire a French general. They had to be content with the Polish General Chrzanowsky. Charles Albert and the democratic opposition could now make a tactical alliance. They both wished to sweep away the conservatives and they both wanted war. The democrats realised that only Charles Albert, as the nominal commander, could maintain the loyalty and cohesion of the regular army,[26] and the King realised that only democratic support could bring about the war which he now saw as his last opportunity to escape from the capital and the frustrations of his new constitutional position.

Led by Gioberti, the democrats assumed power in December 1848. The King sanctioned new elections in which the democratic war party obtained a majority, and with even less reluctance he accepted Gioberti's resignation over the question of the proposed intervention in Tuscany, taking great pains to prove himself a model constitutional monarch. In February 1849, Chrzanowsky was made *generale maggiore* at a ministerial council, but Charles Albert was allowed to accompany the army when war was resumed shortly afterwards. Indeed, the ministers only publicly avoided assuming operational control of the army because they knew that the army was incapable of implementing their full programme which called for the reconquest not only of Lombardy but parts of Venetia as well. They also had a natural wish to dissociate themselves from a war plan which might prove disastrous.

It was disastrous, and the defeat at Novara on 23 March 1849 could have sealed the fate, not only of Charles Albert, but of his dynasty, his army and the whole concept of the *guerra regia.* Yet dynasty, army and concept survived, so that within six years the Piedmontese, still under the House of Savoy, were able to participate in a *guerra regia* in the Crimea, and in just over ten years helped to expel the Austrians from Lombardy and establish their rule over most of Italy. That the Second War of Independence was fought to a successful conclusion under civilian leadership and within the framework of liberal institutions was primarily the result of the solid achievements of the Cavourian decade, but the foundations of this parliamentary monarchy of the 1850s were laid during the militarily disastrous First War of Independence.

No one, of course, could have predicted this on the evening of 23 March. A broken King was preparing to slip away to exile and death, leaving his son the task of restoring the prestige of the monarchy. The army, its morale shattered by recent events, was desperately in need of firm leadership and reorganisation. Radetzky's troops were poised along the frontiers of a country which seemed to be on the verge of civil war. But Anglo-French diplomacy averted an Austrian occupation, Victor Emmanuel showed a greater aptitude for constitutional pretence than his father, and La Marmora was able to suppress the Genoese rising and initiate his army reforms. A retrospective 'spirit of Dunkirk' even began to evolve, but the fundamental importance of the First War of Independence for politico-military developments lay in the widely held conviction that control of the army must never again become the exclusive monopoly of the King and his generals.

III

Emphasis on the Piedmontese contribution to the war effort in 1848 and 1849 is justified from the point of view of future developments, but the campaigns which ended at Custoza and Novara were, of course, only a part of the First War of Independence. For observers like Cattaneo and Mazzini, the performance of the Armata Sarda and the conduct of the Turin government had not only been uninspiring but positively harmful to the Italian cause. Strategic errors and organisational deficiencies could be more readily forgiven than the shameful neglect of the volunteer movement and the grasping dynasticism of Charles Albert. It was this unedifying display of parochialism which had repelled and alarmed conservative as well as democratic opinion in the other Italian states. In the negotiations for the establishment of a customs union just before the war and in the attempts to construct an Italian league in the months that followed, Piedmont had shown no willingness to transcend her narrow particularism. Although the Duke of Genoa, Charles Albert's son, had rejected the crown which had been offered by the Sicilian separatists, Ferdinand II remained intensely suspicious of the expansionist tendencies of the House of Savoy. The attempted absorption of the duchies of Parma and Modena was an unequivocal warning to all those who valued independence or autonomy.[27] Patriots who entered Lombardy and Venetia to fight for a free Italy soon became disillusioned with their Piedmontese ally, many of them turning for inspiration not to Turin but to Manin's Venice or Mazzini's Roman Republic.

The popular risings at Palermo and Milan which had initiated this phase of the Risorgimento did not remain isolated examples of the people's war. Bologna, Messina and Brescia became the scene of similar heroic gestures, but it was the defiance of Venice and Rome which kindled the imagination and, for a time, kept alive the hope that the people could redeem themselves without the assistance of regular armies, princes and diplomats. Even after the Austrians reconquered the mainland and the Sardinian fleet withdrew, Manin's Republic of St Mark fought on in splendid isolation while the rest of Europe was pacified. Bombardment and blockade finally forced her to submit. After the pope had fled to Gaeta, the *Terza Roma,* the Rome of the People prepared to defend itself in the spring of 1849. Rather like the Easter Rising of 1916, this was essentially a symbolic act and as such, Mazzini's exalted phraseology and Garibaldi's generalship were just what were needed to turn a forlorn hope into an unforgettable drama. The French decision to intervene in favour of the pope was a shattering blow, but the defenders of Rome continued the struggle and Garibaldi's initial successes against this new enemy provided the Italians with a national hero who was also their most capable general.[28] His eventual defeat and miraculous escape did nothing to tarnish his reputation and probably enhanced it.

By comparison with such daring exploits the performance of the Piedmontese army was depressingly unspectacular. But the people in arms had been defeated, and defeated by regular armies, and whereas their military formations had melted away after defeat, the Armata Sarda was still in existence. Although battered and demoralised it remained the only disciplined body of troops capable of meeting the Austrians on the field of battle. Its possible rival, the Neapolitan army, had made only a tentative appearance in northern Italy, and after Ferdinand's *coup* of 15 May 1848 had been ordered to withdraw to resume its more traditional role of suppressing internal disorder. Apart from a few officers and men who deserted with General Pepe, Ferdinand II found his army a loyal instrument in his reconquest of Sicily and the reimposition of Bourbon absolutism throughout his kingdom. This garrison army with its multifarious police duties was clearly unequipped to become the nucleus of any future army of liberation even if the Bourbon dynasty dropped its allegiance to pope and emperor.

The military theories of the inter-war years had been put to the test in 1848-9 and found wanting. Mutual distrust between the regular army and the volunteer or partisan movement made co-operation difficult even when things were going well and when the military situation deteriorated, accusations of treachery were voiced by both sides. These bitter recriminations culminated occasionally in armed clashes like that at Genoa and left behind a legacy of hatred which made any future collaboration seem a very remote possibility. But when the smoke of battle had cleared away, the Piedmontese army discovered that it had at least one invaluable asset. In Italy, as elsewhere in Europe, moderate opinion had become alarmed by the implications of such phenomena as the June Days in Paris or the Genoese riots. As the embodiment of social order and political stability, the Piedmontese army was infinitely preferable to Radetzky's troops for those Italians who wished to preserve their self-respect as well as their property and privileges.

Notes

1. Stato Maggiore dell'Esercito *L'Esercito Italiano* (3rd ed., Rome, 1962), p.56.
2. F. Lemmi, *La politica estera di Carlo Alberto nei suoi primi anni di regno* (Florence, 1928), p.77.
3. D'Azeglio, p.341.
4. For a discussion of the 'legend' and those who contributed to it see A. Omodeo, *La leggenda di Carlo Alberto nella recente storiografia* (Turin, 1940).
5. This point perhaps needs labouring as the legend still tends to be uncritically accepted today. See, for example, G. Martin, *The red shirt and the cross of Savoy* (London, 1970), p.311.
6. P. Pieri, *Le forze armate nella età della Destra* (Milan, 1962), p.12.
7. Ibid., p.11.
8. L. Cadorna, *Il Generale Raffaele Cadorna nel Risorgimento* (Milan, 1922), p.9.
9. *Stato Maggiore,* p.58.
10. *Proposta d'un programma per l'opinione nazionale italiana,* quoted in G. Candeloro, *Storia dell'Italia moderna,* vol.III (Milan, 1960), p.61.
11. E. della Rocca, *Autobiography of a veteran* (London, 1899), p.46.
12. Ibid., p.46.
13. A. Colombo, *Dalle riforme allo Statuto di Carlo Alberto* (Casale, 1924), p.86.
14. H.W. Smyth, 'Piedmont and Prussia: the influence of the campaigns of 1848-1849 on the constitutional development of Italy', *American Historical Review,* LV (1950), pp.484-5. Much of what follows rests heavily on this illuminating article.
15. F. Racioppi and I. Brunelli, *Commento allo Statuto del Regno,* vol.I (Milan, 1909), p.253.
16. Candeloro, III, p.181.
17. F. Carandini, *Manfredo Fanti* (Verona, 1872), p.159.
18. La Marmora said later: 'It was a great mistake not to use him. I do not believe he is a Republican in principle. . . When there is another war, he is a man to employ. Garibaldi is no common man.' Quoted in C. Hibbert, *Garibaldi and his enemies* (London, 1965), p.31.
19. Troops had to be withdrawn from the French frontier. As the threat of a hostile invasion by republican France began to recede, so Charles Albert began to dread the possibility of a friendly invasion and hence his insistence that *'Italia farà da sè'.*
20. Della Rocca, p.56.
21. Smyth, p.491.
22. As after the second battle at Custoza in 1866 and after Adua, relatively unimportant defeats came to be regarded as national humiliations.

23. There were two Milanese, one minister from Piacenza, a Venetian and two Genoese (Candeloro, III, p.267).
24. Cavaignac refused to allow Changarnier, Bugeaud or anyone else to accept La Marmora's offer. Despite this failure, La Marmora became, from now on, one of the dominant military and political figures in Piedmont, becoming war minister for the first time in October 1848 (G. Massari, *Il Generale Alfonso La Marmora* (Florence, 1880), p.57).
25. Smyth, p.495, f.50
26. For example, Perrone, who became premier in October 1848 and bitterly opposed to war, obeyed the King and fought and died at Novara (A. Moscati, *I ministri del Regno d'Italia,* vol.I (Salerno, 1948), pp.192-7).
27. Gioberti's plans to send the Piedmontese army into Tuscany and the Papal State in February 1849 also alarmed both princes and patriots and provided additional ammunition for the opponents of the House of Savoy.
28. Few people were aware that some of Garibaldi's colleagues regarded him as 'utterly incapable of directing the manoeuvres of masses of men', that 'Garibaldi did not know how to reply to the operations of the enemy or how to direct his attack'. (E. Dandolo, *The Italian volunteers and Lombard Rifle Brigade* (London, 1857), p.235, and Carlo Cattaneo quoted in Hibbert, p.77).

3 LA MARMORA'S REFORM OF THE PIEDMONTESE ARMY

The defeats at Custoza and Novara did not automatically contribute to the growth and consolidation of parliamentary government in Piedmont, thereby ensuring the supremacy of the civilians over the military. Defeated armies do not necessarily feel such shame and remorse that they willingly agree to play a submissive and subordinate role in society. They can just as easily turn viciously on those whom they regard as being responsible for their military failure, accusing them of culpable negligence or even of a calculated 'stab in the back'. Refusing to act as scapegoats, they point the finger – and sometimes the gun – at the real culprits, perhaps carrying out a *coup d'ětat* in the process.

In March 1849 scapegoats were in plentiful supply. The democratic element in Piedmont accused the conservatives of a 'Savoyard plot', while they in turn accused the left of irresponsible warmongering. Whereas the King, the army and his loyal subjects had soberly resumed the war with Austria, the democrats had ranted and criticised, mistaking their own sound and fury for the din of battle. During this unseemly wrangle the name of General Ramorino began to emerge, the conservatives being quick to realise that he would make an excellent scapegoat. Mazzini's general in the abortive invasion of Savoy, he had been foisted on the King and the army by the democrats, and his incompetence at the river crossing at Mezzana Corti on 20 March had resulted in his being relieved of command of the V division. The conduct of the commander in chief Chrzanowski had been equally deplorable but he was a Pole and therefore unsuitable for victimisation, and any attempt to pillory Charles Albert would weaken the position of the new King. Ramorino's execution, on the other hand, would weaken the democrats. It would also distract attention from other army officers and help Victor Emmanuel's negotiations with the Austrians.

At this meeting with Radetzky at Vignale on 24 March, Victor Emmanuel is supposed to have rejected the Austrian's attempts to secure the abolition of the Statuto, threatening to resume hostilities rather than violate the constitution. This 'legend of the liberal King' was, in fact, fabricated by later historians.[1] It was Victor Emmanuel who took the initiative in declaring to Radetzky his eagerness to crush the democrats. Reporting his conversation with the King, Radetzky explained to Schwarzenberg:

> He frankly declared his firm intention of defeating the democratic Revolutionary party, to which his father had latterly given such free rein that it became a real threat to himself and his throne. He said he only needed a little time for this, but it was especially important for him to avoid being discredited at the outset of his reign, because otherwise he would not be able to find any suitable ministers.[2]

As long as the King intended to uphold the monarchical principles inherent in the Statuto, the old marshal saw no point in humiliating him or his country and no reason for destroying the constitution. Radetzky's conciliatory policies were later condemned by men like Bruck and Bach, who had wanted him to march on Turin to dictate terms.

After signing the armistice, Victor Emmanuel and his new conservative ministry under the Savoyard General De Launay had to make another painful military decision – the subjugation of Genoa. The War Minister, Della Rocca, was preparing to lead troops into the rebellious seaport when he heard that his brother had been shot there. Unwilling – or so he wrote later – to be accused of vindictiveness, he assigned the command to Alfonso La Marmora.[3] La Marmora took this opportunity to become the only Piedmontese general to achieve a total victory in this First War of Independence and, as a result of his successful restoration of order, to become one of the pillars of the politico-military hierarchy in Piedmont, a position he held until his disastrous handling of the campaign of 1866.

Like so many of his fellow officers, La Marmora came from a family steeped in the military tradition. Two of his brothers had fought under Napoleon I and a third, Alessandro, had created the Bersaglieri. Born in Turin in 1804, he was sent to the military academy there twelve years later. A lieutenant in the artillery in 1823, he rose to the rank of captain in 1831 and major in 1843, so it can be seen that even someone with his background and connections did not achieve rapid promotion. The higher ranks were monopolised by senior officers whose outstanding attribute appeared to be senility rather than ability. The test of war in 1848 proved too much for most of them and La Marmora became successively a colonel, chief of staff to the Duke of Genoa, a major general and War Minister. The post of War Minister, which La Marmora held on three separate occasions within twelve months, seems to have been regarded by the generals as the object of an intricate game of pass the parcel. His third term as War Minister, however, lasted for over a decade and won for him a lasting reputation. Not long after his first ministerial appointment he decided to stand for parliament. Like Della Rocca, he discovered that most deputies at first found his Piedmontese dialect almost incomprehensible, but unlike his bluff and rather limited companion in arms, La Marmora proved himself capable of adapting to political life. Indeed, it is primarily as a politician that La Marmora's career should perhaps be judged.

Although the Genoese insurrection had been defeated in the second week of April, La Marmora remained in the city for another six months as *regio commissario,* exercising full military and civilian powers. It was a situation familiar to so many European cities after June 1848. Generals of garrison armies – *eserciti di caserma* as the Italians called them – comprising long-service regulars imbued with *esprit militaire* dispersed the people in arms and restored order. Men like Cavaignac, Filangieri, Oudinot, Radetzky and Windischgrätz, and the type of army they commanded, were seen as the bulwark of civilisation and private property. On a more parochial level, La Marmora played such a role in Genoa. It probably confirmed his belief in the 'army of quality' which appeared to have revealed its superiority, militarily and politically, over the 'army of quantity' and the popular forces raised by the revolutionaries. When he returned to the War Ministry in November 1849, La Marmora determined to end the unsatisfactory compromise between the French and Prussian models which existed in the Armata Sarda. But there could be no real reform programme until Piedmont achieved political stability.

The July elections of 1849 had returned a majority hostile to the Peace of Milan which the government finally signed with Austria on 6 August. This opposition was unrealistic as the army was in no condition to resume fighting but it was none the less disturbing for the King and his new premier Massimo D'Azeglio. It was decided to call new elections and on 20 November the King issued the Proclamation of Moncalieri which had been written by Azeglio. It contained the warning that if the electors persisted in returning opposition members the King would be obliged 'to save the nation from the tyranny of parties'. The appeal was heeded, the constitution was saved by his threat to abolish it, and the army was not called in to execute a *coup d'état.* However, no sooner had the threat from the left begun to recede than the conservatives launched their drive for the restoration of absolutism. The appointment of Count Siccardi as Minister for Justice and Ecclesiastical Affairs in December, and of Count Cavour as Minister of

Agriculture and Commerce in the following October, proved that they had seriously miscalculated. Azeglio had not escaped from democratic domination to become the prisoner of the right. Piedmont's anti-clerical legislation and free trade policies clearly indicated the government's intention to pursue a vigorous reform programme despite conservative opposition at home and absolutist pressure from her continental neighbours. Not even the army, regarded by many as the last bastion of reaction, was to remain immune.

Within the army La Marmora had built up a wide circle of friends ranging from the Duke of Genoa to Captain Govone and including representatives from the well-known families like the generals Collegno and Valfré, Major Genova di Revel and Colonel Petitti. They formed what Piero Pieri has called 'the most intelligent and dynamic group in the army', and had close ties with the Azeglio brothers and Cavour. This sort of interlocking relationship between certain members of the civilian and the military élites helped to promote a degree of mutual trust which precluded constant friction. Despite the financial stringency following the war, La Marmora found that his political colleagues were prepared to allocate funds for his projected reforms. A commission was appointed to streamline a bewildering array of military laws and regulations, an infantry school was opened at Ivrea, a cavalry school at Pinerolo, and another military academy was established in Turin for engineers and artillery officers. The entry qualifications for admission to the staff were made stiffer in an effort to attract the best officers, but the prejudice against educated soldiers remained powerful, the predominant view being that

> The Thing of Ultimate Effect
> Is Character – not Intellect.

Promotion through merit became much more common and La Marmora supported his brother's efforts to expand the Bersaglieri and build them up into an élitist force which would, they hoped, inspire the rest of the infantry. The war minister's most ambitious and most controversial attempt to professionalise the army was, however, his military law of 1854.[4]

Introduced into the senate as early as 3 February 1851, it was only finally approved by both houses on 20 March 1854. La Marmora patiently listened to parliamentarians who demanded a return to the past or a national militia.[5] Indeed, his strenuous defence of this bill was his most successful action since the conquest of Genoa. The most controversial aspect of the measure was the drastic increase in the length of service for conscripts from fourteen months to four or five years. Afterwards, these men of the so-called 'first category' then spent six years in the reserve. The method of selecting the conscripts remained the same – the drawing of lots, the system of exemption, and the right to provide a substitute. Men in the 'second category' merely underwent a forty day training period and then went into the reserve for five years.

Cavour trusted La Marmora and was content to let him run his own department. With a usually hostile King and Revel waiting in the wings to supplant him, Cavour was grateful for the support of his War Minister and for his guarantee that the reorganised garrison army would not be used to thwart his policies. In a visit to Lyons shortly after the Cavour-Rattazzi *connubio,* La Marmora had found an opportunity to inform Napoleon that he was a staunch supporter of Cavour and his policies.[6] Just as Azeglio and Cavour incorporated *émigrés* into the political and cultural life of Piedmont, so La Marmora retained the services of some five hundred non-Piedmontese officers.[7] Despite the prejudice against them, men like Cialdini and Fanti, both from Modena, were favourably treated and allowed to rise to the highest ranks. It gave this dynastic army a dash of *italianità* which was a useful counterpoise to Savoyard parochialism and raised the hopes of patriots.

The outbreak of the Crimean War in 1854 proved a trying time for both Cavour and La Marmora. The King hoped to use the occasion to eject his overpowering premier, perhaps even to execute a royalist *coup* with the help of his military entourage and all those conservative backwoodsmen who so detested Cavourian liberalism.[8] Aware of the political and diplomatic dangers whether he opted for neutrality or intervention, Cavour twisted and turned and finally chose intervention as the best means of preventing his dismissal. Sending troops to fight Russia in the Crimea when La Marmora admitted that 'he did not have two brigades on a war footing', was a desperate gamble, particularly because there was no popular enthusiasm for the war. The Piedmontese minister in Paris hoped that this bizarre episode would have paved the way for the destruction of the Holy Alliance and lead to *'il risorgimento della nazionalità in Europa'*,[9] and Cavour told parliament that it was their country's task 'to prove that Italy's sons can fight valiantly on battlefields where glory is to be won' and that the laurels won in Eastern Europe 'will help the future state of Italy more than all that has been done by those people who hoped to regenerate her by rhetorical speeches and writing'.[10] This was whistling in the dark but, amazingly, this gamble paid off. Although La Marmora and his 18,000 men only lost thirty men in combat – 2,000 died from cholera – their performance at the Chernaia earned them a reputation for gallantry which proved helpful to Cavour after he had been admitted to the Congress of Paris in 1856.[11] As an official history put it, somewhat grandiloquently, the troops 'had gained practical experience, recovered a sense of confidence, had redeemed the prestige of the army in the country, had raised morale and had offset, at least in part. . .the disastrous memory of Custoza and Novara'.[12] Critics of La Marmora who had accused him of creating 'a pretorian army rather than a national army' began to change their minds and it was perhaps more than a coincidence that both the *Società Nazionale* and the *Rivista Militare* were founded in 1856.

Hoping to exploit the patriotism which the Crimean War and even the Congress of Paris had so unexpectedly aroused, La Marmora introduced an additional military law hoping to tap the still unexploited resources of manpower in the state. This *'legge di sangue',* as it came to be called, alarmed all those who had been able to win exemption under the 1854 law. Although La Marmora sought to incorporate them only in the reservist second category, the imminent prospect of war with Austria made this a dangerous commitment. Apparently patriotism was too important to be wasted in the army. A supporter of this new measure pointed out that as only one man out of fifty-five was being called into the army, the Piedmontese should be grateful that in the whole continent only the inhabitants of Portugal, Naples and the Papal State fared better than this.[13] With Cavour's help the law was passed in the summer of 1857 but, after all the uproar which had been caused, it is ironical that La Marmora only called up the full quotas in the summer of 1859 when the Second War of Independence was already in full swing. It may have been ironical but this laxity was perfectly understandable. An expansionist programme for the army implied increased taxation or at least the reallocation of funds. Even the most patriotic politician would need to calculate the effect this would have on his constituents, and many of the army officers were critical of this programme, advocating that any additional funds which were forthcoming should be used to increase their pay and improve the efficiency of the existing army establishment. Cavour tended to be a big spender but he was a civilian through and through, in spite of or perhaps because of his years at the military academy and in the engineers.[14] Just over 28 per cent of government expenditure went on the armed services and this could not be increased without economies elsewhere.[15] He was also realistic enough to realise that French military assistance was indispensable in any war with Austria, and that although the Piedmontese army must be a respectable partner in any joint operations, it would inevitably be the junior partner. Another argument against military expansion was the shortage of suitable officers and NCOs despite La Marmora's reform of the Military Academy, the establishment of a military college at Asti, and the creation of a *Battaglione dei Figli* designed for the sons of soldiers to ensure that they followed their fathers' profession.[16] With each mile of railway track laid and each convent suppressed, Piedmont began to look more and more like a modern, progressive state, and with the gradual diffusion of new techniques it became imperative for the army to adapt itself to changing circumstances. This required the formation of an officer corps or at least a general staff capable of regarding war as something more than an extension of hunting. It was partly for this reason that the Mezzacapo brothers founded the *Rivista Militare.* In their first issue of March 1856 they expressed amazement at the fact that Piedmont had possessed no military journal.[17] These brothers, who had deserted from the Neapolitan army when their King had withdrawn from the war in 1848, are a good example of the dynamic impact which many of these exiles made on Piedmontese society. Luigi Mezzacapo, for instance, produced a balanced account of the military implications of Piedmont's expanding railway network. In 1848 there were 8 kilometres of track; ten years later there were 850 with another 250 under construction. La Marmora's friend Major Govone began to draw up mobilisation plans involving their use. It was also at this time that the first *grandi manovre* were held, utilising the railways, the 414 kilometres of new *strade nazionali* and the 700 kilometres of *strade provinciali.* Nor could any future war manoeuvres or mobilisation plans ignore the 1,256 kilometres of telegraph lines.

Equally important was the growth of heavy industry, the Ansaldo concerns at Sampierdarena and Sestri Ponente employing over 1,000 workmen by 1861 and capable of producing quantities of locomotives and guns. In the era of free trade, with fierce foreign competition, the survival of such firms depended largely on army contracts. Military demands stimulated industrialisation just as much as industrialisation stimulated military demands.[18] The close relationship between government, heavy industry and the armed forces which originated in the 1850s had important but not always happy consequences in the later development of Italy.

Another important link forged between the military and the civilians was the National Society. One of its founders, Pallavicino, explained its objectives.

> Our view is that the 100,000 men in the Piedmontese army are indispensable for any war of independence. We want to entice, or if need be, force the King to act alongside us. We will entice him by offering him the crown of Italy; or we could force him by the threat of a republican revolution which would deprive him of the crown of Piedmont-Sardinia.[19]

Under La Farina's leadership the society began to abandon republican threats provided Victor Emmanuel and Cavour pursued 'nationalist' policies.[20] Many activists were weaned away from Mazzini and Garibaldi's adherence was the society's most notable recruit. As early as August 1856 Garibaldi had said: 'We must obviously depend largely on the Piedmontese regular army and the Piedmontese volunteers, and hence any decision to act should lie, at least indirectly, with the government'.[21] The failure of the Mazzinian uprising in Milan in 1853, the Pisacane fiasco, and the abortive Genoese revolt in the same year, 1857, all played right into the hands of the National Society and its propagandists.[22]

Meanwhile, La Marmora became involved in the tortuous diplomacy preceding the war of 1859. Indeed, he was one of the small circle of associates to be informed about the mysterious meeting at Plombières.[23] He also helped to transform the Franco-Piedmontese agreements into an alliance early in 1859 but the initiative, as in the Crimean War, came from Cavour and the political element and not from the military. La Marmora, in fact, became afraid that Cavour was being too precipitate and 'altogether too optimistic', and when the French Marshal Niel came to Turin he informed him of his doubts and hesitations. This action infuriated Cavour who, throughout March and early April, was close to despair over the growing international pressure for disarmament or a congress to settle the Italian question.[24] The Austrian ultimatum to Turin on 19 April gave Cavour his war. Despite his reluctance, La Marmora had concentrated troops along the frontier, but readiness alone would not have spared the Piedmontese a bloody encounter if the Austrians had pushed home a determined attack before the French had arrived in Italy. They were spared this because of the cumbrous nature of the Habsburg military machine and by the incredibly bad relations which existed between Buol and Adjutant-General Grünne, head of the central military chancery.[25]

Cavour's preparations had been as thorough as circumstances would allow. In January 1859 the alliance with France had been signed. The following month parliament had approved a 50 million lire loan and on 23 April an enabling act had been passed giving the government the right to suspend the constitution and rule by decree. The National Society had supported this 'royal dictatorship' and had alerted all its members the previous month. War broke out on 26 April.

La Marmora refused command of the army but agreed to accompany the King as minister in the field. Della Rocca was appointed chief of staff under the supreme command of Victor Emmanuel, but after the first two weeks all major military decisions were made by Napoleon III and the French commanders. The Piedmontese were uncomfortably aware that whereas the French had fulfilled their part of the bargain and taken the field with 200,000 men, they had only been able to provide 65,000 combat troops instead of 100,000. The 20,000 volunteers who came in could have helped to redress the balance but they tended to be badly treated by the government and by the regulars. Even Garibaldi and his Cacciatori delle Alpi had been consigned to the periphery and deprived of supplies and first-class equipment. Magenta and Solferino, the decisive battles of the war with Austria, were French victories. At Magenta on 4 June only a single battalion of Bersaglieri took part in the actual fighting and at Solferino on 24 June there were no Piedmontese at all – although it must be remembered that 31,000 of them fought a separate engagement that same day at San Martino. The French determined the shape of the campaign and won the major battles but the Piedmontese contribution was far from negligible.[26] This phase of the Second War of Independence was, of course, a startling contrast to what had happened in 1848-9, but outside Lombardy and in the period after the truce of Villafranca, the same tensions which had developed between exponents of the *guerra regia* and the *guerra di popolo* during the First War of Independence began to reappear.

Notes

1. H. Smyth, 'The armistice of Novara; a legend of a liberal king', *Journal of Modern History,* vol.7 (1935), pp.141-2.
2. Radetzky to Schwarzenberg, 26 March 1849, ibid., p.177. See also A. Filippuzzi, *La pace di Milano* (Rome, 1955), p.29.
3. His autobiography was written long afterwards and published in 1897, the year he died.
4. This is dealt with in the introduction to the documents by P. Pieri, *Le forze armate,* and in his 'Le guerre dell'unità italiana', *Nuove questioni di storia del Risorgimento e dell'unità d'Italia,* vol.2 (Milan, 1961).

5. Pieri, *Le forze armate,* pp.104-9 and 154-62.
6. Candeloro, IV, p.146.
7. Massari, p.106.
8. D. Mack Smith, *Victor Emanuel, Cavour, and the Risorgimento* (London, 1971), pp.49-50.
9. F. Valsecchi, *L'alleanza di Crimea* (Florence, 1968), p.340.
10. C.B. di Cavour, *Discorsi parlamentari,* ed, A. Saitta, vol. XI (Florence, 1957), pp.168-9.
11. C. Rubiola, *L'Armata Sarda in Crimea* (Pisa, 1969), p.53; Stato Maggiore, p.70.
12. Ibid., p.71.
13. Pieri, *Le forze armate,* pp.31-4.
14. R. Romeo, *Cavour e il suo tempo* (Bari, 1969), p.365.
15. Between 1848 and 1859, for instance, public works expenditure rose from 3 per cent to over 14 per cent and interest on the public debt stood at 21 per cent by the end of the decade (Candeloro, IV, p.208).
16. Stato Maggiore, p.71.
17. *Rivista Militare,* vol.1, No.1 (1856), p.iii.
18. For this theme see W. Millis, *Arms and men* (New York, 1956), pp.58-9.
19. Quoted in Mack Smith, *The Making of Italy,* p.217.
20. For the National Society consult R. Grew, *A sterner plan for unity* (Princeton, 1963).
21. As reported by Pallavicino (Mack Smith, p.216).
22. For Pisacane's scheme and other developments see L. Cassese, *La spedizione di Sapri* (Bari, 1969), p.11 and pp.33-84.
23. Massari, pp.204-6.
24. G. Massari, *Diaro dalle cento voce,* ed. E. Morelli (Bologna, 1959), pp.147-8.
25. G. Craig, 'Command and staff problems in the Austrian army 1740-1866', *The Theory and practice of war,* ed. M. Howard (London, 1965), p.60.

4 FANTI AND THE CREATION OF THE ITALIAN ARMY

La Marmora's reforms had not increased the size of the Piedmontese army but they had improved its efficiency. The five year service for conscripts – six years for those in the Bersaglieri, the artillery and the cavalry – produced a better trained fighting force than Charles Albert's army. Promotion through merit and the new emphasis on educational attainments had been bitterly resisted, but there were significantly more professionally competent officers and NCOs in 1859 than there had been a decade earlier. Pay increases, the improvement in the standard of living and other administrative measures had raised morale. Defects in essential services like the supply system and the treatment of the wounded, which had created such a scandal in 1848-9, were being slowly remedied. The entire army was more flexible, more cohesive, and better equippped to fight than ever before. What struck many contemporaries was that it also appeared to be less of a dynastic army. Conservative Savoyards who had for so long monopolised nearly all key positions were less conspicuous. Apart from Garibaldi's volunteer corps, no less than three of the divisional commanders, General Fanti, Cialdini and Cucchiari, were non-Piedmontese in origin. All three came from the state of Modena and had fought in the Spanish civil wars and in 1848-9. A fourth commander, Durando, was Piedmontese but he too had fought in Spain and remained in exile until 1848. The fifth, Filiberto Mollard together with the commanders of the cavalry division and the artillery reserve, General Bertone di Sambuy and Major Giovanni Thaon di Revel, were as 'dynastic' as their names suggest.

La Marmora had not been unduly alarmist, however, when he had warned the over-optimistic Cavour of various weaknesses in the army. The field army was disappointingly small – as the Emperor lost no time in pointing out – and even more serious was the scarcity of reserves and the meagre supply of trained officers. The implications were clear. The French would have to bear an even more disproportionate share of the burden, and both allies would face a severe manpower shortage if casualties were high or if the struggle became protracted. In addition, the Piedmontese would be incapable of opening up a second front or of providing significant military support for any insurrectionary movement. There was also a serious shortage of horses and mules as well as of men.

In the initial stages of the war, the Piedmontese batteries had to be reduced from eight to six guns, and as the allies pushed into Lombardy there continued to be grave deficiencies in the transport system despite and sometimes because of the use of railways.

It was perhaps fortunate that after the arrival of the Emperor neither La Marmora nor Della Rocca were expected to display much initiative. Neither they nor the King were inspired military leaders. It was true that Napoleon III and his entourage were also limited, showing little in the way of strategic or tactical brilliance, but the French army had the reputation of being the finest in the world and this proved to be a tremendous asset. The battles of Magenta, Solferino and San Martino were largely accidental encounters in which both sides fought stubbornly and heroically. The old military virtues of courage, discipline and *élan* were lavishly displayed but there was little evidence of careful planning or intelligent leadership. Franz Josef had written that the 'strength of the army lies not so much in educated officers as in loyal and gallant ones',[1] and MacMahon, the victor of Magenta, had once threatened to 'remove from the promotion list any officer whose name I read on the cover of a book'.[2] This was the type of language which the old Savoyard generals appreciated. Implemented on the battlefield, it led to the carnage of June 1859. 'Rather lose a province than undergo such a horrible experience again!' remarked Franz Josef after Solferino.[3] Napoleon III felt a similar revulsion and this helped the two emperors to agree to a truce on 8 July and to the preliminary peace of Villafranca three days later. Austria agreed to cede Lombardy to France who would then transfer the province to Sardinia, but she insisted on the retention of the Quadrilateral and Venetia. Mazzini had forecast that this dynastic war could only lead to a new Campoformio in which Italian interests would be ignored, and Cavour had become increasingly alarmed by the King's steadfast refusal to allow him to interfere with the conduct of the war or even to keep him informed of military events. Stunned by the news of the sudden ending of the war, Cavour rushed to army headquarters, and when the King sensibly refused to continue hostilities without French assistance, he angrily resigned. La Marmora took over the premiership, and as he stormed back to his estates at Leri, Cavour was prepared to believe that Mazzini's assessment of the situation was correct.

But since the outbreak of the war, much had happened outside Lombardy, Garibaldi's corps had fought a dashing campaign on the Alpine fringe and he remained unconvinced that Villafranca was a tragic event. It enabled Italy to free herself from the suffocating embrace of her French ally, and it enabled *volontarismo* to take over where the regular army had left off.[4] The French alliance had failed to free northern Italy from the Alps to the Adriatic, but in central Italy the situation was very fluid. It had, indeed, been partly as a result of developments in Tuscany and elsewhere that Napoleon had decided to retire from the war.

On 27 April, the day after the outbreak of war, units of the Tuscan army refused to take action against crowds demonstrating in favour of support for Piedmont. The same evening, the Grand Duke Leopold II went into exile. With him went the commander of the 10,000 strong Tuscan army, General Ferrari di Grado, a Venetian in the service of the Habsburgs. He had effectively reformed the Tuscan forces in the past decade, but since the Crimean War had fought a losing battle against the propagandists of the National Society. Leopold's subservience towards his Habsburg relatives alienated the majority of politically conscious Tuscans and anti-Austrian sentiment among the troops proved stronger than loyalty to the grand duke. One of their officers, Major Alessandro Danzini, became a member of the provisional government which assumed power after Leopold's departure from Florence. One of its first acts was to invite Victor Emmanuel to exercise a dictatorship over Tuscany for the duration of the war, but this was vetoed by Napoleon III who allowed him to accept the military and diplomatic protectorate. Boncompagni, Sardinian minister in Florence since 1857, was appointed royal commissioner and a new government was set up with Minister of the Interior Ricasoli as the most powerful of the new men. Afraid that Leopold would return at the head of Austrian troops or that popular risings would take place as in 1848, the Tuscan moderates hoped for Piedmontese military help. However, no troops could be spared; instead, Turin sent General Ulloa. This Neapolitan exile had fought for Manin's republic, but he had also been resident in France and for this reason he was widely suspected of being a Bonapartist. Sent to reorganise the Tuscan army which had unanimously supported the revolution, he only succeeded in creating dissension by some unwise appointments and promotions.[5]

Piedmont had only been able to send Ulloa, Napoleon III was eager to despatch not only his cousin Prince Napoleon but his V Corps. Cavour was convinced that this was the prelude to the establishment of a Bonaparte Kingdom of Central Italy. He failed to prevent French intervention but at least he succeeded in presenting it as an integral part of allied military strategy. He also made sure that it was Victor Emmanuel who sent the orders to Ulloa placing his troops under the command of Prince Napoleon. On his arrival at Leghorn on 23 May, the prince had indeed publicly announced his support for the union of Piedmont and Tuscany but few people were prepared to believe him. Rebuked by the Emperor and treated with suspicion by the Tuscans, he decided to lead his troops northwards into Lombardy. They were, however, too late to participate in the fighting, and the Tuscan troops and volunteers who had accompanied the V Corps were not called upon to emulate the heroes of Curtatone and Montanara, but they nevertheless performed a useful role during the formation of the Italian army in the months which followed.

The old régime had taken longer to collapse in the duchies. It was only after the news of the Austrian defeat at Magenta that the Duchess of Parma and Duke Francis V of Modena finally decided to leave. The duke's army, a brigade strong, loyally followed him into Venetia and steadfastly refused to desert to the national cause.[6] When Luigi Carlo Farini arrived in Modena to assume power on 19 June he was alarmed by the military situation. Having just left Turin, he was convinced that Piedmontese troops could not be spared. Ignazio Ribotti who had been organising his Cacciatori della Magra first in Massa and Carrara and then in Parma, led his forces into Modena but Farini, realising that they would be unable to repel any serious invasion, secured the support of Ulloa and the Tuscan troops now no longer required in Lombardy.

As the Austrian garrisons moved out of the Romagna in the second week of June, a peaceful transfer of power took place in Bologna and the neighbouring cities. On the outbreak of war the pope had declared his neutrality but had not prevented the departure of patriotic volunteers. Many of these had crossed into Tuscany where they were organised by General Luigi Mezzacapo who, like Ulloa, had been despatched by the Turin government. Other volunteers were raised in the Romagna itself by General Roselli and Colonel Luigi Masi. The papal forces tended to disperse or join the insurrection and, for a time, it looked as if Umbria and the Marches would follow the example of the Romagna but this was prevented by the unexpectedly firm action of the papal commander at Perugia on 20 June.

Despite this temporary setback, the revolutionary gains in central Italy had been spectacular. In the opinion of Napoleon III they had been too spectacular, and provided an additional incentive for him to end hostilities as quickly as possible. The preliminary peace signed at Villafranca had serious implications for the patriots in central Italy. The two Emperors agreed that the Habsburg rulers of Modena and Tuscany should return and that an Italian confederation should be established under the presidency of the pope. Napoleon had wanted to insert a clause excluding the use of force in the restoration of Francis and Leopold, but Franz Josef had refused. He did appear willing, however, to allow the Piedmontese to acquire Parma, the dispossessed ruler there being a Bourbon and not a Habsburg. Victor Emmanuel's philosophical attitude during this tense situation was in marked contrast to the hysteria of Cavour, and in ratifying the Franco-Austrian agreement he was careful to add that he did so *'en tout ce qui me concerne'.*

One immediate result of Villafranca was the resignation of Cavour, and another was the withdrawal of all Piedmontese officials from central Italy. With so much political and diplomatic uncertainty the fate of the whole area hung in the balance, and an additional complication was the confused military situation. Contingents of troops comprising regulars, raw conscripts, and enthusiastic but undisciplined volunteers, lay scattered from Parma to Ancona. It was at this point that two outstanding personalities emerged in Florence and Modena. Basing their authority on popular support, Ricasoli and Farini were determined to prevent the return of the Habsburgs. They had very different personalities and frequently disagreed with one another over the policies to be adopted but they both saw the need, however temporary, for some form of central Italian union. They hoped in this way to stifle any revolutionary or reactionary attempt to fish in troubled waters, and also to prepare the region for its eventual fusion with Piedmont. The maintenance of law and order and the defence of the frontiers could only be effectively carried out by a disciplined body of troops. The task of organising and leading this army was given to General Manfredo Fanti. On 10 August 1859 Modena and Tuscany signed a military convention. Farini and Ricasoli, initially apprehensive about committing themselves to the defence of the Romagna, were won over by Marco Minghetti, who persuaded them to allow the Romagna to adhere to this convention. As Parma decided to invite Farini to rule over them a few days later, the new military league embraced all of central Italy except those areas still under papal control. The nucleus of the army of the league was the Tuscan division under Ulloa, but he had never been happy with this command and decided to resign. The name of his successor stunned the moderates for it was none other than Garibaldi, whose motives in accepting this post were not hard to divine. Minghetti again made a crucial intervention and secured the services of Fanti, convincing the La Marmora-Rattazzi cabinet that he would be indispensable. With Fanti as commander of the league, Garibaldi had to take second place, and organisational work was given priority over the invasion of papal territory.

General Fanti, who arrived in Modena on 29 August, was returning home for the first time since his part in the Menotti Conspiracy in 1831 drove him into exile. After a period in France he soldiered in Spain from 1835 to 1848. Joining the regular Spanish army in 1839, he rose to full colonel in 1847 after serving for a time on the general staff. He had married a Spanish girl and seemed to be making a new life for himself when news came of the 1848 revolutions in Italy. He returned and was appointed a major general by the Lombard government. After Custoza he led the Lombard troops back to the Ticino so that they could become part of the Piedmontese forces, and shortly afterwards he was appointed a major general in the Armata Sarda. The following year he was elected a deputy but this second success story almost had a tragic ending when in March 1849 he became involved with Ramorino. He was not shot but he was placed on the reserve list and tried in October 1849.[7] The La Marmora brothers spoke for him and he was found not guilty, but he had acquired a certain notoriety and this, together with his conspiratorial and Spanish past, took him a long time to live down. The chance to reinstate himself came when La Marmora gave him the command of a brigade in the Crimea. When the Second War of Independence broke out he was given a divisional command and took part in the operations around Magenta. What proved to be his greatest opportunity, however, was his appointment as the commander of the league.

By 1859 Fanti was a staunchly conservative regular officer. His flirtation with revolutionary ideas appears to have been brief,[8] and his experiences in the Spanish civil wars, particularly his dealings with the Carlists, led him to despise partisan warfare. It was scarcely surprising, therefore, that his relationship with Garibaldi was uncomfortably tense. Continually frustrated, Garibaldi solved the problem by throwing up his command in November. Fanti's task of building up a disciplined force, modelled on the Piedmontese army, could now proceed more smoothly. Indeed, it had already become accepted practice to number the various units as if they actually formed part of the Armata Sarda, the Tuscan division, for instance, being called the ninth.[9] In this way the military integration of central and northern Italy can be said to have preceded and paved the way for the political integration which followed.

In a matter of months the army of the league was built up into a force of 50,000 men. Three new divisions were formed and commanded by Roselli, Ribotti and Luigi Mezzacapo. Carlo Mezzacapo acted as Fanti's chief of staff and the renowned Piedmontese Colonel Cavalli took charge of the artillery. The Tuscans, who had been so dissatisfied by Ulloa's methods, were reorganised and revitalised by Raffaele Cadorna who arrived in October. Fanti had asked for other Piedmontese officers but La Marmora was finding it increasingly difficult to provide for the three Lombard divisions in process of formation at this time, and was therefore unable to comply. Fanti was forced to employ veterans of 1848 without enquiring too deeply into their political or professional backgrounds, to indulge in a series of rapid promotions which caused problems later,[10] and to institute a crash six month course for officers at the newly founded academy at Modena.

Whatever the military effectiveness of all this, the presence of this army in central Italy acted as a deterrent to supporters of the dispossessed princes and to those who wished to install Prince Napoleon. Mazzini's efforts in these months were also frustrated and his appeals to Ricasoli, Garibaldi and Ribotti fell on deaf ears. But the fate of the whole area rested primarily with Napoleon III. If the negotiations at Zurich led to a decision to implement the Austrian version of the peace of Villafranca it is doubtful if Fanti's troops could have done much about it. But Napoleon upheld his refusal to sanction violence in the restoration of the princes, and La Guéronnière's *Le Pape et le Congrès,* obviously inspired by the Emperor, indicated that the French were not prepared to assist the pope to recover the Romagna. The fact that there were no serious disturbances in central Italy and that there was apparently an almost unanimous desire for fusion with Piedmont, helped to destroy the credibility of Napoleon's schemes for a confederation, although this had been dutifully included in the Franco-Austrian treaty signed at Zurich on 10 November 1859. Further events in the following January brought the annexation of central Italy perceptibly nearer. Britain pressed hard for acceptance of the principle of non-intervention and the successful conclusion of the Cobden-Chevalier treaty led to a brief period of close Anglo-French collaboration. The Piedmontese had additional cause for satisfaction when they heard that the rigidly conservative Walewski, the Austrophile French Foreign Minister, had been replaced by Thouvenel. In Turin itself, of course, the big event of January 1860 was the return to power of Cavour, despite the hostility of the King and Rattazzi. By 21 January, when Cavour announced his new cabinet, it was clear that the European congress on Italian affairs which had been mooted ever since Villafranca would not in fact take place. The problem of central

Italy would have to be solved some other way, and Cavour was soon convinced that only the cession of Savoy and possibly Nice would overcome Napoleon's reluctance to sanction the Piedmontese annexation of Tuscany and Emilia.

Cavour's intentions were clarified by one of his cabinet appointments. Fanti was made War Minister, but was allowed to retain command of the army of central Italy. He did not have to exercise this dual role for long because on 11 and 12 March plebiscites were held in central Italy which revealed overwhelming support for annexation to Piedmont, and on 25 March, the same day that general elections were held throughout Victor Emmanuel's enlarged kingdom, the army of central Italy was officially integrated with the Armata Sarda. It was declared that the army now consisted of thirteen active divisions grouped in five military commands, *Grandi Comandi Militari,* each of which would constitute a corps in time of war. The command centres were Alessandria, Brescia, Parma, Bologna and Turin.[11] The Garibaldini of the Cacciatori delle Alpi became the Brigata Alpi of the 51st and 52nd regiments in May 1860, a significant reminder of Fanti's determination to convert volunteers into disciplined regulars.

Fanti's tenure of the War Ministry from January 1860 to June 1861 marked the period of transition from the Armata Sarda to the Esercito Italiano. Using the Piedmontese army and its traditions as his model, his first task was the consolidation of the various units. He began the controversial process of forming mixed brigades composed of men from different regions, and of moving divisions around from place to place, all in an attempt to break down regionalism. By constructing a truly unified army it was expected that not only would it be more militarily effective, but that it would assist in the unification of the country. In the decades to come the military defects of this system were frequently pointed out, but its defenders could always be relied upon to flourish their trump card, the role of the army in the sacred cause of *italianità.* In this connection, the observations of the pro-Italian Richard Bagot are interesting. Writing in 1912 on the theme of the social unity of the Italians, he first commented on the obligatory teaching of pure Italian in the schools and then proceeded to discuss conscription:

> It was believed that, among the many other benefits conferred by conscription. . .not the least important would be the fusion of the various sections of the Italian people which might be expected to take place under a system which brought young men of all classes and all regions into close contact with each other during their term

> of military service. For this reason conscripts from the northern provinces were drafted into regiments quartered in the south of the kingdom, and vice versa. Unfortunately, the results of this plan were far less than had been anticipated. The soldiers, in their hours of liberty, almost invariably sought the companionship of those belonging to their own particular town or district; and this spirit of clanship is even still a prominent feature of barrack life.[12]

In 1860, however, it was understandable that Fanti and many others tended to exaggerate the part to be played by the army in the formation of national consciousness.

Because the size of the army had been more than doubled, it became necessary to increase and reorganise the staff in the War Ministry. This was begun in May when the ministry was divided into a general secretariat and three departments, *direzioni generali,* and this process of greater specialisation was continued the following year.[13] The general staff was also enlarged but no serious changes were made. But the fundamental need was to augment the size of the officer corps. The Piedmontese army had fought the last war with just under 2,500 officers, including many veterans hastily recalled for active duty. This had proved barely sufficient for the five divisions in the field and when three Lombard divisions were created the situation became desperate. After the revolutions in central Italy, only a handful of northern officers could be spared, and Fanti's various expedients have already been mentioned. In March 1860, when Fanti announced the formation of the army of 13 divisions, most authorities seem agreed that 68 per cent of the officer corps were Piedmontese, 20 per cent were Emilian and 12 per cent were Tuscan.[14] Numerous Lombards, Venetians and Neapolitan exiles must have been included in one of these categories, but whatever their provenance they were all in short supply. This was one of the reasons why Fanti decided to raise the number of companies per battalion from four to six, and lower the number of battalions per regiment from four to three.[15] This, together with a similar rearrangement in the cavalry, slightly reduced the demand for senior officers. La Marmora, who often spoke as if his own reforms were sacrosanct, challenged Fanti over this issue in March 1861 and although he lost the argument on this occasion his views eventually triumphed under Fanti's successors at the War Ministry.

While the plebiscites were being held in central Italy, Cavour was arranging for the transfer of Nice and Savoy to France. Fanti promptly joined in the chorus of disapproval. He did not stress the unconstitutionality of Cavour's treaty with France of 24 March, nor was he emotionally involved in the question of Nice like Garibaldi. His criticisms concerned the strategic implications of the loss of Savoy. The new frontier, he argued, would be indefensible and would leave Turin open to any French offensive. He alarmed Cavour by threatening resignation.

> If Fanti resigns, the present ministry would not last a single day. Fanti is the soul of the army, the only person capable of amalgamating the Tuscan and Emilian battalions with the old Piedmontese regiments. What is more, Fanti is the only one among the present ministers who is regarded sympathetically by the King.[16]

He remained in the government, however, furious at the way in which the French determined the boundary. As a result of the cession, Fanti also had to discharge 12,000 troops who lived in Nice or Savoy. The 300 officers were given the right to choose whether to remain in the service of the King or become part of the French army. Two hundred chose Italy and most of them did remarkably well.[17] In his memoirs, written in French, General Pelloux explained why he and his brother decided to remain Italian while their father chose to become the subject of France. They had just completed their course at the academy at Turin and were convinced that their career prospects were better in Italy; in addition, wrote Pelloux, 'I wished to continue to serve the House of Savoy'.[18] Although Victor Emmanuel had to surrender the cradle of the dynasty there were still enough Savoyard generals on the Italian side of the Alps to serve as a living reminder of the continuity of history. Owing allegiance to the King rather than to the nation, their continued presence at court and at army headquarters was reassuring for a king who was now called upon to adopt an unfamiliar role and who had also lost his favourite hunting grounds.

Despite the outstanding part he had played in the annexation of Lombardy, Tuscany and Emilia, Cavour became the object of vicious attacks for his surrender of Savoy and Nice. His critics lost no time in reviving the accusation that he was merely the most successful of Napoleon III's prefects. The King, Rattazzi, and Garibaldi seemed intent on removing him from power, and it was in this embattled situation that Cavour learnt that insurrections had broken out in Sicily and that moves were afoot in Piedmont to assist the rebels. If the activists became involved in a Garibaldian expedition to the south, they would at least have to cease their hue and cry over Savoy and Nice.

But if they succeeded in implicating the Turin government, the international repercussions could be disastrous, whether it were successful or not. If, on the other hand, they dissociated themselves from the government and succeeded, they would have seized the initiative, registered a triumph for *volontarismo,* and be well on the way to capturing the Risorgimento.

I

Villafranca had brought Garibaldi's Alpine campaign to a premature halt, his attempts to renew the war after his arrival in central Italy had been frustrated by Fanti, and the new society which he had sponsored, *Nazione Armata,* had been dissolved by a government fearful of a movement which might take too seriously the patriotic rhetoric which accompanied the launching of the Million Rifles Fund. The decision to cede Nice was the last of a long line of grievances, and Garibaldi seems to have decided to concentrate all his energies on this issue. But some of his friends like Crispi, Bertani and Bixio were already urging him to command an expedition to Sicily. Garibaldi was reluctant to commit himself. Reports from Sicily in April were conflicting. Fanti and Cavour had rejected his suggestion that he be allowed to recruit volunteers from among the former Cacciatori who were now part of the regular army.[19] Massimo D'Azeglio as governor of Milan, and the Minister of the Interior Farini, both categorically refused to surrender the hundreds of rifles which had been bought by the Fund. It was still with many misgivings that Garibaldi reluctantly gave up his project to intervene in Nice and accepted the leadership of the Sicilian venture.

Cavour would have been delighted if Garibaldi had refused as he had for a time played with the idea of sending his own expedition under General Ribotti, but the diplomatic difficulties seemed too great. He could not afford to arrest Garibaldi or order the police to raid Bertani's headquarters in Genoa. Particularly infuriating was the knowledge that the King was in constant communication with Garibaldi through the agency of Marquis Trecchi.[20] With his political career at stake, and perhaps the fate of Italy, Cavour was forced to move cautiously.

The same could not be said for Garibaldi after his landing at Marsala on 11 May. With his famous Thousand he rapidly over-ran the island despite the presence there of 25,000 Neapolitan regulars. The first skirmish which took place at Calatafimi four days after the landing proved decisive although only thirty were killed on each side. Using the bayonet, as only forty of the thousand or so rifles proved serviceable,

Garibaldi succeeded in forcing a Neapolitan withdrawal, and as the news spread numerous guerrilla bands began to intensify their attacks on the Bourbon lines of communication. The indecisiveness of the young King Francis II, barely a year on the throne, and the ineptitude of the local commanders led to a rapid deterioration of the Bourbon position throughout the island. Palermo fell, more volunteers and equipment arrived from Genoa, and Sicilians continued to acclaim Garibaldi and accept uncritically his slogan 'Italy and Victor Emmanuel'. Soon all the Neapolitan troops had withdrawn to Messina and the rest of Sicily belonged to Garibaldi. The peasant revolt which had played such a significant part in the conquest of Sicily now became more of a liability than an asset. Garibaldi, whose early decrees had been favourable to the peasants, was disconcerted by the failure of his attempted *levée en masse,* and by increasing signs of actual peasant hostility to his 'army of liberation'. He and his lieutenants came to rely more and more on the propertied classes for the further prosecution of the war, and the Bronte shootings were a grim warning that they regarded any attempts at social revolution as unforgivable sabotage of the national cause.

Cavour and his emissary La Farina proved equally troublesome. Whereas Garibaldi wished to use Sicily as a power base whose resources would enable him to liberate all Italy, Cavour wished to detach it from him as soon as possible, and sent La Farina to try to achieve this. Garibaldi soon sent him packing, however, and secured the services of Depretis.[21] Cavour's obstructionism now took the form of trying to prevent Garibaldi from crossing over to the mainland, and, when this failed, to fomenting a revolution in Naples to forestall him there. Garibaldi's followers, now no longer The Thousand but the Southern Army, crossed the straits in the middle of August. A rapid, triumphal march on the capital then followed, Francis II deciding to leave his capital for Gaeta on 6 September. The next day, far in advance of the main body of troops, Garibaldi entered Naples. His military critics might grumble that all this was magnificent but it was scarcely war, yet it was impossible to withold admiration. Even Cavour paid him a handsome tribute.

> If tomorrow I were to fight against Garibaldi, even though most of the old diplomats might approve, European opinion would be against me, and rightly so. Garibaldi has done Italy the greatest service that a man could do: he has given the Italians self-confidence; he has proved to Europe that Italians can fight and die in battle to reconquer a fatherland.[22]

Beside his exploits, the achievements of the Armata Sarda as the auxiliaries of the French in the campaign in Lombardy paled into insignificance. Those who had advocated the *guerra di popolo* were jubilant at the way in which he had seized the initiative from the regular army, and the democratic groups realised that they now had a chance of wresting control from the moderates.

Cavour then proved that he could move as quickly and decisively as any redshirt. Farini and General Cialdini were sent to Napoleon III to secure his sanction for a military intervention on the part of Piedmont which would involve an invasion of Umbria and the Marches. The argument was that only in this drastic fashion could Garibaldi be prevented from attacking Rome and unleashing war and revolution. Next, Fanti was ordered to prepare an expeditionary force of two corps.

Fanti must have derived some slight satisfaction from the fact that his new army, composed of such disparate elements, had held firm throughout the Garibaldian adventure. Only five regular officers had deserted to join the volunteers,[23] and only one unit, the Ferrara brigade, had broken discipline.[24] He was now being given the opportunity to restore the prestige of the regular army. After his entry into Naples, Garibaldi found that a considerable proportion of the Bourbon army was still intact and occupying various strongholds and the line of the Volturno. The demoralisation which had been so apparent in Sicily and Calabria no longer afflicted the loyal troops who rallied to the defence of their young King and Queen at Gaeta. This stiffening of the resistance gave Fanti's two corps commanders, Cialdini and Della Rocca, sufficient time to cut through papal territory and arrive on Neapolitan soil before the Bourbon army had ceased to be a serious military threat. The regular army took over the operations against Gaeta, Messina and Civitella del Tronto. Garibaldi met Victor Emmanuel at Teano on 26 October and laid his conquests at his feet. He had always intended to do this, but only after he had redeemed the whole of Italy. Cavour and Fanti had outmanoeuvred him before he could reach out for Rome and Venice, but rather than commit his Southern Army to a fratricidal war he submitted to the King and postponed his final military objectives. The Southern Army had lost its leader, and Fanti made no secret of his intention to dissolve it as quickly as possible so that the new Kingdom of Italy would possess one army and not two, and that that army was going to be the disciplined force which he had been constructing around the solid nucleus of the Armata Sarda.

Luigi Mondini has rightly called the treatment of the Southern Army, with its 7,300 officers and over 50,000 men, 'the real *puntum dolens* in the development of the unification of the army'.[25] Garibaldi believed that the troops he had led would become Cacciattori delle Alpi, with a strength of five divisions, and grouped around talented officers like Medici, Bixio, Cosenz and Sirtori, all soldiers whose qualities were admired by most professionals.[26] The King and Farini certainly seemed willing to countenance this, but Fanti was adamantly opposed to such a solution. He had warned Cavour that the regular army would not tolerate any preferential treatment for volunteers, and although Cavour had sharply reminded him that he was no longer in Spain and that in Italy the army would obey its commands, he was assured of his support.[27] Grumbling that Fanti treated the Garibaldini like dogs, the King was unable to resist the combined pressure of Cavour and Fanti.

On 16 November it was decreed that all volunteers could choose to sign on in the royal army for two years or be free to return home with six months' pay in their pocket. Over 30,000 of them chose the latter course. A mixed commission of Garibaldini and regular officers was next appointed to decide the fate of the 7,000 officers. It met once in Naples under the presidency of Della Rocca but in January 1861 it was transferred to Turin. By this time only around 3,000 volunteer officers were still interested and they were given until 15 February to present themselves before the commission. As they were refused any allowances, many of them were unable to travel north and those who did found that their claims were treated unsympathetically and that their documents were rigorously examined. About 2,000 managed to satisfy the commission and, after the disbanding of the volunteer corps in February they were dispersed among various depots in northern Italy together with those troops opting to serve in the royal army. The disillusioned Garibaldi determined to raise the issue of the Southern Army when the first national parliament met at Turin. In order to head him off, Cavour established a skeleton corps on 11 April consisting solely of those volunteer officers who had passed the scrutiny of the commission. This naturally failed to satisfy Garibaldi and in April the chamber of deputies was the scene of bitter exchanges between Garibaldi and the government. It was more than a debate about the type of army which the new kingdom should possess. Acceptance or rejection of the concept of the nation in arms was a trial of strength between the democrats and the moderates, and the winners would determine the political, diplomatic and, to some extent, the social orientation of the new Italy.

What increased the bitterness of Garibaldi and his followers was the startling contrast between the way in which the government treated the defeated Neapolitan officers and the victorious Garibaldini. Cavour and the King had hoped to incorporate as many of the Bourbon troops as possible and their officers were invited to join the royal army with the rank they had held on 7 September 1860.[28] Fanti was prepared to accept many of these regular professionals despite their rather dubious political past, whereas he treated the Garibaldini with cold suspicion. Even before the Bourbon strongholds had fallen in the middle of March 1861, Piedmontese military laws were extended to the former Kingdom of the Two Sicilies. As in Umbria and the Marches, the implementation of these laws again preceded political integration. Conscription was introduced in December 1860 and not even Sicily was immune. On 20 March, conscripts in the south were given two months' leave before performing their military service in the royal army. Most of them, in fact, took this opportunity to disappear, many of them swelling the ranks of the brigand bands which infested this part of Italy.

Cavour, Fanti and the moderates defeated Garibaldi in the chamber and on 4 May the Esercito Italiano was formally constituted. Garibaldi then sought to convert the National Guard into a sort of peoples' *Landwehr,* but the deputies were afraid of putting arms into the hands of urban democrats and the regular officers resented any challenge to their military monopoly. On 24 July 1861 Garibaldi was defeated again when the moderates and the army succeeded in emasculating the National Guard.

Worn out by his strenuous labours of the past two years and particularly by his struggle with Garibaldi, Cavour died on 6 June 1861. Fanti resigned and until his premature death in 1865 played no further significant part in the affairs of the army he had helped to create. The original five Piedmontese divisions of 1859 had become thirteen in 1860 with the incorporation of the Lombards and the forces which Fanti had organised in central Italy. After the conquest of Umbria, the Marches and the Kingdom of the Two Sicilies, the number of divisions was raised to seventeen with one reserve cavalry division. A quarter of a million strong, it was composed of Italians from every region, although for obvious reasons Venetia and Lazio were under-represented. Fanti began attempts to turn the army into a vast melting pot. Recruits would enter as Lombards or Sicilians, or even perhaps Pisans or Palermitans, but would leave the ranks as true Italians. The newly formed Umbrian regiments, for example, were given Palermo as their depot, the Abruzzi regiments had their headquarters in Milan and Bergamo, and the

Calabrian in Brescia and Modena.[29] Recruits were not only sent out of their own localities, they were forced to serve alongside soldiers from different regions. The officer corps was predominantly northern, with Piedmontese and Savoyards still in a majority, particularly in the higher ranks, but Lombards, central Italians and southerners were already becoming well entrenched. After all, Fanti himself was from Modena.

Amongst the various organisational changes, Fanti had improved the efficiency of the War Ministry and increased the size and scope of the general staff, the *Corpo di Stato Maggiore.* La Marmora's work in the 1850s must not be ignored, but Fanti deserves the title of *'fondatore dell'Esercito Italiano'.*[30] The army, like Italy, had been created, but now a period of consolidation was necessary. Unfortunately, the army was given no real respite. It was immediately plunged into a desperate civil war and soon afterwards a war with Austria. The effort required in winning the civil war helps to explain why it lost the war against Austria.

Notes

1. Craig, p.54.
2. Alistair Horne *The price of glory* (London, 1964), p.16.
3. C.A. Macartney, *The Habsburg Empire 1790-1918* (London, 1968), p.491.
4. Stato Maggiore, p.79.
5. L. Mondini, 'L'Unificazione delle forze armate', *Atti del XL Congresso del Risorgimento Italiano* (Rome, 1963), p.320.
6. Ibid., p.315.
7. F. Carandini, *Manfredo Fanti* (Verona, 1872), p.159.
8. In 1834 he was protecting a French colonel from a Lyons mob (ibid., p.38).
9. The Piedmontese divisions were numbered 1 to 5, and the Lombard 6 to 8.
10. F. Bava-Beccaris, *Esercito Italiano* (Rome, 1911), p.40.
11. Ibid., p.40. On 9 June 1861 six military commands were established at Turin, Milan, Parma, Bologna, Florence and Naples. A seventh, Palermo, was added in 1862.
12. R. Bagot, *The Italians of today* (London, 1912). p.33.
13. Bava-Beccaris, pp.41, 49.
14. Ibid., p.40; Pieri, *Le forze armate,* p.45.
15. Ibid., p.48.
16. Cavour to Nigra, 24 April 1861, *Carteggio Cavour-Nigra,* III, 269.
17. A. Anthonioz, *Généraux savoyards* (Geneva, 1912).
18. L. Pelloux, *Quelques souvenirs de ma vie,* ed. G. Manacorda (Rome, 1967), p.48.
19. Candeloro, IV, 435.
20. Candeloro, IV, 438.
21. For a detailed analysis of all this see D. Mack Smith, *Cavour and Garibaldi,* 1860 (Cambs., 1954).
22. Cavour to Nigra, 9 August 1860, *Carteggio Cavour-Nigra,* IV, 144-5.
23. Hibbert, p.198.
24. Bava-Beccaris, p.43.
25. Mondini, p.326.

26. Della Rocca, p.197.
27. Mondini, pp.329-30.
28. Mondini, pp.324-6.
29. Stato Maggiore, p.100.
30. Stato Maggiore, p.98.

Part Two: The Consolidation of the Army

5 IL BRIGANTAGGIO

A series of adroit political and diplomatic moves culminating in the deployment of the royal army had enabled Cavour to regain the initiative for the Turin government and to prevent the democrats from utilising the considerable military resources which Garibaldi had at his disposal after his spectacularly successful invasion of southern Italy. In order to achieve this and to 'close the era of revolutions', he had had to accept that part of the democratic programme which called for a united Italy. In a speech to the senate on 16 October 1860 he attempted to allay the fears of his more cautious followers:

> By resolutely seizing the direction of political events in southern Italy, the King and his government prevented our wonderful Italian movement from degenerating; they prevented the factions which did us so much harm in 1848 from exploiting the emergency conditions in Naples after its conquest by Garibaldi. We intervened not to impose a preconceived political system on southern Italy, but to allow people there to decide freely on their fate. This, gentlemen, was not to be revolutionary but essentially conservative.

He went on to justify the presence of Fanti's troops in Umbria and the Marches.

> Even in these provinces, gentlemen, we have not brought revolution and disorder. We are there to establish good government, legality and morality. Whatever people may say, I proclaim with certainty – and this will be confirmed by the impartial voice of enlightened, liberal Europe – that no war has ever been fought with greater generosity, magnanimity or justice.[1]

But even as he spoke, 'magnanimity' was on the decline and a new, more terrible war was just beginning. The papal army had been dispersed, the Bourbon army was soon to capitulate, and Garibaldi's Southern Army was about to be dissolved, when a new enemy arose to challenge the military verdict of 1860. Guerrilla bands, some claiming allegiance to Francis II and Pius IX, began to harrass lines of communication and make nonsense of Cavour's claim that he had established 'good government, legality and morality'.

The first military assignment of the newly constituted Italian army was the suppression of brigandage in southern Italy. *Il Brigantaggio* was the official and pejorative term used by the Turin government to describe a phenomenon which soon bore an ominous resemblance to civil war. The collapse of the Bourbon regime and the brief Garibaldian interregnum increased the opportunities for lawlessness which had been endemic in most provinces for decades if not for centuries. It was land hunger which drove the majority of peasants into acts of rebellion. To secure their active support against the Bourbons both Garibaldi and the southern liberals made promises to partition the land, abolish the *macinato* and lower the price of bread and salt. But the peasantry had already begun to make indiscriminate attacks on property, the recently acquired land of many of the urban liberals being one of their primary objectives. Growing fears of a social revolution which would hamper the war effort and endanger existing property relationships led to such incidents as the Bronte shootings when the Garibaldini turned their weapons against the *cafoni.* On the mainland, as in Sicily, those liberals who regarded the redshirts as an insufficient safeguard against peasant depredations began to long for the arrival of Piedmontese regiments. Many autonomists and even radicals clamoured for unconditional annexation to Piedmont, and, indeed, in some areas like Isernia, the swift arrival of Cialdini's northern troops was a matter of life or death.[2]

From his stronghold in Gaeta, Francis II called upon his people to attack the liberals and to resist the invaders of his territory. When Gaeta fell in February 1861, Francis fled to Rome and continued his appeals from there, even after the last Bourbon stronghold had capitulated. This considerably complicated the issue. Living in the Quirinal as the honoured guest of the pope, Francis set up a central committee to direct the guerrilla warfare in the south. Pius IX had long deplored the anti-clerical legislation of Piedmont, and in 1859-60 the Romagna, Umbria and the Marches had been seized by this infidel power. Finally, with the fall of Naples and Gaeta, the entire peninsula fell prey to the *Risorgimento scomunicato,* except in Venetia and Lazio where Austrian and French bayonets kept it at bay. It was scarcely surprising that the Vatican was prepared to assist Francis and his adherents. Resistance to the Piedmontese aggressor was a holy duty. Clergy and Catholic laity, shocked by the brusque implementation of anti-clerical laws, were prepared to make life as uncomfortable as possible for the soldiers and administrators of Victor Emmanuel. But Francis II's flight to Rome did more than give a religious aspect to the war in the south. The 'Southern

Question', as it was soon to be called, became inextricably bound up with the Roman Question.

The French troops, who had garrisoned Rome since 1849, protected what was left of the temporal power. Cavour had sent the army south to prevent any clash between them and Garibaldi. But after February 1861 these troops not only protected the pope but also Francis and his followers. Armed bands were able to elude the Italian army and cross into pontifical territory to recuperate and to rearm themselves. In March, Cavour publicly proclaimed that Rome must one day become the capital of Italy, and secretly prepared the ground for this by initiating a series of complicated negotiations with both Rome and Paris. The official severance of diplomatic relations between Paris and Turin in September 1860 over the Piedmontese invasion of Umbria had not alarmed Cavour. He regarded this and the reinforcement of the French garrison at Rome as merely a tactical move on the part of Napoleon to placate Catholic opinion at home and abroad. With the proclamation of the Kingdom of Italy in March 1861, Cavour waited impatiently for French recognition, hoping that when it came there would be a Roman settlement associated with it. A swift solution to this problem seemed imperative when Cavour learnt of the gravity of the situation in southern Italy. Rome had become the headquarters of the Bourbon reactionaries and the brigand movement. As long as the pope continued to champion the rebel cause behind a screen of French bayonets, the Italian government would be unable to restore order in the southern provinces. Any prolongation of this anarchy would threaten the stability of the new kingdom and play into the hands of the activists, and failure to produce an agreement over Rome would enable Garibaldi to rally his supporters and unleash a radical revolution. Napoleon's response was that he felt disinclined either to recognise the new kingdom or to negotiate over Rome until the Italian government had proved its ability to maintain order within its new frontiers.[3] This argument proved a godsend to all those governments who hesitated to follow the British lead and accord full recognition to the new kingdom.[4] Cavour's premature death in June had the effect of separating the question of French recognition from the Roman issue. Afraid that Italy might now fall apart, Napoleon was willing to extend recognition but not to withdraw from Rome.

When Ricasoli succeeded Cavour as premier he found that the Roman question and the southern question had become almost inextricably interlocked and that the civil war gave credence to all those who prophesied that the new regime would speedily collapse. Even Massimo

D'Azeglio had doubts about the feasibility of forcing the southerners into an unnatural union.[5] The very structure of the new state as well as its international standing seemed to depend upon the restoration of law and order in the south.

Disbanding Garibaldi's Southern Army had prevented dualism, but it had also deprived the government of a garrison force which might have been able to prevent the rapid spread of brigandage in the critical period of the spring and summer of 1861. The government and military were, however, anxious to employ officers and NCOs from the Bourbon army. A mixed commission under the ex-Bourbon General de Sauget examined 3,600 cases in two months, and by February 1861, 2,191 officers had been admitted to the royal army, although many of them preferred to retire.[6] This generous treatment of officers and NCOs helps to explain why so few of them joined the brigands. The rank and file, described by La Marmora as *'canaglia'* were unceremoniously disbanded and many of these helped to swell the number of brigand bands.[7] The introduction of conscription, Piedmontese style, also led to a widespread exodus to the hills.

After the brief dictatorship of Garibaldi, the Turin government established a *Luogotenenza Generale* to administer the Neapolitan provinces. The civilians sent down from the north were appalled by the task confronting them. Hoping he would repeat his successes in Emilia, Cavour appointed Farini to supervise their activities, but he proved to be the first of a long line of officials to tarnish his reputation by failing to solve the problems of the south. Farini was suspicious of the Garibaldini and southern liberals, and of the National Guard which they appeared to dominate, so he turned to the officials of the old régime. They were delighted by this turn of events and were very willing to pay lip service to their new masters in Turin, but they were most unwilling to take energetic measures against Bourbon sympathisers. This was another reason why brigandage was able to assume such formidable proportions in so short a time. In the parliamentary inquest of 1863, General Arnulfi estimated that two thirds of all the mayors in the southern provinces were 'Bourbons'.[8]

With such unreliable allies, it was easy to see why the civilian administrators despatched by Turin came to rely more and more on the support of the regular army, despite any initial misgivings they may have had. It was reported that on his death-bed Cavour had muttered that anyone could govern by martial law but that he would govern them with liberty,[9] but, in common with so many frustrated northerners and Piedmontese generals, he had sometimes referred to the south as 'the weakest and most corrupt part of Italy', and instructions had been sent from Turin that 'some rough military treatment would be a salutary medicine'.[10] The generals scarcely needed this advice. Instead of being treated as liberators when they marched into Neapolitan territory, the peasantry saw them as alien conquerors, and the church, so often the bulwark of law and order, regarded them as atheists in the service of an excommunicated King. Commanders who were accustomed to the uniformed carnage of the Crimea or the Lombard plain, were bewildered and outraged by guerrilla warfare in which they were soon involved. For General Cialdini, moving in from the Marches with his IV Corps, this was no novel experience. Like Fanti, he had fought in the Spanish civil wars, and he had acquired a fanatical hatred of partisan movements. On 21 October 1860 he informed the governor of Molise that he had begun shooting all peasants carrying weapons,[11] and yet outside the walls of Gaeta he chivalrously ordered his men to cease firing when the young Queen of Naples appeared on the battlements. Neapolitans in uniform and under the command of regular officers, were usually treated with respect, particularly after they had been captured or shot, whereas 'brigands' were regarded as beasts to be hunted down and then exhibited as trophies of the chase.[12] In November 1860 General Pinelli posted notices on the walls of Avezzano threatening to shoot all those found with weapons, and all who aided insurgents or spoke disrespectfully of King Victor Emmanuel.[13] Fanti sanctioned the formation of extraordinary military tribunals on 23 October, and in view of the arbitrary shootings which soon took place, this could perhaps be regarded as a liberal measure. The politicians in Turin winced, but most of them soon pretended that it was not really happening and that all atrocity stories were fabricated by Bourbon sympathisers. *'Fusillez mais point de tapage'*, was the advice received by Ricasoli from Vimercati, the King's agent in Paris.[14] It was advice which Ricasoli, and his successors Farini and Minghetti, often felt constrained to accept. This helped to create a strange double standard in Italian political life and perpetuated the differences between the north and the south.

For a time, the war in the south appeared to be a dynastic struggle, a desperate attempt by the exiled Francis to regain his throne. In an interview with Odo Russell, Britain's unofficial observer in Rome, Francis admitted that most of his supporters were led by brigands, but he remained convinced that 'in course of time his adherents would organise a guerrilla war in the mountains which, if only supported by 8,000 men, would be sufficient to render the establishment of the

Piedmontese terrorism impossible', and lead to his restoration.[15] Foreign mercenaries, willing to fight for the legitimist cause, presented themselves at Rome, and were sent across the frontier to contact brigand leaders like Chiavone and Crocco. Borjes, an idealistic Catalan, joined up with Crocco but he was captured by Bersaglieri and shot in December 1861. Another Catalan, Tristany, was instructed to assume control of the rebel movement, and, having failed to secure the co-operation of Chiavone, he succeeded in capturing him and executing him for disloyalty. De Cathelinau, De Trazéquies, Karl Mayer and many others enlisted under the Bourbon banner. They were all totally disillusioned by their reception, by the suspicious and calculating response of brigand chiefs who jealously guarded their independence, and by the type of warfare they were forced to conduct. Those who were not killed or captured by the security forces, soon decided to leave, especially after the Italian army began to improve its anti-guerrilla methods. General Pallavicini, who captured one of Crocco's friends, Caruso, agreed to release him on condition he scouted for the army and taught them guerrilla tactics.[16] Another factor hastening the departure of legitimist mercenaries was the replacement of General Goyon, the commander of the French garrison at Rome. Goyon had done little to prevent the rebels from using papal territory as a haven, but his successor, Mirabello, began to concert with the Italian forces in a drive against brigandage.[17]

Gradually the Bourbon network which had been set up by the central committee in Rome began to disintegrate. The agents of the gullible Francis fleeced him unmercifully so that the financial situation of the exiled court deteriorated, and the Italian government succeeded in unmasking several leading conspirators, including Cardinal-Archbishop Sforza of Naples, who was forced to flee in July 1861.[18] More and more the struggle in the south took on the appearance of a social war. 'Bread and work' was the commonest slogan among the dissident southerners, their main demands being the redistribution of land and lower taxes. Bourbon landowners, who had supported the rebel bands in the early stages of the war, now felt threatened by these demands and relied on the Italian troops for the protection of their property.

Growing evidence of the social and economic nature of peasant unrest made no perceptible difference to the conduct of the war. In July 1861 the appointment of General Cialdini as military commander in Naples and, a little later, as Luogotenente, concentrated formidable military and civilian powers in his hands. It was a clear indication that the Ricasoli government sought to resolve the southern crisis as swiftly as possible, even if this meant giving the military a considerable amount of latitude. This decision coincided with the visit of General Fleury to Turin, bearing Napoleon III's congratulations to Victor Emmanuel as King of Italy. He brought a letter with him in which the Emperor explained that circumstances compelled him to retain his troops in Rome to ensure that the remaining papal territories were not invaded by 'regular or irregular forces'. He concluded by cautioning the King against any excessive haste in building up his kingdom, adding that 'political transformations are the work of time, that complete unity cannot be lasting unless it has been long prepared by the assimilation of interests, ideas, and customs; in a word, I think that *unity* ought to follow and not precede *union*'.[19] This was disturbing enough, but worse was to follow when on 21 July the Emperor sent an open telegram to Fleury in which he bitterly criticised the conduct of Italian troops in the south.[20] Ricasoli responded by accusing the French of condoning brigand depredations by the support given to them by the Emperor's garrison in Rome. Ricasoli's argument that the restoration of order in the south was dependent upon solving the Roman question led to a vicious circle of accusations and counter-accusations which came near to disrupting relations between the two countries. The Emperor's assumption, shared by so many other rulers, that the Italians had bitten off more than they could chew, stimulated them to greater efforts. It was clear that international opinion would withold recognition of Italy's great power status until she was victorious in the south.

Cialdini declared that with only 20,000 men under his command he could not guarantee victory. By the end of August this had been increased to 40,000, and by the end of the year there were over 50,000, excluding the forces in Sicily, but still victory eluded the Italian forces. The Luogotenenza was dismantled in October 1861, La Marmora was substituted for Cialdini, new techniques were developed – a combination of base camps and flying columns – but still the war dragged on. The young Italian army began to feel the strain. Lieutenant Negri's complaint that in order to fight this war of intrigue and treachery it was necessary to cease being a soldier and to become a police agent instead, became a widely held belief.[21] Politicians, particularly those in opposition, began to discover the 'Southern Question'. Giuseppe Ferrari, who had just returned from a visit to the ruins of Pontelandolfo, destroyed by the army as a reprisal for the killing of fifty Bersaglieri, gave a moving account of the escalating horror of the war in a speech to the chamber on 2 December 1861. One reason why Ricasoli had removed Cialdini had been the mounting criticisms of his brusque behaviour, and a steady stream of complaints about the military usurping civilian functions, thus making nonsense of the liberties guaranteed by the Statuto. The National Guard, which could have taken over many of the duties of the army, was regarded with suspicion by Turin, was sadly lacking in equipment, and was composed largely of men whose political allegiance and military expertise were highly suspect.[22]

The generals had sufficient problems without having to face a barrage of criticism from humanitarian politicians or armchair strategists. They had no topographical maps of the area, for instance, and it was only in February 1862 that the war ministry began to remedy this, but it was estimated that it would cost 2 million lire and would take approximately eight years, as only 12,000 out of the 92,000 square miles had ever been adequately surveyed.[23] The heavy equipment of the troops – carrying over 60 lb plus weapons – was unsuitable for partisan warfare, and their long lines of communication and widely scattered detachments were vulnerable to sudden attacks by large brigand bands. As coffee and rum was the sovereign remedy for malaria, and sanitary regulations were lax, disease began to take a heavy toll. No newspapers were allowed and no correspondence, so few people in the north realised that companies were reduced to half their strength in a matter of weeks after arrival, that equipment deteriorated rapidly in the scattered garrisons, and that at least six pairs of boots per man were needed for a two month period. Above all, Fanti's successors at the War Ministry, Della Rovere and Petitti, imposed their rigid and limited strategic and tactical views on commanders who seemed only too willing to observe them. There were some, like General Cadorna, who realised that traditional methods were useless, that night attacks and an effective intelligence system would begin to produce results, but they were largely ignored and unorthodox officers were posted elsewhere before they had time to perfect their techniques. Cadorna also preached the unpopular doctrine that in a war of this type, the regulars needed a superiority of ten to one. In 1862-3 the Italian army pitted around 100,000 men against an estimated force of 25,000 guerrillas, a superiority of only four to one, but even so it absorbed over two fifths of the entire army. In a farewell address to his troops in July 1862, Cadorna stressed the need to maintain an *esprit de corps* despite the fact they all came from different regions. In that way, he added, the army would become *'il vero simbolo della concordia'*.[24] He did well to stress this aspect, because there were fears that the civil war was producing discord not concord, that young conscripts, inadequately trained, were being thrown into the struggle, and that this disillusioning experience was converting them into hostile critics of united Italy. Azeglio's warning that it was unwise to force the unification of the peninsula at the point of a gun was still remembered. It was, ironically, the situation in the south which convinced the Turin government that any schemes for the decentralisation of power, along the lines of Minghetti's *regioni,* would play into the hands of disruptive elements.[25]

In the course of 1862 it became apparent that the government would sooner or later have to admit that the southern question was something more than mere brigandage which could be contained by the deployment of a few regiments. The government, for obvious reasons, preferred to keep silent over the disturbances in the south, hoping that Cialdini or La Marmora, or someone would find a way of ending the war quickly. But in that year, Garibaldi's 'Rome or death' expedition which led to the tragi-comedy of Aspromonte focused attention on the south so effectively that the government's conspiracy of silence could no longer be maintained.

Garibaldi's campaign emphasised that the southern question and the Roman question were still largely inseparable. It also indicated that Fanti's triumph over the volunteers in 1860-1 was not to pass unchallenged. Garibaldi's appeal, and the equivocal attitude of the King and Rattazzi's government, were a real threat to the discipline and morale of the army, especially among units in the south, but it seems that desertions were few. Only seven volunteers apparently were executed as deserters after Aspromonte,[26] and Pallavicini's regulars had not hesitated to fire on the redshirts. Nevertheless, the whole episode was soon regarded as something of a national humiliation, a civil war within a civil war.

La Marmora, still in charge of the suppression of brigandage used Garibaldi's expedition as a pretext for putting into effect something which the politicians had strenuously opposed for a long time, the proclamation of a state of siege giving the military authoritarian powers throughout the south. The tensions of August 1862 gave the Rattazzi government little alternative, and La Marmora made sure that the state of siege was prolonged after the Garibaldian crisis was ended.[27] It was only on 16 November that Rattazzi finally insisted that it be lifted as parliament was about to reassemble. Rattazzi, at this time, spread rumours of a *'partito militare'* led by La Marmora and Cialdini – a rather unlikely combination – and made sure that this story appeared in the columns of the influential *Opinione.* But this must be seen as one of a series of manoeuvres executed by Rattazzi who was fighting hard to extricate himself from a very difficult political situation. La Marmora's insistence on prolonging the state of siege had certainly weakened Rattazzi's government and his refusal to enter the ministry and share political responsibility created still more bitterness between the two men. Rattazzi was well aware that if there was a 'military party' worthy of the name its headquarters lay not in the command posts of La Marmora and Cialdini but in the royal palace. Cavour's death had encouraged the King to pursue his own policies, even if they conflicted with the official governmental programme. Victor Emmanuel believed that the Venetian question should have priority, and with the help of military courtiers and other 'King's friends' he made contact with activists who were willing to stir up trouble in the Habsburg Empire. In the early summer of 1862 the King, with the connivance of Rattazzi, had hoped that Garibaldi would land somewhere in the Balkans.[28] Instead he had landed in Sicily and then had tried to take Rome; Rattazzi could scarcely divulge all this in order to silence his critics, so he spread rumours of a different sort of conspiracy, and when this failed, he agreed to submit the southern question to a parliamentary commission. After a long debate which had begun on 20 November, Rattazzi presented the so-called 'La Marmora Report' as a basis for discussion.[29] The commissioners appointed to examine it felt that the report was not sufficiently comprehensive and called for a full parliamentary enquiry. In a secret session on 16 December, a commission of enquiry was established, by which time Rattazzi had already resigned and the Farini-Minghetti ministry was in power.

The nine members of the commission, which included three from the right and three from the left, one follower of Rattazzi and two Garibaldian generals, Bixio and Sirtori, toured regions in the south in the first months of 1863. In March and May some of their findings were read out and in August a selected amount of information was published. But the rightist majority in the chamber succeeded in preventing most of the report from being made public. The government was anxious not to stress criticisms of the army or the government and sought to avoid any general discussion of economic problems, and so it laid the emphasis on Bourbon and clerical conspirators. So effective was their interpretation that it became the basis for the *Legge Pica,* which enabled the government to suppress southern brigandage without being unduly restricted by the constitutional guarantees of the Statuto.

The Legge Pica, which was in force from August 1863 until 31

December 1865, permitted the establishment of military tribunals in those provinces which were declared by royal decree to be *'in stato di brigantaggio'*. Military tribunals, appointed by generals commanding the various war zones, consisted of a colonel or lieutenant colonel as president, five judges (two superior officers and three captains), and four clerks. *Giunte provinciali* composed of the prefect, the president of the tribunal, the royal procurator and two provincial councillors, dealt with vagabonds, *camorristi* and all those suspected to be in contact with the brigands, and had powers to confine them all to house arrest. In addition, local volunteer forces were to be raised so that they could assist in the anti-guerrilla warfare. A few days after the Legge Pica became law, practically the whole of the south was declared to be in 'a state of brigandage'. Military tribunals, which already existed for purely military offences, were given additional powers, and the War Minister Della Rovere established eight more, making twelve in all.[30]

Giving soldiers the right to shoot all brigands caught bearing arms and to bring in to the provincial councils all suspects, was to place excessive power in the hands of the military and to suspend individual liberties for a large proportion of the Italian people. It caused embarrassment to members of the right who had objected to La Marmora's prolongation of the state of siege, and it alarmed the democrats who saw that this could become a precedent. *'Gegen Demokraten helfen nur Soldaten'*. The turmoil in the south, however, had become such an embarrassment, and the moderates manipulated the findings of the commission of enquiry with such unscrupulous skill, that the Legge Pica acquired parliamentary consent *'a tamburo battente'*.

La Marmora now felt able to assume the offensive against the brigands. The army, now adapting itself to guerrilla warfare, carabinieri and volunteer forces, began a series of drives. General Pallavicini, who had captured Garibaldi at Aspromonte, was particularly successful in breaking up the larger brigand formations, and by 1865 the war was virtually won, although smaller bands of genuine criminals were never completely eliminated. The military tribunals, dispensing summary justice, do not appear to have been as harsh as some critics have suggested.[31] But, inevitably, many injustices were committed, and the new Kingdom of Italy became for many peasants synonymous with martial law. In 1863 2,901 cafoni[32] were summoned before the courts and 261 were condemned to death or long prison terms; in 1864 there were 4,523 with 822 condemned, and in 1865 3,242 and 1,035 condemned. There are no accepted figures for the number of brigands and regulars killed in action, but for the period from 1861-5 Molfese estimates that well over 5,000 brigands were killed. Jaco puts the number of brigands killed in Basilicata alone between 1861 and 1863 at 3,000, so his total for the entire south over a longer period would be considerably higher.[33] The troops killed seem to have been around 400, but in 1863-4 at least 1,000 died, mainly from typhus and malaria. Casualties among the civilian population as the result of reprisals and counter-reprisals cannot even be approximately estimated, but it is certain that the loss of life in this long, brutal civil war was many times greater than the overall total of casualties for all of the wars of the Risorgimento put together.

It was ironical that a commission of enquiry whose frame of reference included an examination of socio-economic problems should have resulted in the establishment of a state of siege over a vast area of southern Italy. Several of the generals engaged in the war admitted that economic problems were the fundamental cause of discontent. Stressing socio-economic factors, General Govone believed that the existing *political* crisis was only *'la causa determinante occasionale'*, a view which was shared by his chief of staff Captain di Saint Jorioz.[34] Bixio, the Garibaldian general, declared that 'in the south all those that have a cloak want to kill those without one', and Enea Pasolini, the soldier son of the well-known politician, wrote: '. . .it is a real civil war of the poor against the rich'.[35] Major Pieri described the brigands as 'those with nothing to lose'.[36] But although they may have been aware of the problem, the majority of officers had the kind of class background which precluded any radical solution to the economic problems of the south. La Marmora also succeeded in maintaining the cohesion of the officer corps, emphasising that their role was the preservation of order and the destruction of brigands. When General Sirtori, who had been chief of staff to Garibaldi and commander of the Southern Army for a brief period, arrived at his headquarters with other members of the parliamentary commission, La Marmora persuaded him that any exposure of military misdeeds would be disastrous for the army and for the cause of unity.

Because the Legge Pica would cease to be valid on 31 December 1863, many deputies who disliked its implications could console themselves with the thought that it was only a temporary measure, and that parliament had the right to refuse to extend it. At the end of the year, however, it was extended to the following February and then a similar law was sanctioned allowing the military regime in the south to continue until the end of April. This, in turn, was prolonged until the end of 1865 when La Marmora, who was Prime Minister at the time, allowed it to expire. This method of renewing the extraordinary legislation every few months made it difficult for opponents to accuse the government of flagrantly unconstitutional behaviour, but it was also an interesting indication that parliament was not prepared to surrender its powers for an unlimited period. Evidence of clashes between the civilians and the military began to accumulate over the months. Prefects in the south complained that their functions were being usurped. When, however, they appealed to sympathetic ministers like Peruzzi, a threat of resignation on the part of La Marmora was sufficient to prevent the government from taking any action.[37] The government could not, however, prevent a big parliamentary debate on this issue between 4 and 12 January 1864. The whole question of the constitutionality of the repressive laws and their effectiveness in combating brigandage was discussed, and Crispi accused the ministers of illegally extending them to Sicily. The government held firm and enough supporters were found to sanction the continuation of the military tribunals.

Unlike the left-wing deputies, most right-wing members were not unduly alarmed by the threat of unconstitutional behaviour by the army leaders. The military élite, with few exceptions, had the same social background as the political élite. Carlo Cadorna, for instance, entered politics and became a minister, while his brother Raffaele entered the army and became a general. Yet their roles were interchangeable; Carlo discussed armistice terms with the Austrians after Novara, and Raffaele was elected to parliament in 1849 where he remained until he entered the senate in 1872. Although La Marmora's reforms, and the increasing pace of technological change, tended to encourage the professionalisation of the officer corps, it was a slow process; and although increased specialisation made it more difficult for civilians to be given high commands without having undergone extensive training, there was nothing to stop soldiers from entering politics or administration. Around 40 officers sat among the deputies in 1861, and throughout the remainder of the century there was a substantial group of them in both houses.[38] It was only in 1907 that the first civilian was appointed War Minister, so they always had a representative in the cabinet, and usually more than one.[39] The number of officers in politics who were on the active list certainly declined, but retired generals and colonels could always be relied upon to continue the tradition of what has been called 'the civilian-military state'.

There is no evidence to suggest that the military ever sought to take advantage of the deplorable situation in the south to effect a putsch or even to apply great pressure on the civilian government. They really had no need to try. They were of the ruling élite and so they could work within the system. Italy became neither a 'praetorian state' nor a 'nation in arms' as long as the right-wing and their liberal descendants maintained the middle course set by Cavour. The young Kingdom of Italy with its new army survived the testing period of the civil war in the south without collapsing and without abandoning the Statuto. But in order to survive it had been necessary to suspend constitutional liberties for a time, to overburden the economy, and to make great demands on the army.

Notes

1. Quoted in Mack Smith, pp.326-7.
2. F. Molfese, *Storia del brigantaggio dopo l'unità* (Milan, 1964), p.14.
3. J.R. Whittam, *Ricasoli as prime minister* (University of Reading, 1971), pp.12-13.
4. The Prussian government, for instance, used this argument to justify its indecision (Loftus to Russell, 13 July 1861, FO 64/512).
5. Azeglio to Matteucci, 5 August 1861, *DDI*, series I,I, p.322, f.1.
6. Molfese, p.33.
7. Ibid., pp.34-5, f.65.
8. Ibid., p.39, f.78.
9. C. Seton-Watson, *Italy from liberalism to Fascism 1870-1925* (London, 1967), p.14.
10. Mack Smith, *Italy*, p.70.
11. Molfese, pp.64-5.
12. See, for example, the photographs in A. de Jaco, *Il Brigantaggio Meridionale* (Rome, 1969), where soldiers pose beside their 'catch'.
13. Ibid., pp.24-5.
14. Molfese, pp.65-6. In January, Della Rocca had written to Cavour informing him that he was discouraging the taking of prisoners (ibid., p.66).
15. Odo Russell to Russell, 10 April 1862, FO 43/86A.
16. Jaco, p.33.
17. Battaglini, *Il Crollo militare del Regno delle Due Sicilie*, vol. II (Modena, 1938), p.131.
18. Ibid., II, 130.
19. 12 July 1861, *DDI*, I,I, p.243.
20. Ibid., I,I, p.269, f.1.
21. Jaco, p.26.
22. *Archivio Centrale dello Stato*, Ispettorato della Guardia Nazionale, busta No.2, 308.
23. Molfese, p.215.
24. L. Cadorna, *Il Generale Raffaele Cadorna del Risorgimento Italiano* (Milan, 1922), pp.204-9.
25. Passerin d'Entrèves, 'La politica nazionale nel giugno-settembre 1861', *Archivo Storico Italiano* (1955), pp.215-30.

26. Petitti, forced to hold an enquiry, issued a circular urging all officers to stick together, a move which roused parliamentary criticisms in both houses. R. Mori, *La Questione Romana* (Florence, 1963), pp.389-90.
27. Molfese, p.201.
28. Mori, p.128.
29. The report was, in fact, composed in Turin on the basis of information received from La Marmora.
30. Candeloro, V, pp.200-203; Molfese, pp.342-8.
31. *Archivio Centrale dello Stato,* Tribunali militari di guerra per il brigantaggio, busta 1 fasc.15, busta 54 fasc.17. Even so, the record makes sad reading. At the end of the depositions there appear the struggling signatures of the condemned or, as frequently, their marks. Whether they understood what it was all about seems doubtful.
32. Peasants head the list of those condemned. In 1864, the list reads peasants 564, operai 86, negoziati 39, possidenti 33, National Guard 17. In 1865 there were 717 peasants as against 235 from all other categories (Molfese, pp.348-9).
33. Jaco, p.26.
34. A. di Saint Jorioz, *Il brigantaggio alla frontiera pontificia dal 1860 al 1864* (Milan, 1864), quoted Molfese, p.133.
35. Jaco, p.45.
36. Molfese p.133.
37. Ibid., p.361.
38. Ibid., p.232.
39. Stato Maggiore, p.288.

6 VENICE AND ROME

The deployment of over 100,000 troops in southern Italy was a constant drain on the military and financial resources of the state. Burdened with debts, it was nevertheless impossible for the Italian government to avoid spending millions if it hoped to make the unification of the peninsula a reality. The role of the army in this process was fully appreciated, yet if necessary public works were to be financed, the military budget which accounted for almost 40 per cent of the total expenditure in 1862, would have to be reduced. In the following three years, the cost of the armed forces fell to 34 per cent, then to 31 per cent and, in 1865, it was down to 23 per cent.[1] This was dictated by the economic situation, not by any relaxation in international tensions or increased internal stability. Aware of the need for financial stringency, the army leaders were nevertheless alarmed by this situation. It gave the government an additional incentive to press forward with schemes to solve the Roman question, acquire Venetia and end the war in the south. For political reasons as well, it was vital for the Destra to resolve one or preferably all of these outstanding issues, because the Garibaldian activists and the democrats constantly threatened to seize the initiative by a march on Rome or Venice, often with the tacit support of the King. The government, and probably the state, would be unable to survive a series of Aspromontes.

The Franco-Italian September Convention of 1864 was a partial solution of both the Roman and the Southern question. The French agreed to withdraw all their troops from Rome within two years provided the Italian government agreed to respect the inviolability of Rome and Lazio. As proof of good faith, the capital of Italy was to be transferred from Turin to another Italian city other than Rome. Prime Minister Minghetti, himself from the Romagna, knew that although this move would be welcomed by all those who advocated *'la spiemontesizzazione dell'Italia'*, it would meet with opposition from the King and the Piedmontese. It was for this reason that he hoped to bring La Marmora into his ministry. La Marmora refused to take office, but he agreed to go on a diplomatic mission to Paris. La Marmora was not against the transfer of the capital but he was aghast at the stipulation that the Italian army should prevent any invasion of papal territory. He tried to convince the Emperor that this could only be fulfilled if the frontiers were redrawn, but the argument was rejected. Victor Emmanuel, very unhappy at the prospect of leaving Turin, then sent General Menabrea to Paris, urging him to emphasise that Turin and Piedmont was *'le berceau de la Monarchie, le foyer naturel des idées d'ordre'*, and that it would cause trouble in the army because 'all the superior officers came from the old provinces'.[2] His mission too was unsuccessful, and on 15 September the convention was signed in Paris.

Although the clause dealing with Turin was supposed to be secret, news of it leaked out, leading to serious rioting in the capital where 30 demonstrators were killed and over 100 injured on 21-2 September. Disgusted by the government's handling of the situation, the King called on Minghetti to resign and appointed La Marmora as premier on 28 September. It is interesting that both supporters and opponents of the transfer used military arguments. Men like Sclopis, president of the senate, argued that if Florence became the new capital, it would be open to attack from a landing at Leghorn. Supporters pointed out that Turin was too close to the frontiers to be defensible. A commission of war set up on 18 September, including Cialdini, Durando, Della Rocca, De Sonnaz and Admiral Persano, decided in favour of Florence for strategic reasons. All except Cialdini were Piedmontese.[3]

La Marmora, who had suppressed the Genoese rising in 1849 and had been fighting a bitter guerrilla war in the south, was called upon to perform yet another unpleasant duty. Acting as his own foreign minister, with Petitti at the War Ministry, Lanza at the Ministry of the Interior and Sella in charge of finances, La Marmora restored calm in the capital and steered the convention through both houses. He had to preside over further reductions in the military budget and answer criticisms that the September Convention had barred the way to Rome, while supervising the arrangements for the mammoth task of transferring the government to Florence. He and his colleagues handled all these problems firmly and competently.

The September Convention and then, on 8 December, Pius IX's Quanta Cura and Syllabus of Errors, had concentrated attention on Rome. It was, however, the Venetian question which soon came to absorb more and more of La Marmora's attention. The speeches and polemics during the October elections of 1865 reflected the major preoccupations of the Italians. Venice was still a peripheral issue. Sella's gloomy financial statements, the failure of Vegezzi's attempt to secure an agreement with the pope, and the implications of the codifying legislation passed by the last parliament, were obviously the dominant themes. In the midst of a growing political and economic crisis, when the chamber and public opinion seemed absorbed in domestic problems, the Venetian question began to attract a certain amount of attention, and rumours of a possible Italo-Prussian accord began to circulate.

There was nothing new in this concept. Cavour had often spoken of the desirability of joint action with Prussia, and had commented on the similarity of their aims. 'We march at the head of the great national party of Italy', he had written to his envoy in Berlin, 'just as the Prussian government is placed at the head of German nationalism.'[4] Bismarck, who was then the Prussian ambassador at St Petersburg, wrote that he was convinced 'that the creation of a strong Italian state in the south between France and Austria is beneficial to Prussia'.[5] Unfortunately for Cavour's plans, Berlin remained unresponsive, as La Marmora found out when he went on a courtesy visit in January 1861.[6] It was only a year after Cavour's death that Prussia finally decided to recognise the Kingdom of Italy, and it was in the autumn of that same year, 1862, that Bismarck became minister-president of Prussia. Unlike his predecessors, Bismarck refused to allow legitimist scruples to thwart any form of co-operation with the usurper King Victor Emmanuel The argument of the military that Venetia must remain in Germanic hands to safeguard southern Germany also failed to impress him. During the Schleswig-Holstein affair of 1864-5 he began to hint that an accommodation between Prussia and Italy would be to their mutual advantage.[7]

La Marmora was no professional diplomat but he had worked alongside Cavour for a decade and was acute enough to realise that an alliance with Berlin would have its dangers as well as its advantages. He was justifiably suspicious of Bismarck who promised war with Austria one day and signed the Convention of Gastein with her on the next, and was afraid that Italy might become a pawn in a dangerous diplomatic game. Prussia might use an Italian alliance to threaten Austria and then withdraw at the last moment leaving Italy to fight alone. La Marmora was determined not to commit himself until he received some form of positive encouragement from France. He also seems to have tried to turn the tables on Bismarck by using a Prussian alliance and French friendship to induce Austria to sell Venetia.[8] In her desperate financial situation, with her military budget being drastically cut, a peaceful solution to the Venetian problem was obviously to be preferred. But by February 1866 La Marmora was under considerable pressure to make an agreement with Prussia. Victor Emmanuel was impatient to launch a war which would cover him with glory, help to consolidate his kingdom, and round off his possessions in the Po valley – the traditional area of expansion for the House of Savoy. The King had maintained his contacts with Garibaldini and Hungarian *émigrés* and was now prepared to further their schemes for the dismemberment of the Habsburg monarchy with or without the approval of La Marmora's government.[9]

Bismarck was pleased to hear of this bellicose attitude. His own master, William I, was obstinately pacific and Bismarck had the task of convincing him that war with Austria was essential. At a council meeting on 28 February General Moltke, the Prussian chief of staff, insisted that an Italian alliance was necessary to guarantee success against Austria. A few days later Bismarck wrote to Florence inviting an Italian general to Berlin to discuss the terms of a military alliance. La Marmora decided to comply. His political situation was precarious, and a diplomatic success might reinforce his authority. His negotiations with Austria had achieved nothing, and, most important of all, the Italian minister in Paris, Nigra, was sending report after report urging him to make terms with Prussia because Napoleon III was in favour of such a move.

General Govone, one of the most talented officers in the army, was chosen for the mission to Berlin, and Count Arese, a close friend of the Emperor's, was sent to Paris to ensure French support. Napoleon welcomed a general agreement between Prussia and Italy, hoping that it would enable Bismarck to overcome William I's hesitations and lead to an Austro-Prussian confrontation in which he could eventually act as arbiter and perhaps acquire some territorial compensation in the process. But La Marmora instructed Govone and Barral, Italian minister at Berlin, to avoid any vague and unspecified commitments and to concentrate on a precise military and political pact.[10] It was this which apparently disturbed Napoleon who feared that Austria might attack and defeat Italy while Prussia stood aside. If Italy collapsed and the Austrians reoccupied Lombardy, France might have to intervene. He hoped to avoid this eventuality by attempting to secure the peaceful cession of Venetia and by urging the Italians, even after they signed their alliance with Prussia, to fight only a token war.

In Berlin, the negotiations which began on 14 March resulted in the formulation of an offensive and defensive alliance. Venetia and the Quadrilateral were to be ceded to Italy and an equivalent territory to Prussia, and the alliance would become void if Prussia failed to act within three months.[11] La Marmora sought to include the Trentino but Bismarck could only give a verbal promise that this could be arranged after the war.[12] It was still unclear whether Prussia would assist Italy if Austria attacked her first, and Napoleon was still irritatingly vague about defending Italy if Austria were the aggressor, but despite his hesitations La Marmora allowed his representatives to sign the alliance on 8 April 1866. Afraid that it might develop into a 'brutal friendship', La Marmora avoided signing a military convention which would have enabled the two armies to co-ordinate their movements. In his apologia some years later, he justified his attitude by referring to his experiences in the Crimean War and in 1859 when the Italians found themselves virtually under foreign command.[13] Moltke's projected visit to Florence never materialised and the Italians were wary of informing the Prussians of their military plans although Bismarck was quite prepared to discuss those of his own general staff – or what he claimed to be their plans. The reason for La Marmora's unwillingness, said his critics later, was that he never expected to fight the war at all. The cynical argued that Italy had no war plans to divulge.

Austria began concentrating troops in Venetia in response to a threatening Italian build-up in Bologna and a Garibaldian raid on Rovigo.[14] La Marmora denied these Austrian accusations and, despite French advice to avoid counter measures, he announced that Italy was placing her army on a war footing.[15] Most of the moderates in Italy were now clamouring for a firm stand and the life of the government would have been very short had La Marmora refused to react. Bismarck made alarming statements about the April alliance not committing Prussia to participate in an Italian war, and it was in this atmosphere of mutual suspicion and confusion that La Marmora received a telegram from Paris announcing that Austria would surrender Venetia to France who would in turn cede it to Italy if Florence broke her agreement with Berlin.[16] There arose the possibility that disloyalty to a disloyal ally would lead to the peaceful acquisition of Venetia. La Marmora withstood the temptation. *'Ma première impression est que c'est une question d'honneur et de loyauté de ne pas dégager avec la Prusse.'*[17] But he also hoped to avoid war by any means short of dishonouring the name of Italy, and asked Nigra about the possibility of a congress. For the remainder of the month of May the British, Russian and French governments attempted to arrange a European congress to deal with the questions of Germany and Italy. Berlin and Florence announced their willingness to participate but Bismarck certainly had reservations about it. Any hesitation on the part of La Marmora became superfluous on 1 June when Austria declared it would only attend on condition that no power acquired any additional territory. With Venice and

Schleswig-Holstein struck from the agenda, the whole exercise became pointless. As in 1859, Austrian diplomacy ensured that the problems of the day would have to be solved by force. There was a strange ending to this complicated series of negotiations which had begun six months previously. In order to secure French neutrality, Austria promised Napoleon III that Venetia would be surrendered whether she won or lost the war. France promised to restrain Italy if she could and hinted to the Italians that if their duty compelled them to begin hostilities, they should not fight too energetically.

As Prussia's troops crossed the frontiers of Austria's German allies, La Marmora prepared to relinquish the premiership and assume the post of chief of staff. The appointment of Ricasoli and the formation of a new ministry delayed the Italian declaration of war, which alarmed and irritated the Prussians. La Marmora was a tired and embittered man as he shouldered his new responsibilities. Bismarck had sent Bernhardi, a military expert but a civilian, to Florence to discuss strategy with the Italians. La Marmora resented being told how to conduct the war, particularly as Bernhardi's suggestions were similar to plans which the Garibaldini and Hungarian exiles had drawn up. Even Usedom, the :he Prussian minister, urged their acceptance.[18] La Marmora resented this interference, and as he had made plain to Govone, he thought that any joint operations with the Prussians were unnecessary and a threat to the independent status of Italy.

The Italian declaration of war was sent on 20 June. The brief and inglorious Third War of Independence followed, and the conduct of the war in many ways reflected the tortuous and often ambiguous diplomacy which had preceded it. The contents of the secret Franco-Austrian agreement of 12 June were soon known in Berlin and Florence. Bismarck's fears that Italy would try to evade her treaty obligations help to explain the insistence with which Prussia urged La Marmora to commence hostilities. Even during the diplomatic exchanges which led to the alliance of 8 April, both parties had been reluctant to make any pledge which would commit them to take the initiative in the war against Austria. Italy appeared to have won this particular duel, but in the last days of peace Bismarck tried hard to push her into war. Technically, Bismarck won this round, because although Prussia began operations on 16 June, it was only on 21 June that he declared war officially on Austria, one day after Italy. Prussian doubts about whether Italy would act even though she had declared war were quickly dispelled. On 23 June La Marmora crossed the Mincio, and the following day lost the battle of Custoza.

'J'ai le coeur gai et beaucoup de foi dans l'avenir', Victor Emmanuel wrote to the French Emperor four days before Custoza, and he had reason to be optimistic.[19] In Italy, it was a popular war – at least with the propertied classes; France appeared to be benevolently neutral, and so did Britain and Russia. His ally Prussia had struck hard at her enemies and was entering Bohemia to take on the main field army of the Austrians. Because of this Prussian threat, Austria only allocated 190,000 men to the southern theatre, of whom only 75,000 were actual combatants. Italy, with over 250,000 men, had an imposing numerical superiority. With 452 guns against Austria's 152, she also possessed greater fire power, and her cavalry was more numerous. In addition, the Italian fleet outclassed the Austrian in the number of ships and guns. Victor Emmanuel also believed that Italian nationalism would help him to accomplish his dynastic ambitions. His army included men from all regions of Italy, and in 1866 only just over 1 per cent of those eligible had failed to answer their military summons – a remarkably low estimate in view of the fact that in Basilicata and Sicily draft evasion had become a seasonal occupation – and mobilisation had progressed very smoothly.[20] Franz Josef, on the other hand, had to struggle against the forces of nationalism and rely upon the loyalty of an international army. Victor Emmanuel had his problems in the south, but Franz Josef faced a formidable separatist movement in Hungary.

As La Marmora left for the front on 17 June, he was less confident than his King. His low spirits were not merely the result of the late nights and the strain imposed by 'diplomacy by telegram'. The financial crisis had led to the resignation of his friend General Petitti in December 1865 and he had virtually to compel General Pettinengo to fill the vacancy at the War Ministry. The mobilisation plans of 1863 and the orders for additional guns had to be drastically revised because of the economies the government had to enforce. Plans to reorganise and improve the services in the army had to be dropped for the same reason. The fact that in 1865 40,000 men of the class of 1845 were simply not called up revealed the full extent of the crisis. Being War Minister in such circumstances was a thankless task, and it was perhaps fortunate that the government at this time was headed by a general. A civilian in charge of such a programme would have generated much greater tension among the military.

On his way to the front, La Marmora stopped at Bologna to hold discussions with General Cialdini. On paper, the Italian army appeared to be a successful amalgamation of the various regions. Its officer corps seemed well balanced as between Piedmontese and non-Piedmontese, ex-Garibaldini and orthodox regulars, progressive officers and the more traditional variety. But just below the surface, and frequently above it, lurked sectional conflict, personal animosities and partisan hatreds. Evidence of this is not hard to find. After the September Convention, General Della Rocca was put in charge of quelling the riots in Turin. He was known to favour the dismissal of the Minghetti cabinet and his critics argued that it was unconstitutional for one of the king's aides-de-camp to be in command of the troops in the capital. After Minghetti's dismissal, Della Rocca was accused of playing a political role. La Marmora, succeeding Minghetti, agreed with these criticisms, and urged the King to remove him from Turin. Della Rocca responded by challenging La Marmora to a duel, but, to avoid an open scandal, the King prevented it.[21] General Pianell, a capable officer and one of the few whose reputation was enhanced by the battle of Custoza, was widely rumoured to be in the pay of the Austrians because he had held command in the old Bourbon army.[22] General Sirtori, once Garibaldi's chief of staff, clashed with his officers as divisional commander at Catanzaro in 1863, and was later reprimanded by La Marmora for constantly invading the civilian sphere of authority. Sirtori petulantly resigned over this issue. On his reinstatement, he argued with the Neapolitan general Nunziante over the way in which the manoeuvres were being held, and again resigned, taking his complaints to the War Ministry where a commission heard his case and decided against him. Incorrigible as ever, he disagreed with Pianell and La Marmora after Custoza – he had issued an order of the day praising his own troops and criticising the others – and, after he had been removed from his command, he asked for La Marmora and three corps commanders to be summoned before a council of war for mismanaging the battle.[23] Before resigning from the service, he wrote a letter to the Prime Minister Ricasoli complaining of a *'camorra militare'* which threatened the stability of the throne and the army, and dishonoured Italy![24] Every army has its unstable characters and personal conflicts, but the way in which the Italian army had been created only five years before undoubtedly helps to explain the high level of intolerance to be found inside the officer corps.

The real threat to the cohesion of the army did not come from men such as Della Rocca, Pianell or Sirtori; nor was Garibaldi, who was put in command of 38,000 volunteers with the Trentino as his objective, much of a problem to La Marmora. It was General Cialdini, the man La Marmora visited on his way north on 17 June, whose attitude could and did present the most serious difficulties. Since his return from Spanish exile, Cialdini had played a leading part in all the military episodes of the Risorgimento, and had become something of a popular hero, the Garibaldi of the regular army. To most of those who knew him well, however, he was 'overbearing, suspicious, of unstable temperament. . .more prone to command than to obey, yet afraid as he was of great responsibility, he shied away from the supreme command. In effect, he did not want to command and did not know how to obey.'[25] One of La Marmora's greatest mistakes was to accept a suggestion made by Petitti in May that the army should be divided into two groups, one under the King and La Marmora in Lombardy, and one under Cialdini in Emilia. As Cialdini had refused to act as chief of staff, La Marmora should have insisted on his unconditional obedience instead of making such a fatal compromise, virtually allowing him an independent command. Whatever the two generals may have said to each other at Bologna on the eve of war, they certainly failed to clarify their respective roles in the forthcoming campaign.

La Marmora showed great weakness in his handling of Cialdini, but the root of the trouble lay in the deficient organisation of the supreme command, and in the absence of any clearly defined plans for an offensive against Austria. It was only after the war, in 1867, that the *Comitato di Stato Maggiore* was established, and only in 1882 that Enrico Cosenz became the first *Capo di Stato Maggiore* and capable of exerting an influence comparable to that of Moltke's in the Prussian supreme command. In 1866, whereas Moltke had had eight years in which to establish his authority and his sphere of competence, La Marmora held the post of chief of staff just three days prior to the declaration of war! Victor Emmanuel's title, *Comandante Supremo,* was purely nominal. To the relief of his generals, who had a low estimate of his military ability, his presence on the battlefield would be primarily ceremonial. La Marmora had the task of co-ordinating the army and giving it a sense of direction, but in order to do this he would need to show a genius for improvisation, and to be assured of an intelligent response from his subordinates. Evidence of both was conspicuously lacking on 24 June.

As had been agreed earlier, there were two armies waiting to begin operations against Austria, the Army of the Mincio which consisted of three corps under La Marmora and the King, and the Army of the Po which consisted of one large corps, eight divisions strong, under the command of Cialdini. La Marmora believed that the main thrust should be across the Mincio towards Verona, whereas Cialdini favoured an assault across the Po. Each imagined that the other's role was primarily diversionary, and when La Marmora was crossing the Mincio on 23 June, Cialdini was unaware that this was anything more than a military demonstration.[26]

The Italians thought that the Austrians would stay on the defensive behind the Adige, and La Marmora pushed forward with six divisions, leaving the other six to cover the fortresses of Peschiera and Mantua. General Cerale, commanding the first division, was informed about dust clouds in the distance but failed to investigate or report the news to headquarters, although there were over 50 squadrons of cavalry at the disposal of the three corps. Sirtori, commanding fifth division, received information that an Austrian corps was heading west but he too failed to report.[27] La Marmora himself gave no orders to scout for the enemy and he allowed his formations to become too spread out. These were serious errors because Archduke Albert and his three corps were not passively waiting behind the Adige but close at hand hoping for a chance to hit the left flank of the advancing Italians. The armies blundered into one another on 24 June but at least Albert knew what he was looking for, and his troops were in close order and therefore in a better position to take advantage of this chance encounter.

So spread out were the Italians that 'the account of the battle is an account of isolated encounters'.[28] Where serious fighting took place, the Austrians were usually numerically superior, more mobile and more skilfully led. La Marmora, when he realised that he had a battle on his hands, tended to rush about from one point to another without informing anyone of the location of his headquarters. There was consequently no central control, and even the King was unable to find the chief of staff at one crucial moment when a counter attack could have saved the day. The orders which La Marmora gave were confused and often ambiguous, and it was obvious that he had no clear picture of the battle as a whole. He became convinced of his defeat before he knew the real situation, sent off a series of alarmist messages, and grossly exaggerated the extent of the Austrian success. In the evening, still verging on panic, he wanted to withdraw the army back as far as the Adda, and only the intervention of Govone appears to have persuaded him to halt instead at the Oglio. In this far from decisive battle the Austrians lost 1,170 dead to the Italians' 714. It was not the battle itself, which the Italians came near to winning despite an almost total lack of coherent orders, but the decisions taken by La Marmora afterwards which turned Custoza into a military disaster. One of the most bizarre aspects of this whole episode was La Marmora's pathetic attempt to induce Cialdini to cross the Po and take some of the pressure off the Army of the Mincio, which he believed to be in danger of disintegration. Because of the devastating news from the battlefield, Cialdini was not prepared to risk his eight divisions in a hopeless gamble. If the twelve divisions of the other army had been dispersed, his corps was the only organised force capable of resisting an Austrian invasion. Far from attacking, he began retreating towards Modena. In fact, less than half of La Marmora's divisions had played an active part in the conflict and even these were capable of launching a counter attack on the following day if the order had been given. The Austrians did not pursue either army so they were allowed to retire unmolested. The next few days were taken up with polemics between La Marmora and Cialdini. The chief of staff had implored Cialdini to move forward when he should have commanded him, but by granting him almost autonomous power over IV Corps La Marmora had really cut the ground from under his feet before hostilities had commenced. In a few hours, La Marmora destroyed a reputation built up over the past two decades. He spent the rest of his life trying to justify his actions, and in prolonging memories of Custoza did his country a disservice.

Meanwhile, the Prussians were menacing the main field army under Benedek, and on 3 July won the crushing victory of Koniggrätz.[29] Napoleon III accepted Austrian requests to act as mediator and was delighted to be offered Venetia, and he immediately wrote to Victor Emmanuel asking him to end the war.[30] The King and Ricasoli's government however, were not prepared to accept Venetia as a gift from the French Emperor. The Foreign Minister Visconti-Venosta thought it would be harmful to Italian prestige, La Marmora described it as an 'insupportable humiliation', and Ricasoli was convinced that Italy must conquer Venetia by her own efforts to erase the infamy of Custoza.[31] For a few hours on 5 July Napoleon toyed with the idea of intervening against Prussia, but the moment passed, and, for a time, the war continued on both fronts.

As Archduke Albert withdrew in order to assist the French attempt to secure an armistice – Venetia having become technically French territory as a result of Franz Josef's cession of it to Napoleon – the Italian army began to advance at last. The bulk of the Austrian forces in Italy, apart from garrisons in the Quadrilateral, were evacuated to fight on the northern front, so when Cialdini crossed the Po his progress was largely unopposed. Garibaldi's volunteers, whom La Marmora had ordered to fall back after Custoza, were now instructed to occupy as much of the Trentino as possible, and General Medici was detached from Cialdini's forces to assist them. By the end of the third week in July, Italian forces were in sight of Trent, had surrounded Venice and were in a position to march on Trieste and Istria. But on 20 July two events took place which doomed Italian attempts to acquire more than Venetia. The Prussians signed a truce with the Austrians without consulting their ally, and the Italian navy suffered defeat at Lissa.

The Austro-Prussian preliminary peace signed at Nikolsburg on 26 July freed Austrian troops for action in Italy and as neither Prussia nor France were willing to back Italian claims to Trent and Trieste, Ricasoli reluctantly agreed to an armistice two days later. Garibaldi was ordered to retire from the Trentino and on 8 August the armistice of Cormons was signed. But there were to be further humiliations for Italy. The Austrians refused to allow her to participate in the Austro-Prussian talks which resulted in the Peace of Prague on 23 August. Instead, a separate Austro-Italian peace was signed at Vienna by General Menabrea and Count Wimpffen on 3 October. As had been agreed at Prague, Austria ceded Venetia to Napoleon on the understanding that he would then surrender it to Italy. After laborious haggling the French and Prussians succeeded in reducing the indemnity which Austria demanded from Italy, and in scaling down the public debt to be borne by Florence. Austrian recognition of the Kingdom of Italy, her surrender of the iron crown and the overwhelming plebiscite in Venetia in favour of union with Italy – only 60 voted against – were triumphs which had to be set against the defeats suffered on land and sea and the cavalier way in which Italy had at times been treated by her ally Prussia and her patron France.

The Italians showed an almost British propensity for self-castigation. The reverses at Custoza and Lissa were magnified into catastrophic defeats, and seen as evidence of serious defects in the new Italian state, which was true, and in the Italian character, which was not. When General Pollio wrote his account of Custoza in 1903, he remarked that the defeat of 1866 still weighed down on the army like a 'leaden cloak'.[32] In 1894 General Corsi, the official historian of the campaign, was writing to the octogenarian General Cadorna, explaining that he had written his account 26 years previously but that 'for reasons which are certainly known to you', its publication had been somewhat delayed.[33]

While the generals wrangled and the politicians debated, the public demanded a scapegoat and found one in Admiral Persano, who had lost the naval encounter off Lissa.[34] But amidst all the harsh criticisms and the deplorable *sauve qui peut* of all those with reputations to salvage, there were a few voices which called for understanding and a reassessment of the situation. In September 1866, Pasquale Villari praised the army as *'la Nazione perfezionata'* and argued that it was the nation which was unworthy of the army and not the army which was unworthy of the nation.[35] Others spoke of the importance of the army's role in peacetime as the *'Fattore della nostra unità nazionale e scuola commune dei nostri populi'*, arguing that it was as a social institution rather than a military institution that the army could best serve the interests of the country.[36] The army and society must become more fully integrated. It was in 1868 that De Amicis wrote his *Vita Militare*, but the implementation of such a programme was regarded with suspicion by the military and with indifference by the public.

Victor Emmanuel had acquired Venetia, but not in the glorious manner he had so confidently predicted. He felt humiliated and threatened by the way in which critics like Carlo Cattaneo spoke of *'la guerra finta'*, hinting that Persano was not the only culprit who should be hauled before the senate.[37] For officers, *'avide de gloire et de grade'*, the war of 1866 had been a disappointment.[38] There had been scant opportunity for heroism and the low casualty figures precluded rapid promotion. A nation on the verge of bankruptcy, which had just spent over 330 millions for the war, was not likely to be over-generous towards an army which appeared to have failed so lamentably. Not only were there insufficient funds to support a large army and fleet, it had become more difficult to justify their existence on purely military grounds. The Austrians had left the Quadrilateral, where they had been a permanent threat to the new regime, and the Austrian Emperor had recognised the new state of Italy, thereby dashing the hopes of the dispossessed princes. On 11 December 1866, the last French troops left Rome in accordance with the September Convention, although they left behind the Antibes Legion, controlled by French officers. Austria was temporarily weak, Napoleon III had lost his opportunity to regain the initiative, and Prussia remained superciliously friendly towards Florence. There was no immediate danger of an attack, no likelihood of Italy launching a war of aggression, and therefore no real need for a massive army which she could ill afford.

The army was still needed, however, for the maintenance of internal security. Taking advantage of the war in the north, there had been a recrudescence of *brigantaggio* in the Neapolitan provinces, but a much more serious situation had developed in Sicily. In September

1866 a rising in Palermo had to be put down by military force. General Cadorna was sent out and the day after his arrival he declared a state of siege, to the annoyance of the Prime Minister Ricasoli, who had wanted martial law to be proclaimed only as the last resort.[39] Order was restored, but several thousand bayonets were obviously necessary to prevent further outbreaks. Two years later, Cadorna received a similar assignment but this time in Emilia where, in January 1869, popular opposition to the detested *macinato* tax led to rioting and attacks on property. Cadorna believed that a show of force was necessary, so seven peasants were shot at San Giovanni in Persiceto, and a few days later he announced that the emergency was over.[40] However critical the moderates might be of the military prowess of the army, they quickly realised that they could not rule without it.

Victor Emmanuel was of the same opinion. When Ricasoli's attempts at compromise with the Vatican broke down in early 1867, the King seriously thought that it might be necessary to resort to a royal *coup d'état.* He felt isolated in Florence, and since the Turin riots of 1864 he felt that he had lost the support of his loyal Piedmontese. Dissatisfaction with the conduct of the recent war, and the current financial crisis, were creating a very ugly mood in the country. The King dissolved the chamber when Ricasoli fell and Prince Eugenio wrote to Ricasoli suggesting that the Statuto should be reformed in an authoritarian sense.[41] Foreign diplomats and leading politicians began to anticipate a royal dictatorship backed by the army.[42] According to the Austrian ambassador, the King asked Generals Cialdini and Durando for their views, but they were opposed to any unconstitutional moves.[43] As there was no significant support among the generals or the political leaders, the King had to abandon the idea of a *coup.*

After the elections of 1867, with the financial situation and Rome as the major issues, the King appointed Rattazzi and events began to bear an uncanny resemblance to those in 1862. In that year Rattazzi had succeeded Racasoli amidst talk of a palace *coup,* and Aspromonte had followed shortly afterwards. Garibaldi's intervention in the 1867 elections, when his gross anti-clericalism had offended even hardened veterans of the left, made it virtually impossible for Rattazzi to ignore the Roman question. Garibaldi advocated, as he had five years earlier, a forcible solution and he soon began to organise volunteers for an assault on Rome. If 1862 were about to be repeated, the Italian army had to be ready to prevent this, for despite the evacuation of the French garrison, Napoleon had clearly indicated that if the pope were threatened he would send his troops back again.

Rattazzi spoke glibly of remaining loyal to the September Convention, but his propensity to run with the hare and hunt with the hounds was well known. The Italian army succeeded in preventing a Garibaldian invasion in the summer, and more troops were despatched to watch the papal frontiers. On 24 September Garibaldi was arrested at Sinalunga. He had just attended the peace conference at Geneva, and being elected honorary president of the assembly he had surprised delegates by justifying a warlike policy to liberate the oppressed Romans. He was briefly held in the fortress of Alessandria and then deported to Caprera, but he refused to promise to remain there and invited Rattazzi to allow the royal army to collaborate with the Garibaldini in the conquest of Rome. Indeed, when armed bands began to cross into Lazio at the end of September, they met with no opposition from the regular army.[44] Rattazzi's apparent willingness to comply with Garibaldi's suggestion alarmed Victor Emmanuel and on 19 October, two days after the French had decided upon intervention, the King forced him to resign. The following day, Garibaldi appeared in Florence and no one dared to re-arrest him. General Cialdini, whom the King had asked to form a new ministry, failed to dissuade him from embarking on his hazardous enterprise. A special train was provided to remove him from the capital, and on 23 October he assumed command of the volunteers at Terni. They began to converge on Rome where an insurrection had been planned to coincide with their invasion. The insurrection failed, however, and Garibaldi decided to retreat, a decision which lost him 2,000 men who promptly deserted. Cialdini's attempt to form a ministry having failed, the King called on General Menabrea, who succeded in constructing a right-wing government by 27 October, the day on which the King issued a proclamation condemning Garibaldi's enterprise. Three days later, French troops began disembarking at Civitavecchia. Garibaldi's forces were attacked by papal troops at Mentana on 3 November, but the arrival of two French battalions equipped with their formidable *chassepot* rifles, deprived the Garibaldini of a probable victory. Garibaldi and some of his followers retreated and surrendered their arms to units of the regular Italian army. Menabrea's government ordered his arrest and by the end of the month he was back in Caprera, the French were back in Rome, and Italian troops who had crossed into Lazio were back on their side of the frontier. Mentana now had to be added to Custoza and Lissa in the growing list of Italian humiliations. The events in November 1867 'mark the end of the Risorgimento, seen as the activities of heroic minorities of conspirators and fighters, just as the lethal fire of the chassepots marked the end of the Garibaldian and revolutionary tactics which relied on the decisive results of an assault with the bayonet'.[45]

That the French intended to stay in Rome was emphasised by Rouher's speech in December, which he concluded by saying that *'Italie ne s'emparera pas de Rome! Jamais. Jamais la France ne supportera cette violence faite à son honneur et à la catholicité. Jamais!'*[46] France had now taken Austria's place as the most intransigent opponent of Italian nationalism, and foreign troops were again on Italian soil. Anti-French sentiment became even more pronounced, but the King steadfastly refused to sever his close ties with Paris. Count Vimercati, his agent in Paris, sent him glowing reports of the French army, and convinced him that it would be disastrous for Italy to abandon France for Prussia.[47] The Hungarian exile, General Türr, was sent on a secret mission to Vienna to explore the possibilities for a triple alliance of Italy, France and Austria.[48] The King had been unable to execute a *coup d'état,* but he was determined to pursue his own foreign policy, and for this he still needed an army.

The campaign of 1866 had shown conclusively that the Italian army was in need of reform. It was true that there was a widespread demand for disarmament or at least a reduction in the armed forces.

> Disarm disarm was a universal cry; this alone was the panacea for the anaemic financial situation. And this cry was the inevitable reaction to Custoza and Lissa. . . The constant repetition that the army is a parasite, costly yet unproductive, has begun to make even the best officers think that their profession is not of great impor-importance for the development of modern society.[49]

Lieutenant Colonel Guarnieri was perhaps being unduly pessimistic, but his book, published in 1868, is a useful guide to officer opinion in these years. He noted how many of the most intelligent officers were leaving the service as they saw little hope of glory or promotion, how all the political parties seemed determined to dismantle the army, and how the military deputies in parliament seemed too exhausted and dispirited to make strenuous objections. War Minister Bertolé-Viale, like his predecessor Revel, was perturbed by this widespread dissatisfaction. He realised that lack of funds as well as popular disenchantment prevented any large-scale reforms, but some progress was made. The general staff was reorganised and a *Scuola di Guerra* established in Turin, modelled on the *Kriegsacademie,* and an attempt was made to equip the infantry with a weapon comparable to the Prussian needle guns and French *chassepots.* It was particularly frustrating for War Ministers like Bertolé-Viale and Govone – and for the restless King – to see further projects for army reform vitiated by the ruthless economies of the new premier Lanza. This may, however, have been a blessing in disguise because it strengthened the hand of the more realistic Italians determined to keep their country neutral if war broke out in Europe.

When the Franco-Prussian War broke out in the summer of 1870, the King's efforts to rush to the assistance of his old ally of 1855 and 1859 were easily repulsed. The state of the economy and the armed forces precluded any serious intervention on behalf of either combatant. When the French garrison was recalled from Rome in August, however, the Italian government very cautiously made its preparations for a more limited form of intervention, the invasion of Lazio. Apart from setting up an observation corps in central Italy under General Cadorna, the government made no move until the news arrived of the establishment of a republic in France. The cabinet then decided unanimously on the immediate occupation of the Papal State including Rome.[50] As in 1860, the government heralded its invasion of papal territory by claiming that the presence of the army was necessary to prevent disorders. Cadorna crossed the frontier on 12 September, halting just outside Rome while last minute attempts at a compromise with the pope were conducted by the Prussian minister. When these failed, Italian guns breached the walls at the Porta Pia on 20 September, and at the cost of 49 deaths on the Italian side and 19 among the papal forces, Rome was occupied. The casualty list was low because the pope had ordered only token resistance. It was an unheroic ending to the 'military Risorgimento'. Many of the leading personalities of the past decades had participated in it. Bixio and Cosenz, ex-Garibaldini, both commanded divisions; La Marmora was made provisional lieutenant of Rome and it was fitting that this should be his last official post because despite his mistakes in 1866 he had played a key role in the creation of the Italian state and army. But amongst these figures of the past were some of the men of the future; Ricotti, the new Minister for War who ordered Cadorna into Rome, remained in this post for six years and initiated important reforms, and a young artillery officer at the Porta Pia, Pelloux, was destined to play a controversial role in the future history of army/state relations. But the absentees were equally notable. Mazzini was a prisoner in the fortress of Gaeta – a strange reversal of roles, for in 1849 he had been in Rome and the pope in Gaeta. He was soon released, but as he passed through Rome on his way north he felt so dispirited by the way in which Rome had become the capital of Italy that he stayed in his lodgings until it was time for his train to depart. Garibaldi, the only popular general of the Risorgimento, was also absent, fighting his last campaign in the Vosges against the Prussian military machine and desperately trying to keep alive the concept of the people's war. Victor Emmanuel was another absentee and seemed most reluctant to visit his new conquest. Quietly and unofficially, he eventually visited Rome on the last day of 1870 to survey the damage done by the flooding of the Tiber. Carducci later poured scorn on the whole episode of the taking of Rome.

Oche del Campidoglio, zitte! Io sono
L'Italia grande e una.
Vengo di notte perché il dottor Lanza
Teme i colpi di sole. . .
Deh, non fate, oche mie, tànto rumore
Che non senta Antonelli.

Once in Rome, however, the imperial monuments of the past began to assert a silent attraction, beckoning many Italians to pursue a policy of grandeur she could ill afford. The papal monuments too provided a constant reminder of the presence of the infallible 'prisoner of the Vatican', inducing the secular rulers of Italy to assert their own claim to greatness.

Notes

1. Candeloro, V, 254, f.82.
2. Mori, p.225.
3. Ibid., p.231.
4. F. Chabod, *Storia della politica estera italiana dal 1870 al 1896. Le Premesse* (Bari, 1951), p.8.
5. O. Pflanze, *Bismarck and the development of Germany* (Princeton, 1963), p.141.
6. A. La Marmora, *Un po più di luce* (Florence, 1873), pp.1-28.
7. La Marmora to Nigra, 4 August 1865, La Marmora, p.41.
8. Ibid., pp.51-7. By December 1865 it was apparent that this attempt had failed, but La Marmora remained interested in an Italo-Austrian agreement over Venice even after signing the Prussian alliance. See his defensive remarks concerning the Landau affair in June 1866 (ibid., pp.57-8, f.1). After the war his critics were quick to condemn such

'disloyal' negotiations. They seemed to explain why the Italian war effort was so feeble.

9. J.W. Bush, *Venetia redeemed* (New York, 1967), p.41. The King told Usedom, the Prussian minister at Florence, that he favoured war (Usedom to Bismarck, 16 February 1866, ibid.).
10. La Marmora, p.102.
11. Ibid., pp.109-10.
12. La Marmora to Barral, 28 March 1866, ibid., pp.111-12.
13. Ibid., pp.132-6
14. Barral to La Marmora, 23 April 1866, ibid., p.165.
15. Diplomatic circular of La Marmora, 27 April 1866, ibid., pp.180-1.
16. Nigra to La Marmora, 5 May 1866, ibid., p.204.
17. La Marmora to Nigra, 5 May 1866, ibid., p.206.
18. Usedom to La Marmora, 17 June 1866, ibid., pp.345-8.
19. Bush, p.78.
20. Stato Maggiore, p.106.
21. Della Rocca, pp.225-30.
22. General Alberto Pollio, *Custoza 1866* (Rome, 1935), p.164.
23. C. Agrati, *Giuseppe Sirtori* (Bari, 1940), pp.229-59.
24. Sirtori to Ricasoli, 9 July 1866, ibid., p.263.
25. Cadorna, p.217.
26. La Marmora to Cialdini, 23 June 1866, Pollio, pp.30-31. He spoke of occupying several points but failed to indicate the scale of the crossing.
27. Ibid., p.57.
28. Ibid., p.107.
29. Benedek has been described as 'an opponent of any kind of staff work done at the green table, and above all of any kind of scholarly activity by soldiers' (Craig, p.63).
30. Bush, p.86.
31. Ibid., pp.86-8.
32. Pollio, p.293.
33. Cadorna, p.236.
34. *Archivio Pellion di Persano,* Archivio Centrale dello Stato. A. Iachino, *La campagna navale di Lissa* (Milan, 1966).
35. Stato Maggiore, p.111.
36. Ibid., p.112.
37. Candeloro, V, 295. On the King and the war see Mack Smith, *Victor Emmanuel,* pp.303-35.
38. R. Girardet, *La société militaire dans la France contemporaine 1815-1939,* (Paris, 1953), p.157.
39. Ricasoli to Cadorna, 3 October 1866, Cadorna, pp.283-4.
40. Ibid., pp.320-21.
41. R. Mori, *Il tramonto del potere temporale* (Rome, 1967), p.109.
42. Ibid., p.110.
43. Mori, *Il tramonto,* p.111.
44. Candeloro, V, 329.
45. Ibid., p.334.
46. Mori, *Il tramonto,* p.285.
47. Ibid., pp.354-5.
48. Ibid., p.361.
49. A. Guarnieri, *Otto anni di storia militare* (Florence, 1868) pp.704-6.
50. S. Castagnola, *Diario storico-politico del 1870-71* (Turin, 1896) pp.26-40; Mack Smith, pp.408-10.

7 THE REFORMS OF RICOTTI MAGNANI

The brief bombardment at the Porta Pia was indeed insignificant compared to the momentous events taking place to the north of the Alps. The Prussians defeated both the imperial army and, with less aplomb, the partisan units which attempted to embody the *'forze vive'* of the French nation. 'How could we prevail against the Prussians? We have learned so little, and they are such a studious people.'[1] This was said by Benedek after his defeat in 1866, and the French commanders of 1870-1 could have said the same. The Franco-Prussian War, which established German predominance in Europe, was a triumph for Moltke's general staff. By adopting new managerial techniques soon to be emulated in the civilian sector, it had been able to organise and control a mass army of conscripts and reservists. Despite the conservatism of the Junker officer corps, the general staff had succeeded in keeping the army abreast of the latest technological innovations. Without decrying the traditional military virtues and the role of the 'heroic leader', Moltke had asserted the primacy of the 'military manager'. As M. Janowitz writes:

> As the military establishment becomes progressively dependent on more complex technology, the importance of the military manager increases. He does not displace the heroic leader, but he undermines the long standing traditionalism of the military establishment, and weakens its opposition to technological innovation.[2]

The French had shown a bravery which may have been magnificent but which was certainly no substitute for intelligence. Without the thoughtful deployment of the available men and materials, the impetuous cavalry charge or acts of personal bravery were extravagant gestures which modern armies could ill afford. Italy, and any other nation with pretensions to military greatness, had to ponder the lessons of the Franco-Prussian War. Making due allowances for Italy's individual social and economic structure, her military establishment decided to model itself on the triumphantly efficient German army.

Between 1870 and 1876 General Ricotti Magnani largely reorganised the Italian army. He was born in Novara in 1822, not long after the abortive military *coup* which had tragically divided the Piedmontese army, and he died in 1917, the year of Caporetto. In the war of 1848-9 he fought as an artillery officer and was promoted to captain. Also a participant in the Crimean War, he fought the Second War of Independence with the rank of lieutenant-colonel, rising to divisional command in 1861. In 1866 he commanded the twelfth division in Cialdini's unwieldy IV Corps. Appointed Minister of War by Lanza in 1870, he retained his post under Minghetti from 1873 to 1876.

Since 1866, army reform had been an insistent demand, but the '*battaglia del bilancio*' and the policy of 'economy to the bone' had prevented any large-scale reforms. Indeed, successive war ministers had been compelled to impose drastic cuts in expenditure. Whereas in the early 1860s the armed forces had accounted for around 40 per cent of the total expenditure of the state, in the late 1860s this had dropped to below 20 per cent. The lowest point was reached in 1872, but this was followed by a steady climb, until in 1877 the total cost of the army rose above the 200 million lire mark. Except in freak years like 1887 – when it rose to over 37 per cent – the percentage remained close to 20 per cent.[3] It was against this background of financial stringency that Ricotti introduced his military reforms.

Despite La Marmora's tenacious opposition and his attempts to influence opinion by his *Quattro Discorsi,* Ricotti introduced his 'modifications' of the military law of 1854 on 19 July 1871. Many of the exemptions of La Marmora's law were abolished, but the duration of active service for conscripts of the first category was reduced to four years, with nine in reserve. The second category remained in reserve for nine years and their period of training increased. The Prussian system of one year volunteers was introduced, and military districts were created which became centres for the enrolling of troops, the training of the recruits, and for mobilisation in time of war.[4] In the following year, Ricotti instituted 15 companies of Alpini to defend the northern frontiers, and by his law of 30 September 1873 he established the peacetime strength of the army at 224,000 men and the wartime strength, with the addition of the reserves, at 800,000. The peacetime army contained 130 generals, 1,223 superior officers, 10,834 lower officers, 16,431 NCOs, and 193,000 troops, grouped in ten corps each of two divisions.[5] The law of 7 June 1875 reduced the term of service yet again, this time to three years. It also established a third category, to incorporate those exempted from service in the first two. Conscripts of the first category served for three years in the army, then passed into the reserve, the mobile militia and the territorial militia.

These fundamental reforms were completed by Mezzacapo, who became Minister of War in 1876, and Ferrero, who held the post between 1881 and 1884. The law of June 1876 decided upon the abolition of the National Guard and its official replacement by the territorial militia. This took place gradually, the National Guard being finally superseded only in 1885. In 1882 the army was raised to 25 divisions grouped in 12 corps. This spate of military legislation between 1871 and 1882 reconstructed the Italian army and gave it the form it preserved until the First World War.

Ricotti's reforms, completed by Mezzacapo and Ferrero, marked a decisive move away from the French model but did not result in total acceptance of the Prussian; Italy did not possess the resources to do so even if this had been her aim. The establishment of three categories, the first line, the mobile militia and the territorial militia, was an attempt to maintain as large an army as possible, as cheaply as possible. An army of ten and later twelve corps was no mean achievement for a state which only just managed to balance its budget for the first time in 1876. Unlike the German system, these corps were not based on regions, but were composed of recruits from all over Italy. This had many grave defects, particularly if the need to mobilise quickly should arise, but the Rome government was still afraid of the divisive power of regionalism and hoped that this national system would help to forge a united nation. Political and social advantages were believed to outweigh any military disadvantages.

The creation, and expansion in the following years, of the Alpini reflected concern over the northern frontiers of the kingdom. As their name suggests, these troops were intended to fight in the mountains, to hold the passes and prevent the enemy from descending into the plains. The loss of Savoy and Nice in 1860 and the acquisition of Venetia in 1866 made it imperative for the Italians to construct new defences in the north west and north east and it was the task of the Alpini to operate in and around them, because in view of the speed and hitting power of modern armies, an enemy breakthrough into the Po valley would have disastrous consequences.

The widely held opinion that the Prussian schoolmaster had played a central role in Moltke's victories had already led the Italians to found the *Scuola di Guerra* in 1867. Ricotti improved the teaching in the military schools and academies, extended the examination system for promotions, sent officers to study abroad, and established *grandi campi di istruzione*. One of the most serious defects of the Italian army, its cohesion as a fighting force, could be remedied by holding realistic peacetime manoeuvres. Unfortunately the financial situation had virtually prohibited this, but as the state of the economy improved, Ricotti was able to begin holding them. Great military parades were also allowed, and in 1875 the Austrian Emperor and the German Emperor took the salute at the military camps of Vogonza and Milan. *'Reichbegabts Volk',* was Moltke's terse comment.[6]

Lack of large deposits of coal and iron and the narrow industrial base of the new state made the modernisation of the Italian army difficult and expensive. The railway network, which was being rapidly expanded at this time, was largely financed from abroad, the bulk of the raw materials needed were imported and foreign technicians helped to supervise its construction. In the equipping of the Italian armed forces a similar pattern can be detected. For the past two decades, the Piedmontese and later the Italian army had been heavily dependent on the Second Empire of Napoleon III. Money, advice, arms and military assistance had from time to time been made available by the Emperor. Many Italians had resented French tutelage, the surrender of Savoy and Nice, and the continued presence of French troops in Rome. During the 1860s, despite the usually amicable relationship between Napoleon and Victor Emmanuel, the two countries began to drift apart. The Prussian alliance of 1866 and the Mentana episode the following year created bitterness on both sides and helped to ensure Italian neutrality in 1870. But until the news of Sedan, Italian military opinion had continued to revere the martial qualities of the French army, although there were some dissentient voices. On the collapse of the Second Empire, Italy lost an exacting patron but quickly realised that freedom and independence presented their own problems.

General Ricotti's military reforms were a response to this new situation. To maintain her independence in the period of armed peace just beginning, Italy needed an army capable of waging modern warfare along the lines indicated by the Prussians. But this required more than the reorganisation of the military structure and an increased emphasis on universal national service. It required the importation or manufacture of the latest weapons and a willingness on the part of the officer corps to handle them as effectively as possible. Technical innovation had produced a military revolution. Essen, Potsdam and Berlin had forged a formidable weapon which had transformed the balance of power in Europe.

Not until the turn of the century was Italian industry capable of supplying the army with a large proportion of its basic equipment, but steps were taken to reduce its dependence on German, British and French armaments. An arms factory was established at Terni, the foundary at Turin was enlarged and a powder factory set up at Fontana Liri.[7] It was a great day for Italian technology when the cruiser *Duilio* was launched at the shipyards of Castellammare in May 1876, but it also underlined another problem confronting the government. Because of her geographical position and her very long coastline, Italy had to consider her naval role in the Mediterranean. Acrimonious disputes between northerners and Neapolitans and the humiliation of Lissa marked the inauspicious début of the Italian battle fleet, but in the 1870s improvements began to take place. As the much richer Germans found out in the 1900s, the maintenance of a large navy as well as a large army was a costly business, capable of generating intense rivalry for funds between the two services.

Despite the 'battle of the budget' in the early 1870s, Ricotti succeeded in steering his reforms through parliament. He also re-equipped the army. The infantry received the 1870 Wetterly and the Bersaglieri the Remington, while the artillery – a speciality of the Italians since Cavalli's experiments in the 1840s – was provided with more powerful guns. In addition, Ricotti began an extensive programme of fortifications, barrack buildings and the construction of other military establishments including the Ministry of War at Rome.

With the new emphasis on mass armies and universal conscription, managerial techniques and technical efficiency, the question of what would now be called public relations began to assume greater importance. Except for a number of officers who freely mingled with politicians, businessmen or professional people, the serving soldier of most countries was largely isolated from civilian society. The army became something of a state within the state, an enclosed world with its own code of conduct and beliefs. A French officer expressed this clearly in 1868.

> *Dans l'organisation de l'armée tout concourt à isoler complètement celle-ci de la nation; les lois particulières, des traditions, des usages, des préjugés même habilement entretenus, tendent au même but: briser les liens qui unissent l'armée à sa source, tous jusqu'aux plus tenaces. . . .*[8]

The regular army in Italy was part of *'Italia legale'*, and, however detached they might sometimes feel, the officer corps and the men they commanded were indispensable guardians of the existing state structure. Most officers possessed sufficient property to qualify them for full political rights, so they were an integral part of the state they were pledged to defend, but the same was not true of the conscripts or the volunteers in the ranks. As Ricotti's reforms did not abolish the system of substitutes, the majority of the rank and file were members of *'Italia reale'* with less commitment to a state which denied them the political rights enjoyed by their officers.[9] Since the French Revolution, universal conscription had become associated with universal male suffrage, but as Italian governments were unwilling to concede a democratic franchise until just prior to the First World War, it was more difficult to justify compulsory military service. The suffrage law of 1882 reduced the minimum voting age from twenty-five to twenty-one, lowered property qualifications and extended the vote to those with a certificate of primary education, but this only increased the electorate from 600,000 to over two million or from 2 per cent to 7 per cent of the total population. That still left many millions who were obliged to bear arms but who were refused the right to vote.

The martinet's answer to the problem of ensuring the loyalty of these members of the army, whether they were short-term conscripts or long-term volunteers, was simple. These recruits from *'Italia reale'* must be bludgeoned, verbally or physically, into unconditional obedience to *'Italia legale'*. More sophisticated methods were attempted. In 1868 the military authorities were alarmed by the growth of anti-militarism. Particularly disturbing was the appearance of Iginio Tarchetti's novel, *Una nobile follia,* the first of a projected series of volumes under the general title of *Drammi della vita militare.* Tarchetti rejoiced over the defeats of Custoza and Lissa because they had freed Italy from the incubus of militarism, and he announced his intention to portray the life of the barracks as it really was. *L'Italia Militare,* the official organ of the Ministry of War, was fortunate at this time to secure the services of a talented young lieutenant, Edmondo De Amicis. He wrote a number of short stories for this newspaper and for others like *La Sentinella,* the *Gazzetta d'Italia* and the *Nuova Antologia* and they proved very popular. Rather in the style of Alfred de Vigny's *Servitude et grandeur militaires,* which had appeared thirty years previously, De Amicis described the daily life of the soldier, his hardships, his satisfactions and the silent service which he rendered to society in peacetime, as in the cholera epidemic of 1867. Some of his stories provided the basis for a reading book 'for use in army schools'; the fight against illiteracy was proclaimed as one of the most important functions of the army. With the title *La Vita Militare,* all his sketches were published in 1868, and various other editions appeared shortly afterwards.[10]

Mazzini had declared that only a nation in arms, prepared to fight a *guerra di popolo,* could make a soldier feel that 'he is not a machine but part of the people and the armed apostle of a sacred cause'.[11] This concept had been rejected in the course of the Risorgimento despite the exploits of Garibaldi, but this did not prevent the authorities from trying to raise the morale of the soldier by convincing him that the army was the embodiment of the nation and that it was a privilege to defend the frontiers of Italy and to prevent internal enemies from disrupting society. Except on ceremonial occasions, however, it is doubtful whether many NCOs or Savoyard generals felt sufficiently dedicated to pursue and develop these arguments.

For the middle classes who were busily consolidating their positions in the state, there was much about the army which they disliked, particularly if they or their sons fell into its clutches. Yet however expensive and unproductive it might appear, it was a necessary evil.[12] The French army, despite its defeat by the Prussians, had saved society by destroying the Commune, repeating the role it had played in June 1848. While Ricotti was introducing his military reforms in Rome, the national assembly in Paris was expressing faith in the army as the regenerator of France, the *'grande école des générations futures'.* The *rapporteur* of the French military law of 1872, the Marquis de Chasseloup-Laubat, explained that by submitting young Frenchmen to the discipline of the camps and the barracks they were ensuring *'le triomphe définitif des grands principes d'obéissance et de soumission',* and preventing the outbreak of another Commune.[13] In a passage reminiscent of De Amicis, he went on to declare that in the ranks of the army, representatives of all regions, classes and political opinions would mingle together to form a *'union nationale'* as they would all have to live under the same rules, share the same privations and become increasingly aware of *'un grand intérêt commun'.* Italian deputies did not need any prompting from their French counterparts in this particular line of argument. The early 1870s saw a series of disturbances provoked by followers of Mazzini or Bakunin and although the police usually managed to cope, it was comforting to realise that the army was there ready to deal with fanatical socialists or reactionary clericals. It was significant that the mobs who protested about the *macinato* in the late 1860s or attacked existing property relations, all denounced the institution of conscription. They too saw the army as the chief bulwark of the *status quo.* It was the task of the officer corps to ensure that the young men under their command would, if necessary fire on their fathers if so ordered.

Anti-militarism inevitably became an established part of the doctrine of the left and particularly of the socialist groups which sprang up as industrialisation developed. The large number of young men, especially in Sicily and the south, who evaded service, was a clear indication of the mass appeal of an anti-militarist programme. But it also made an impact on elements of the literate middle classes. The concern with which the military authorities viewed the publication of Tarchetti's novel is proof of this, and they must have been relieved when he died in 1869 before being able to write the sequel. *L'Italia Militare* served a useful purpose, but it was basically for those in the service, just as the *Rivista Militare,* founded by the Mezzacapo brothers, was intended primarily for military specialists. Army propagandists needed to reach a wider public. The military themselves, however, had made this more difficult by the cavalier attitude they usually adopted towards journalists and sometimes civilians in general. The *Corriere Italiano* was apparently one of the first Italian newspapers to carry full reports from the battlefields in 1866.[14] The role of the war correspondent, however, was not widely appreciated by the generals. The Crimean War and the extention of telegraphic communications had produced this new type of journalist. Theoretically it became possible to give the public an almost blow-by-blow account of military engagements shortly after they had taken place. What had once been mysteriously remote could now be given an immediacy which enabled civilians to feel a sense of participation. Blundering generals were not slow to see the disadvantages of this; the fog of war, the mystique, the arcana, were often invaluable elements in the preservation of military reputations, and war correspondents might look for the spectacular and the outrageous to satisfy their readers back home, even if this led to exposures which lowered the morale of their own troops and encouraged the enemy. Petrucelli della Gattina, acting as correspondent for *Journal des Dèbats* during the campaign of 1866, was treated with scant deference by the authorities. 'I received him coldly,' wrote Genera Della Rocca. 'In time of war I have little sympathy with these gentlemen, who, for the sake of sending a few columns of news to their papers, are capable of altering truth in a most dangerous manner.'[15] General Cadorna was even more outspoken. While at La Storta, on the even of the capture of Rome, he lashed out at the irresponsible journalists who were following him around with their interminable questions. He longed for these gossip writers to be under military discipline and was presumably itching to have them shot.[16] If this was impossible, there were other ways of silencing unwelcome critics. The young lawyer, Felice Cavallotti, who had harshly criticised the military establishment in 1869, was challenged to a duel and wounded by Cisotti, one of the editors of *L'Italia Militare.*[17] The duel and the more sophisticated trial for defamation of character became a recurrent feature of the next decades as the army strove to defend its honour. A more positive attitude towards the press and the intellectuals would have deprived anti-militarists of many opportunities for damaging attacks on the army.

The task of these critics was made easier still if the army itself was seen to be divided. Two accusations which were frequently made – that the army was perpetuating the ascendancy of Piedmontese officers and that the officer corps despised ex-Garibaldini – were not altogether without foundation but there were many professional reasons for this. There were certainly prejudices and regional loyalties in the army but men like Ricotti were trying to eliminate them rather than perpetuate them. Another major accusation was that the army was the praetorian guard of the ruling class, and the prevalence of this view has already been mentioned. There were few, however, who accused the army of unequivocal support for any particular political grouping. But this did become an important issue in 1876 when the Destra fell from power and the Sinistra, under Depretis, took office for the first time.

Minghetti's resignation in March 1876 led to the appointment of new ministers, and the November elections which were a great triumph for the government filled Montecitorio with new deputies. Meanwhile, Minister of the Interior Nicotera, one of four southerners in the new cabinet – the highest number since unity – was busily purging the administration from the prefects down. It seemed that, not to be outdone, the new War Minister General Luigi Mezzacapo was also intent upon radical changes in army personnel. Thirteen generals were retired, including Cadorna and Petitti, allegedly because of their age, but it was pointed out that ten of them happened to Piedmontese. The War Minister's brother Carlo was made a corps commander, General Nunziante became president of the committee of the army of the line, Colonel Primerano became secretary at the War Ministry. They were all southerners and they were seen by some as representatives of a new Bourbon administration. It was true that Depretis was Piedmontese but his government relied upon southern support, and this 'slaughter of the generals' smacked of politics, as well as of regionalism.[18] It was argued that Cadorna was being punished for an adverse vote in the senate and because his brother, the politician Carlo Cadorna, refused to collaborate with the new government.[19] Italy, it seemed, was becoming like Spain where the army had become intimately bound up with politics. There was, however, little cause for alarm. Mezzacapo continued with the reforms of Ricotti, and his professionalism was reassuring for all but those officers who read about their retirement in the newspapers. For those at the bottom or middle of the military hierarchy of the officer corps the prospects of promotion looked brighter. Perhaps the real significance of events after 1876, as far as the army was concerned, was the willingness of the Sinistra not only to maintain the existing military establishment but to enlarge and strengthen it. This was one reason why Victor Emmanual accepted the 'parliamentary revolution' with equanimity. With new men in the saddle, this political veteran felt that he would be able to reassert his authority in the sphere of foreign policy and consolidate his control over the army. He revealed his prowess by achieving the remarkable feat of securing the appointment of General Cialdini as ambassador at Paris despite the understandable reluctance of the French and the bewilderment of Depretis.[20] As many of the old landmarks were swept away by the political events of 1876, events in the Balkans began to cause concern. But the King who had fought in the three wars of liberation was still on the throne, convinced that he was more capable than any politician of leading Italy through the difficulties which lay ahead. *Les Ministres passent. Le Roi reste.*

Notes

1. Craig, p.64.
2. M. Janowitz, *The professional soldier* (New York, 1964), p.22.
3. L. De Rosa, 'Incidenza delle spese militari sullo sviluppo economico italiano', *Atti del primo convegno nazionale di storia militare* (Rome, 1969), pp.212-17.
4. Pieri, *Le forze armate,* pp.461-4
5. Stato Maggiore, p.187.
6. Stato Maggiore, p.188
7. Ibid., p.189.
8. Girardet, p.88
9. See A. Berselli, *La destra storica dopo l'unità. Italia legale e Italia reale* (Bologna, 1965).
10. L. Gigli, *De Amicis* (Turin, 1962), pp.83-90.
11. 'Cennie documenti. . .', *L'Italia del popolo* 1849-50.
12. A hundred years after Sedan, the West German president Heinemann called the Bundeswehr a 'necessary evil' in a speech to conscientious objectors. The

right immediately attacked him for calling the military evil and the left for calling them necessary *(New Society,* 8 April 1971).

13. Girardet, p.163.
14. Gigli, p.90.
15. Della Rocca, p.236.
16. Gigli, pp.157-8.
17. Gigli, p.122.
18. *Perseveranza,* 21 May 1877, quoted in Cadorna, p.358.
19. Ibid.
20. Chabod, p.669.

8 THE TRIPLE ALLIANCE, THE ARMY AND DIPLOMACY

In January 1878 it was the ministers who remained and the King who left. A few days after learning of the death of La Marmora, Victor Emmanuel died, his ambition to fight one last glorious war still unfulfilled.[1] Perhaps because he was so small in stature he had tried to by every inch a King and, in particular, a Warrior King. As Queen Victoria had quickly seen, he was a social misfit who was never completely at ease unless in the company of his officers. His son, who assumed the title of Humbert I, was not so militaristic nor such a colourful character. The circumstances of his accession were not as daunting as they had been for his father on the evening of Novara, but serious enough for some of his advisers to cast around anxiously for someone like La Marmora. Twenty years later, during another tense period, General Pelloux was to be summoned. In January 1878, however, he was a young colonel in charge of supervising the late King's funeral procession to the Pantheon. As a reward for his services he was not on this occasion called upon to save the monarchy.[2] Later he described the situation in these years as resembling *'une vèritable lanterne magique'*, with one weak government succeeding another in rapid succession.[3] This political instability was unfortunate because with a young and inexperienced King on the throne both the domestic and the international scene was far from reassuring.

When he was Minister of the Interior in Cairoli's ministry of March 1878, Zanardelli's formula of *'reprimere, non prevenire'* tended to encourage the growth of subversive republican movements. The 'Barsanti circles', named after a corporal shot for attempted insurrection in 1870, appeared particularly menacing as one of their prime objectives was to incide the troops to mutiny. Equally disturbing was the continued growth of irredentism, the *Italia Irredenta* association organising various demonstrations throughout Italy in the summer and autumn. The most notorious incident took place in the December of the following year when General Avezzana, who had been chairman of the association, was given a state funeral which degenerated into a riot. This affair created a tense diplomatic situation between Austria-Hungary and Italy as the Emperor consistently adopted a very harsh attitude towards anything resembling official patronage of irredentist claims to Habsburg territory. In addition to these movements, anarchist bombs were exploded in Florence and Pisa and, in November 1878, the first attempted assassination of the King took place. The way in which the politicians handled these crises did not inspire great confidence and, at the same time, neither did the performance of Italian diplomats. The Eastern Crisis of 1875, which had encouraged Victor Emmanuel to believe that his day of glory was at hand, had finally been resolved by the Congress of Berlin. Foreign Minister Corti, representing Italy, had been instructed not to make any territorial demands unless Vienna formally annexed Bosnia. As the Austrians were content merely to occupy this area of the Balkans, Corti was content to allow his 'clean hands' policy to become synonymous with an empty hands policy. Seemingly unresponsive to tempting offers of Albania, Tunis or Tripoli, the Italian delegates were regarded by the other representatives at the congress with contemptuous incredulity. On his return home, Corti found that public opinion believed him to be responsible for a national humiliation comparable to Custoza or Lissa. But worse was to follow. In 1879 the Dual Alliance was signed between Germany and Austria-Hungary, in 1881 the Three Emperors League re-established friendly relations between the central powers and Russia, and in May of that year the French brushed aside Italian interests and established a protectorate over Tunisia. Internal unrest combined with a dangerous diplomatic isolation alarmed the King, his generals and a large section of the political élite in Italy. The need for security, internal and international, made some diplomatic arrangement with the Dual Alliance seem a tempting prospect. During his visit to Germany in 1877, Crispi had found Bismarck unprepared to consider any Rome-Berlin agreement direct against Vienna. A treaty with Germany any time after 1879 involved one with the 'hereditary enemy' also. This was an unpalatable fact of life for many Italians, but there were those like the young deputy Sidney Sonnino actively promoting a triple alliance. At the end of May 1882 he wrote an article in the *Rassegna Settimanale* in which he dismissed Italian claims to Trieste, and although he admitted that the Trentino was unquestionably Italian he argued that 'the interests which we might have in Trent are slight compared to those we have in establishing a sincere friendship with Austria'.[4] Without it, the Italian armed forces would be permanently immobilised and Rome would continue to be ignored in the other capitals of Europe. Sonnino had emphasised the international implications of isolation but in December 1881 Alberto Blanc, the Secretary General at the Foreign

Ministry, had stressed the domestic perils. In a conversation with the Austrian ambassador he advocated an Austro-Italian agreement in order to safeguard the monarchy and the existing *status quo.*[5] One of the many ironies in the situation was that the central powers would only negotiate if Rome not only agreed to abandon irredentism but accepted the French protectorate over Tunisia as well. After considerable delays these terms were accepted, serious negotiations followed, and the Triple Alliance was finally signed on 20 May 1882. Italy, no longer isolated, had joined two powerful military monarchies. King Humbert, now described by his radical critics as 'the Austrian colonel', became the partner of Franz Joseph and William I, the combined weight of their three armies being more than sufficient to curb French or Italian republicanism. Perhaps for the first time in his reign the King began to feel secure although the Oberdan crisis later on in the year demonstrated how easily Austro-Italian tension could be revived.

'We must hold to the Austrian Empire. We must not place ourselves between two enemies, one on our right and the other on our left'.[6] The words were Crispi's but they expressed the sentiments of the military establishment during the 1880s. Since 1866 army leaders had regarded the Austro-Italian frontier in the north-east as a strategic and tactical nightmare with the Habsburg army holding all the advantages. The alpine frontier with France was, on the other hand, a much more manageable proposition. From the point of view of the army, therefore, it was an advantage to have a friendly Austria and a hostile France rather than the reverse. The closer links which were likely to develop between the Italian and the German armies were also welcomed by the officer corps, especially by the newly reorganised general staff, from September 1882 until December 1893 under the direction of General Enrico Cosenz. Naval commanders like Saint Bon and Benedetto Brin were naturally less sanguine. Although for the next few years the Italian navy ranked third in tonnage behind the British and the French, it was incapable of providing adequate defence for the numerous ports and exposed cities along the western coast of Italy against a French attack.[7] This was, of course, the basic reason for Italian determination to emphasise that the Triple Alliance was not directed against Britain. Only the British could neutralise French naval power in the western Mediterranean.

After a preamble stressing the 'essentially conservative and defensive nature' of the alliance and the desire of the signatories 'to assure the unimpaired maintenance of the social and political order in Their respective States', the articles which followed dealt with the specific commitments which had been agreed upon by the three powers. If France attacked Italy, Austria and Germany were 'bound to lend help and assistance with all their forces to the party attacked'. If France attacked Germany, Italy promised assistance, but if Russia attacked Austria, Italy promised only benevolent neutrality unless France joined in the war. To this treaty, which was to remain in force for five years, there was attached a ministerial declaration dated 22 May 1882 in which Rome stipulated that the treaty was in no way directed against Britain. Rumours that a military convention had also been signed proved to be false, the nearest approach to this being article V which stated that if war threatened 'the High Contracting Parties shall take counsel together in ample time as to the military measures to be taken with a view to eventual cooperation'.[8] In fact, it was not until 1888 that an Italo-German military convention was signed, after the Triple Alliance had been renewed and successfully renegotiated by Count Robilant the previous year.

In later years army officers tended to look back on the 1880s as a golden age when promotion was swift and the military career looked attractive enough to induce even the sons of the rich bourgeoisie to enter the academies.[9] Garibaldi had died in 1882, an event which seemed to symbolise the passing of an era just as the signing of the Triple Alliance seemed to inaugurate a new one. In his farewell address to the Peruvian people, San Martin had warned that 'the presence of a fortunate soldier. . . is dangerous to newly constituted states', and in view of her military record over the last decades, Italy had only one such claimant. Despite his humiliations at Aspromonte and Mentana, and his sometimes grotesque political interventions, Garibaldi had become a living legend because of his exploits in South America,[10] Rome and Sicily. Alive, he was a constant embarrassment to the civilian and military élite; dead, he became a valuable asset and an army of statues could now be raised up to honour the man who had failed to create a Nation in Arms. The future of the army lay in the hands of men like the Neapolitan General Cosenz. He had fought in the defence of Venice in 1849 and served under Garibaldi in the Alps and in Sicily, but despite this unorthodox and southern background Cosenz had proved remarkably adaptable. Entering the royal army, he had commanded a division in 1866 and again in 1870 and his appointment as Chief of Staff in September 1882 had not created consternation among the entrenched military dynasties of northern Italy. A dedicated professional, his presence disarmed those critics who attacked the officer corps for being politically and regionally exclusive.

In the 'golden age' of the 1880s there were, however, other targets for these critics. Under War Minister General Ferrero (1881-4) the army grew from ten to twelve corps, and the military estimates grew accordingly. Economy-minded deputies were appalled by this extravagance and claimed that the size of the Italian army was being dictated by her partners in the Triple Alliance. Supporters of increasing armaments like Crispi argued that Ferrero had introduced his measures in November 1881, over five months before the signature of the alliance, and Pelloux in 1890 claimed that without the alliance military expenditure would have been even higher to compensate for Italian isolation.[11] These arguments were not entirely convincing, and not only because the secret military convention of 1888 could not for obvious reasons be brought into the debate. By joining the Triple Alliance, whether she remained in it or tried to escape from it, Italy, unlike Spain, had become identified as one of the six great powers. Therefore 1882 was an important turning point, and in a period of armed peace with huge armies watching each other Italy was compelled to play a role which ensured that her military establishment would play an important, perhaps even a preponderant part in the life of the nation.

Although no longer a member of the military establishment, Count Robilant was determined to use his considerable diplomatic skills to assist the efforts of men like Cosenz and Ricotti to consolidate Italy's great power status. Robilant, who had lost a hand at Novara and had later risen to the rank of lieutenant-general, had rapidly outclassed Menabrea and Cialdini as a soldier turned diplomat after his appointment to the embassy at Vienna in 1871. As ambassador, he had signed the Triple Alliance in 1882 but had been critical of the way in which the Foreign Ministry had handled negotiations. In 1885 Depretis offered him the post of Foreign Minister. Initially he was reluctant to accept but the King insisted and he gave way, because, as he put it, 'an old soldier like me does not discuss the orders of his sovereign'.[12] When the time came to renew the Triple Alliance, Robilant intended to renegotiate some of the terms so as to include Balkan and North African considerations. Bismarck was supposed to have said that in the event of war he would be content if 'one Italian corporal with the Italian flag and a drummer at his side should take the field on the western front against France and not on the eastern front against Austria'. It was this sort of attitude on the part of the central powers which made Robilant's task difficult. That he succeeded in his renegotiations was due primarily to his patient awareness that the European diplomatic situation was changing in Italy's favour. The

Bulgarian crisis from 1885-7 resurrected fears of Russian expansionism and Boulangism in France of a war of revenge along the Rhine. After a few friendly gestures in the direction of Paris, a hint here and there of the non-renewal of the alliance, and the statement that 'the Italy of 1887 was not the same as the Italy of 1882; with her new financial and military strength she could offer her allies more and could ask more from them', Robilant sat back and waited for Bismarck to act.[13] Bismarck decided to accede to Italian requests and put pressure on the reluctant Austrians to make concessions, even threatening a separate agreement with Italy if they proved recalcitrant.[14] It was, ironically enough, news of Italy's disaster at Dogali in eastern Africa, which hastened the signature of the new alliance – as well as Robilant's downfall. Bismarck feared that a shaken Italy might throw herself into the arms of France and Russia to seek compensations denied her by the central powers. 'It is annoying', wrote the Austrian ambassador at Berlin after the signing of the treaty on 20 February 1887, 'but nevertheless true that the Italians, who gain a province after every defeat, are now to be enabled to gather in booty without having fired a shot.'[15] Austria had just committed herself to an agreement with Italy whereby any change in the Balkan *status quo* would necessitate prior consultations 'based upon the principle of a reciprocal compensation. . .'[16] Germany had committed herself to protect Italian interests in North Africa. If war broke out between France and Italy in this area this would 'constitute *ipso facto*. . .the *casus foederis* of the aforesaid treaty of May 20, 1882, as if such an eventuality were expressly contemplated therein'.[17]

Shortly after Robilant's fall, the first Mediterranean Agreement was signed between Britain and Italy, with Austria acceding in March, and Spain becoming an associate member in May. Apart from securing British protection against a naval attack from France, Italy had also succeeded in associating Britain with the Triple Alliance. Her value as an ally of Germany and Austria was thereby enhanced and her own position in the Mediterranean strengthened. The achievements of the past few months, however, were not appreciated by the majority of Italians.

Dogali had revived that mood of disillusion and masochism which had been so noticeable after 1866. Colonialism became a contentious issue. 'Africanists' argued that colonialism must be seen as an integral part of the Risorgimento, while opponents declared that it was a betrayal of the Risorgimento and a dangerous diversion, distracting attention from the fundamental problems of Italy. Alfredo Oriani, who wrote *Fino a Dogali* in 1889, presented an interpretation which became popular among the nationalists of future decades.

> Italy, too easily crushed during the revolutions of 1821 and 1831; defeated in 1848. . .; barely victorious in 1859. . .miserably beaten in 1866. . . Italy, into which Garibaldi could not breathe his courage, Mazzini his genius and Cavour his good sense, which entered Rome on the sly in 1870. . .needed a contingent of its soldiers (the men of Dogali) who, becoming heroes, proved that the Latin blood still coursed in the veins of its people. . .that the revolution was being continued in Africa. . .. But the tragic solemnity of Dogali has not been able to raise the nation from the political mud.[18]

'War is an inevitable struggle for existence and blood will always be the best warm rain for great ideas.' This and similar sentiments marked the beginning of nationalist rhetoric which did so much to obscure the real achievements of the 1880s and led to false assumptions about Italian military strength. Those who reacted to events like Dogali with gloom and despondency and those who reacted with an exalted nationalism, both did a disservice to their country. It was a time for cautious consolidation, along the lines of Benedetto Brin's attempts to lay the foundations of an armaments industry based on a consortium of foreign and domestic banks, and linked to Schneider in France and Armstrongs in Britain. It was a misfortune that at this particular moment Francesco Crispi rose to power.

Crispi regarded himself as the Bismarck of Italy although Lord Salisbury thought he was more like Randolph Churchill. For a decade his personality seemed to dominate Italy and her policies. It has been said that his 'vision of the military possibilities of the Triple Alliance betrayed his revolutionary, popular past. His role in the Postrisorgimento might be described as that of uniting the nation through mass military rather than political action'.[19] Like Cavallotti, one of his severest critics, he thought in terms of a 'bloody baptism' and a successful war which would eradicate the painful memories of the 1860s and render any prolonged examination of the *rivoluzione mancata* unnecessary and irrelevant. In many ways he resembled neither Bismarck nor Randolph Churchill but rather Victor Emmanuel and was perhaps the nearest approach to a militarist to assume power in nineteenth century Italy. Becoming Prime Minister as well as Foreign Minister on the death of Depretis in the summer of 1887, Crispi was delighted to receive an invitation to visit Bismarck at Friedrichsruh in

October. In their conversations, Crispi outlined Italy's position in much the same way that Mussolini was to do in his talks with Hitler.

> I replied by outlining the conditions of Italy. Although we have not quite a million soldiers, our army is now sufficiently strong and compact to answer for the obligations implied by the two alliances. . .
>
> Our country is quiet; we do not fear subversive parties. . . In case of attack from the outside, all classes would unite in defence, and in case of an expedition to a foreign country, we should be able to use all our strength, having no fear of an insurrection at home.

He went on to promote the signing of a military convention.[20] When he returned home he told the astonished Austrian ambassador that if Russia attacked Turkey he would send 100,000 men to co-operate with the Austrian army.[21] In such a warlike atmosphere even Britain decided that the time had come to send a military attaché to her embassy at Rome.[22] The military convention sought by Crispi was signed in February 1888, the Italian agreeing to send an expeditionary force of five army corps and three cavalry divisions to fight on the Rhine if the Triple Alliance went to war with France and Russia.[23] As disciples of Clausewitz, officers of the general staff approved of this strategy which aimed at a battle of annihilation against the French in the opening moves of the war. Transporting the expedition to the Rhine, perhaps by violating Swiss neutrality, was to provide some intriguing problems for these same staff officers in the next two decades.

Crispi took a personal interest in the military bills passing through parliament at this time which raised military expenditure in 1888-9 to an unprecedented 560 million lire, compared to 256 million in 1880 or even to 498 million as late as 1909-10.[24] He also felt competent to intervene in technical matters, explaining to his War Minister Bertolè-Viale his views on mobilisation.

> . . .allow me to call your attention to the system of mobilisation which Italy alone of all the great powers continues to practise, which is both slow and expensive, and in times of war might prove a source of much danger.
>
> I have discussed this point with General Cialdini who is in favour of the Prussian method, but who would not be adverse to the adoption of the French system, which would appear to be a compromise between the Prussian method and our own.

Cialdini was apprehensive about the political repercussions and particularly the impact the Prussian system might have on regionalism. Crispi, however, was confident that 'the national sentiment is profound in all classes of the population, and the different elements have been so thoroughly mingled by twenty-nine conscriptions that their fusion is now complete'.[25] There were few who shared his optimism and Crispi had to admit his scheme was premature. Even more distressing was the news a few weeks later that the desertion rate among the Alpini was increasing and they were the crack troops of the Italian army and, moreover, organised on a territorial basis.[26]

Crispi's dynamism was, for a time, remarkably infectious and the court, the army, the diplomats and even foreign governments were whirled along at an unwonted pace. But a tariff war with France and the escalating cost of armaments led to demands for a less frenetic tempo or even a change in direction. For the army, the new commitments had serious implications. General Ricotti had argued during the 1880s that quality was more important than quantity and that the army establishment should be reduced from twelve to ten corps. After the convention with Germany in February 1888 such a programme was virtually impossible. Pelloux, one of Ricotti's chief critics in this decade, supported the retention of twelve corps but hoped to economise by keeping the peacetime strength of companies as low as possible. His whole argument was based on the premise that the Italian army was a defensive and not an offensive army like the French or the German. Behind the rampart of the Alps the Italians could hold off the invader while they brought their companies up to wartime strength. Crispi's attempts to inject an offensive spirit into the Triple Alliance destroyed Pelloux's premise.[27] Recruitment, strategy and organisation would all become involved if this change of emphasis became permanent. Crispi's fall in 1891, in part the result of a growing awareness that Italy could not afford his grandiose foreign policy, did reduce tension. Pelloux, who became War Minister under Crispi's successor Di Rudini, had been a member of the budget commission of the chamber in 1890 and had seen the necessity to reduce military expenditure. He thought, however, that economies could be effected without 'material or moral harm to the strength of Italy' and he appointed himself 'the watch dog of the army of twelve corps'.[28] By making sacrifices he hoped that the army would retain 'that sympathy and affection' which was so essential for the well-being of the armed forces.[29] The King was a staunch supporter of Pelloux's policy and when Rudini attempted to reduce the size of the army his administration was doomed. Giolitti who replaced him was astute enough to realise that defiance of the King on this issue would be tantamount to political suicide. He therefore retained the services of Pelloux. Without reducing the number of corps, Pelloux cut costs by various expedients such as calling up conscripts in March instead of in November of the previous year, thereby allowing companies to dwindle away almost to nothing during the winter months. The number of civilian labourers employed on construction work for the forces was reduced from about 14,000 to 6,000 and the 'horse allowance' to infantry captains was withdrawn.[30] The golden days of the 1880s were indeed over! Between 1891 and 1893 it proved possible to save over 27 million lire and Pelloux considered one of his most significant achievements had been the 'consolidation of the war budget' at 246 million lire. This was regarded as the minimum figure compatible with the efficient functioning of the army, and it was part of Pelloux's programme for attempting to remove military affairs from the political arena. Unlike Bismarck and Moltke he failed to secure a *'quinquennato'* which would have guaranteed the income of the army for years in advance but he did manage to kill an attempt to establish a *'consiglio di tutela sul ministero della guerra'* which would have enabled politicians to supervise closely the structure of the army. In this period, neither the civilians nor the military made any serious attempts to encroach very far into one another's domain. Parliament's financial control appeared to be a sufficient safeguard against any military bid for supremacy. But economic problems and, in particular, the Banca Romana scandal, began to make life very difficult for Giolitti and, with his fall, the stage was set for a turbulent era which has been aptly called 'the crisis of the liberal state'.[31]

Notes

1. Crispi to Depretis, 27 August 1877, *The memoirs of Francesco Crispi,* ed. T. Palamenghi-Crispi, vol.II (London, 1912), p.9.
2. Pelloux, p.102.
3. Ibid., p.106.
4. G. Volpe, *L'Italia nella triplice alleanza* (Milan, 1941), pp.30-3.
5. L. Salvatorelli, *La triplice alleanza* (Milan, 1939), p.61.
6. L. Albertini, *The origins of the war of 1914,* vol.I (Oxford, 1952), p.67.
7. P. Halpern, *The Mediterranean naval situation 1908-1914* (Harvard, 1971), pp.187-8. See also Ufficio storico della marina militare, *La marina militare nel suo primo secolo di vita, 1861-1961* (Rome, 1961).
8. A. Pribram, *The secret treaties of Austria-Hungary 1879-1915,* vol.I (Harvard, 1920), pp.65-9.

9. G. Licata, *Notabili della terza Italia* (Rome, 1968), p.69.
10. Recently well summarised in J. Ridley, *Garibaldi* (London, 1975).
11. Pelloux, p.15.
12. Chabod, p.631, f.3.
13. Pribram, II, p.54.
14. Ibid., p.60.
15. Ibid., p.76.
16. Ibid., I, p.109.
17. Ibid., I, p.113
18. J. Thayer, *Italy and the great war* (Wisconsin, 1964), pp.136-7.
19. Ibid., p.37.
20. Crispi, *Memoirs,* II, pp.213-14, 217.
21. Salvatorelli, p.140.
22. Kennedy to Salisbury, 19 May 1887, FO 170/382; and Pauncefote to Savile, 19 October 1887, FO 170/387.
23. *DDI*, 2nd series, XXI, p.520.
24. L. De Rosa, 'Incidenza delle spese militari sullo sviluppo economico italiano', *Atti del primo convegno nazionale di storia militare* (Rome, 1969), p.126.
25. Crispi, *Memoirs,* II, pp.390-1.
26. Crispi, *Memoirs,* II, pp.391-2.
27. Pelloux, p.xix.
28. Ibid., p.xxvii.
29. Ibid., pp.145-6.
30. Ibid., p.xxxi.
31. Seton-Watson, p.165.

Part Three: The Testing of The Army

9 THE ARMY AND THE CRISIS OF THE LATE 1890s

When Crispi returned to power in December 1893 he had to cope with problems in Europe, Africa and Italy itself, which differed considerably from those confronting him during his first ministry. The international situation was much more menacing. His friend Bismarck had been out of office for nearly three years and the Russo-German Reinsurance Treaty of 1887 had been allowed to lapse on his departure. The growing *rapprochement* between Russia and France became a military alliance. Europe was dividing into two armed camps and Italy, as a member of the Triple Alliance, would have to accept the consequences of this or try to extricate herself. Britain under the Liberals had shown no interest in renewing Salisbury's Mediterranean Agreement, and, even more ominous, Anglo-German relations were beginning to deteriorate. The rioting at Aigues-Mortes, the fortification of Bizerta, and the assassination of the French president by an Italian anarchist revived Franco-Italian bitterness in the years 1893-4. All this diplomatic uncertainty in Europe threatened the Italian position in East Africa.

As the Ras of Shoa, Menelik had welcomed an understanding with the Italians pushing out from Massawa. After the death of John of Ethiopia in a battle with the Mahdists, Menelik had proclaimed himself Emperor and in 1889 had signed the Treaty of Ucciali. The Italians believed that it established their protectorate over Ethiopia, but Menelik, as he consolidated his power, disputed this and in 1893 denounced the treaty and looked to the French and Russians for support. Colonel Arimondi's victory over the dervishes at Agordat in December 1893 'united Italy's first authentic military success',[1] and General Baratieri's defeat of Ras Mangasha drew the Italians irresistibly forward, but at the same time enabled Menelik to unite the tribes against this dangerous invader. High above the Red Sea, General Baratieri, born in the *terra irredenta* of Trentino and a survivor of Garibaldi's Thousand, was poised either for a great victory or a great defeat.

Faced with a disastrous political and economic situation at home, Crispi deperately needed a great victory. During his first ministry Crispi had been an energetic and authoritarian Minister of the Interior. He had been particularly severe with the irredentists. In a letter to the King he wrote: 'Today, in all the cities where such existed, those associations which bore the names of Barsanti and Oberdank have been simultaneously dissolved. The police officials were equal to their duty, and consequently the operations were successful.'[2] 'Irredentism', he declared the previous year, 'is the most dangerous of those errors by which Italy is today distracted', and he made determined efforts to suppress this and other subversive movements.[3] Although irredentism was still very much alive during his second ministry, it was temporarily eclipsed by the Sicilian *fasci* and by uprisings in the Lunigiana and elsewhere, prompted by the severe economic crisis which was causing widespread discontent. This was a far more formidable threat to the stability of the country than irredentism, a fact recognised by Crispi who allowed Alberto Blanc to run the Foreign Ministry so that he himself could devote more attention to his tasks as Minister of the Interior. Both in the maintenance of order at home and of Italian prestige in Africa, the army had an important role to play. If Crispi failed, and he was now seventy-five years old and at long last beginning to show his age, there could be anarchy or perhaps a military takeover. 'The only cement holding Italy together.' This was the comment of Domenico Farini, president of the senate from 1887 to 1898, on the role of the army, and a thoroughly frightened *'Italia legale'* tended to agree with him.[4] In this state of emergency, when banks were crashing and socialism seemed to become an irresistible tide, men of property were prepared to accept Crispi's plea for a 'truce of God'. When the internal crisis receded in 1896, they used the news from Africa to drive him out of politics. They feared De Felice or the anarchists' bomb more than Menelik. The victory of an Ethiopian tyrant enabled them to defeat Crispi before he established himself as an Italian tyrant.

Crispi's efforts to conciliate his fellow Sicilians were overtaken by events. During his first month in office, 98 peasants were killed by police and soldiers. He swiftly complied with the growing demand for stern measures, and, as so often in the past, he detected a Franco-Jesuit plot. Their aim was to detach Sicily from the kingdom and so ruin Italy. Between January and August 1894 Sicily was declared in a state of siege, reservists were called up and General Morra with 40,000 troops was sent to the island. 'I have done today what I did in 1860,' said Crispi as the arrests, deportations and trials by court-martial began.[5] It was a confession that over 30 years after the Bronte shootings the peasants were still unreconciled to the kingdom. In the summer, laws against anarchism and 'incitement to class hatred' were passed by parliament and in October 1894 Crispi suppressed the Socialist Party which had rather belatedly announced its solidarity with the Sicilian workers. The non-socialist left and many moderates now began to react against arbitrary government. For the socialists and many radicals, arbitrary government had become associated with the maintenance of the Triple Alliance and the twelve corps army, and before long Africanism was to be added to the list.

Mancini had described Massawa and its coastline, or Eritrea as it became officially in 1890, as providing the keys to the Mediterranean. For Crispi and the activists, colonialism became the substitute for a war with France, for irredentism, for radical reforms at home. It also provided that poetry of the Risorgimento which had been lost since Custoza and Mentana. In the Abyssinian highlands, old Garibaldini and those too young to have shared their triumphs, could relive the heroic past. Writing from the Plain of Monkeys in December 1887, Colonel Baratieri thanked Crispi for posting him to Africa and reminded him of their comradeship under Garibaldi's leadership.[6] The names of those appointed to commands in Eritrea, however, suggest that Garibaldi types were in a distinct minority. Piedmontese professionals who had been attached to the general staff predominated. The King, an enthusiastic Africanist, might be expected to welcome requests from the more adventurous staff officers. In April 1889, when Crispi suffered one of his rare defeats in the cabinet over military policy in the colony – it was indeed rare for him even to inform them of such matters – he wrote to the War Minister Bertholè-Viale that he was still a Garibaldian and that 'in spite of my sixty-nine years I see things differently from the tacticians educated in military academies'. The War Minister replied that the daring of old Garibaldians was laudable but 'in Africa, even more than elsewhere, daring must be accompanied by prudence and foresight'.[7] Perhaps this is why lukewarm Africanists like Bertolè-Viale or Pelloux made no strenuous objections to sending so many Piedmontese officers out to waste their talents on the desert air. Cosenz, although an old Garibaldian, was also a professional and the chief of staff. Officers from the academies who had passed through the general staff must restrain their less cautious fellows, and would be able to implement some of their war theories under more realistic conditions without disturbing the farmers of the Val d'Aosta, where manoeuvres were frequently held. The leader of the first Massawa expedition in 1885 was Saletta, a Piedmontese professional, a staff officer who became chief of staff between 1896 and 1908. De Cristoforis, commander at Dogali, was Piedmontese and had been attached to the general staff. General Baldissera, who favoured a policy of cautious penetration in East Africa, had been an officer in the

Austrian army (he was born in Padua) before joining the Italian army after 1866. He fought in the African campaigns from 1887 to 1889 and returned in 1896 to assume full civil and military powers in the colony. The generals at Adua, under Baratieri, were Dabormida, Arimondi, Albertone (who had signed the military convention with Schlieffen in 1888), and Ellena, all Piedmontese professionals. Arimondi and Dabormida had been through the general staff, Albertone and Dabormida had taught at the *Scuola di Guerra* and Ellena had been in the learned branch of the artillery rising to Director General of Artillery and Engineers.[8]

Adua was not inevitable with such leaders and the men under their command, but financial stringency, Crispi's behaviour and Baratieri's temperament increased the chances of an unhappy encounter if the Italians continued their advance into the interior. Menelik was able to assemble 100,000 warriors, many of them equipped with Italian weapons, a legacy of his co-operation with them while Ras of Shoa. Russian and French arms were also rumoured to be in his possession.

Owing to the economic plight of Italy, Brin had watched – and as Foreign Minister under Giolitti from an elevated vantage point – his battle fleet of heavy cruisers being surpassed by the Russians and even being challenged by the infant German fleet. Italy was dropping from third place to fifth in terms of naval power, a dangerous development if she wished to exert influence in the Mediterranean and the seas beyond. His brother-in-law Pelloux was appalled when Mocenni, Crispi's War Minister, agreed to a 15 million lire reduction of the 246 million lire consolidated military budget. 'The defeat of Adua', wrote Pelloux, 'was the immediate consequence of the situation which was then created.'[9] These economies, which Crispi's cabinet colleagues Sonnino and Saracco insisted upon, were not really compatible with a forward colonial policy.

It was at this point that Crispi's Garibaldian heritage began to have unfortunate consequences. Because the great redshirt had won Sicily and Naples on the cheap, there seemed no reason to doubt that Baratieri could sweep aside Ethiopian savages despite his slender resources. Arimondi's victory at Agordat, Baratieri's occupation of Kassala in July 1894 and his subsequent defeat of Ras Mangasha fostered this belief. But Baratieri, the new national hero, had some misgivings, and on his return to Italy in the summer of 1895 he asked for reinforcements. Crispi, Blanc, Mocenni and Sonnino all gave him evasive answers. Menotti Garibaldi hailed him as the man who had 'renewed in Africa the splendour of Garibaldi's victories',[10] but, as

Pelloux warned Baratieri, rhetoric was no substitute for reinforcements. Pelloux, now commanding V Corps at Verona and commander designate of the Army of the Rhine in case of war, advised him not to go back to Africa without first securing a firm government guarantee to meet his more pressing demands.[11] Crispi did promise more money for Eritrea and sanctioned the recruitment of more native troops, but both he and Baratieri underestimated the strength of Menelik. With dissension in his cabinet, Crispi could not in any case contemplate any massive reinforcements, and with the applause of the veterans of The Thousand still ringing in his ears, Baratieri now imagined them to be unnecessary. When the true seriousness of the situation was finally realised and 20,000 troops were despatched, they arrived a month too late.

In December 1895 and January 1896 the Italian outposts of Amba Alagi and Makalle were overcome. Crispi oscillated dangerously between ordering a retreat and ordering an advance. Because he needed some dramatic success to extricate him from his domestic problems, he decided in favour of an advance. On 7 January, Baratieri was informed by Crispi that Italy expected another victory 'and I expect a complete victory'.[12] Baratieri himself, hesitating between retiring behind the Mareb or pushing towards Adua, held a conference which decided in favour of attack. Hints of cowardice and the knowledge that General Baldissera was on his way to replace him, obviously unsettled him. It was decided that their force of 16,000 should advance on Adua to await Menelik's response. If he failed to be drawn they would retreat. Somehow the columns became dispersed during a night march and on the following day, 1 March, the Italians and their Eritrean askaris were decisively routed by Menelik.

> One speaks – and this is no rare occurrence when tragic events kindle the passions – of the incapacity of the commanders, of weaknesses, of indiscipline, of disobedience; it was, instead, only a fatal coincidence of fortuitous and unpredictable circumstances.[13]

The insertion of the word 'only' makes this interpretation too charitable. The Italians might have won a significant victory but they would have had to achieve this despite Baratieri, despite Crispi and despite the unfavourable economic climate of Italy at this moment. Battles won or lost do tend to be a reflection of the strengths and weaknesses of society as a whole, although a certain 'coincidence of fortuitous and unpredictable circumstances', such as the exploits of a military genious or the chance death of key officers, can distort the reflection. An Italian victory at Adua would have been such a distortion. There was a divided cabinet led by a man who was torn between romance and reality, a divided military command in Africa led by a man whose background and temperament predisposed him to take risks; and yet, ironically, it may have been the 'professional' Arimondi who finally convinced Baratieri to make the provocative march on Adua.[14] There was, above all, a divided society, which economic depression had accentuated. It was difficult to find homogeneity anywhere. The metropolitan army was split between colonialists and anti-colonialists, and capitalists were divided over the relevance of imperialism.[15] Socialists, Catholics, liberals and conservatives were at odds with one another, and even within individual parties and groupings there were few issues which produced general agreement. Menelik too had his problems. His large army, riddled with tensions, had virtually exhausted its supplies and the weather was about to break. One severe setback and his power might disintegrate. But he was 'the king of kings' in personal command, unencumbered by any Crispi, unaware of many of the economic and political problems which beset the European states, and it was the Italians who made the false move.

Unquestionably 'tragic events kindle the passions'. News of the fall of Khartoum set the eighteen-year-old Beatrix Potter wishing that 'some lunatic had shot old Gladstone 12 months since'. The British and the French certainly had their fair share of colonial disasters, but these were more than offset by their successes. For the Italians there were no counterbalancing victories for the Adua defeat, and almost immediately 1896 was seen as another 1866, another year of shame and humiliation. The cries of 'Viva Menelik' voiced more than contempt for Crispi. The oppressed, the masochists, the moralists and political opportunists welcomed this national defeat, some because they saw it as a judgement on Crispi's megalomania, others because it revealed him as a failed megalomaniac and they could not tolerate a broken Coriolanus.

As in 1866, a military defeat was quickly transformed into a national disaster by the public outcry which followed. Of Baratieri's force of 16,000, 4,000 Italians and 2,000 askaris were killed, and 1,500 were taken prisoner. Baldissera and the new reinforcements relieved various garrisons in the following month and stabilised the situation north of the Mareb, thereby ensuring the safety of Eritrea. The retreat from the highlands was formalised by the Treaty of Addis Ababa in October 1896. Uccialli was scrapped and the independence of Ethiopia recognised, but Menelik accepted the Mareb as his frontier. King

Humbert greatly resented that fact that he, 'the descendant of a glorious line with eight centuries of military renown', was forced to make peace with 'an African ape', but Rudini, Crispi's successor, insisted.[16] Eritrea became a 'quiet colony' like the Italian Somalian protectorate until Mussolini decided that the time had come to seek 'revenge for Adua'.

Arimondi and Dabormida received gold medals for valour, posthumously. Crispi was hounded out of public life, and Baratieri was brought to trial. He was not shot like Ramorino but like Persano was branded with incompetence. Crispi and Baratieri were scapegoats, and because of their errors very credible scapegoats, for a ruling class which had blundered badly. Anti-militarism threatened the army, republicanism the monarchy, socialism the factory owners of Milan, peasant lawlessness the southern landowners. In such circumstances, which bore a close resemblance to the situation in 1849 or 1866, there was the danger that, in order to avert anarchy, some form of authoritarianism might be instituted. This could only be attempted with the support of the army and under the leadership of a trusted Savoyard or Piedmontese general. But, as on past occasions, the army showed a distinct disinclination to assume political power and the generals proved to be most reluctant militarists. Parliamentary government, despite scandals and widespread rumours of corruption, showed itself to be stronger and more resilient than most people imagined.

Unable to maintain Crispi in power, the King at least hoped to appoint one of his former collaborators. Senator Saracco was approached but he hastily suggested that a general like Ricotti might be a more appropriate choice. Ricotti, perhaps the least militaristic of all the generals, was frowned upon by court circles and most of the military because of his scheme for reducing the army by two corps. But in this March crisis of 1896, when anti-militarism and anti-monarchical feeling had reached a dangerous pitch, an army reformer like Ricotti who had consistently opposed Crispi's adventurous policies had much to recommend him. Through Domenico Farini, the King attempted to persuade Ricotti to accept the premiership and to leave the army intact. However, as Gastone Manacorda remarks in his excellent introduction to the memoirs of Pelloux, the King was in no position to impose conditions because 'it was he, or rather the monarchy itself, who needed General Ricotti'.[17] On 7 March he presented his 'ultimatum' to the King which called for the reduction of the army. It was to remain twelve corps strong but the number of infantry companies, cavalry squadrons and artillery batteries was to be reduced by about a quarter. Although later denying this, the King accepted these conditions. Ricotti thereupon agreed to serve as War Minister under the premiership of Rudini.

By reducing the number of military units from 1,920 to 1,506 and by increasing the annual intake of conscripts by at least 20,000, Ricotti hoped to produce a cheaper, younger and more efficient army.[18] In other words, he hoped to construct an 'army of quality' rather than an 'army of quantity', a fundamental reform which he had advocated for the past 20 years. In June the senate approved his measures, but the King, supported by Rudini and the majority of the military establishment, was determined to kill the reform. If Pelloux had remained a deputy he would have undoubtedly led the opposition in the chamber. In his absence, the Neapolitan General Afan de Rivera was delegated to lead the whispering campaign against Ricotti. Pelloux, who was in contact with Afan de Rivera (soon to become his Under-Secretary at the War Office), Rudini and the German military attaché Engelbrecht, played a far from insignificant role in this conspiracy although he was rather unstrategically placed in distant Verona. As commander designate of the Army of the Rhine, he had received the Grand Cross of the Red Eagle when William II visited Venice in April. This enabled him to act as something of a spokesman for Italian military commitments to the Triple Alliance at a time when German opinion tended to view Ricotti's reforms with misgiving.[19] Becoming aware of the plot against him and disgusted by Rudini's dilatory tactics, Ricotti resigned on 11 July 1896. When Rudini reshuffled his government, few people were surprised when Pelloux became War Minister. This has been described as a blatant example of militarism. To a certain extent this is true, but this rather underhand manoeuvre was essentially limited and defensive in character. The issue at stake was the organisation of the army, the civilian premier Rudini supported the conspiracy, and there was no comprehensive plan to usurp the political functions of the government or legislature. It is significant that Pelloux himself, after he had become premier in June 1898, came into conflict with his War Minister General Mirri. The events of June 1896 were, however, an indication that a military *coup*, if it had the King's support and the approval of leading personalities of the political and military élite, was a distinct possibility.

As War Minister between July 1896 to December 1897, Pelloux dealt with two important issues, the retirement of elderly officers and the system of mobilisation. The problem of senior and sometimes senile generals had been recognised by both Pelloux and Rudini in 1891 but nothing tangible had resulted. As long as generals were retired only at their own request or by some complicated intrigue, the upper echelons of the army remained clogged by veterans who prevented the rise of younger, abler officers. By his law of 1897, Pelloux did something to solve this problem by fixing an age limit for retirement.[20] For a man who took very seriously Italy's military commitments to her Triple Alliance partners, the method of mobilisation was of supreme importance. It was generally agreed that the existing system of national recruitment was slow, expensive and inefficient. Each infantry regiment received recruits from two different regions and mobilisation in time of war would follow the same pattern. This meant that Piedmontese might be summoned to join their regiment down in Naples or Sicily, and that southerners might be required to journey up to Venice or Milan. Regional recruitment and mobilisation had much to recommend it from the military point of view and it was in fact practised along the northern frontiers. But the existing method which had been adopted since the foundation of the Italian army was justified on political grounds. Apart from 'school of the nation' theories, there was also the argument that the maintenance of order was supremely important and that to recruit regionally would make the troops unreliable. Called upon to suppress disorders in their own locality, they would be more prone to disobey, and in a period of mounting social tension this argument found many willing supporters. Pelloux himself was unconvinced that Italian unity was sufficiently secure to abandon the existing system despite its military disadvantages. He therefore advocated a mixed system, 'national in recruitment, regional in mobilisation'. The obvious objection, that the troops would have to serve in units unknown to them under officers and NCOs who were unfamiliar, was answered by Pelloux's argument that there would be sufficient time between the outbreak of war and the active engagement of the majority of units to enable them to become integrated.[21] The inadequacies of this system were to be revealed in 1915 and the whole episode illustrates the fact that the socio-political role of the army was believed to be more important than its purely military role. In the increasing turbulence of the late nineties this belief seemed to be amply justified.

Despite the economic revival which began after 1896 and the emigration of well over 300,000 Italians each year – which was something of a safety valve – internal unrest grew rapidly, defeating Rudini's hesitant attempts at progressive reforms. Socialists, anarchists and Catholics became more militant, and on the right Sonnino launched his famous, but embarrassing, *Torniamo all Statuto'* calling for greater powers for the executive. The disastrous harvest of 1897, the outbreak of the Spanish-American war which further increased the price of wheat, and the death of Cavallotti in a duel which removed a man who might possibly have kept radicalism on negotiating terms with Rudini, all helped to build up an atmosphere of crisis. Pelloux, who resigned in December 1897 after the government had been defeated over a question of army reform, was no longer a member of the government when, in May 1898, it lost its head and ordered in the troops to restore order in Milan, the industrial capital of Italy.

General Bava-Beccaris, not long after the fiftieth anniversary of the glorious *Cinque Giornate,* proclaimed martial law, shot and killed over 80 Milanese, suppressed newspapers and made mass arrests. Bava-Beccaris was publicly congratulated and decorated by the King for his brilliant campaign in the streets of Milan against a largely imaginary revolutionary army. The government, the King and Bava-Beccaris had so obviously over-reacted that a public outcry ensued. The Rudini government fell on 18 June.

Meanwhile, Pelloux's response to the crisis had been sensible and restrained. When Rudini and the new War Minister San Marzano had given full powers to all military commanders in charge of disaffected provinces, Pelloux had been sent to Bari with responsibility for Puglia, Basilicata and Calabria. In an exchange of telegrams with Rudini he expressed his conviction that it was unnecessary for him to proclaim the state of siege in his area and that he would be able to maintain order by simply enforcing existing laws. He was most relucatant for the army to assume the role of the police. If the army were to remain a symbol of unity, its participation in civil disturbances could only damage its reputation and promote the cause of anti-militarism.[22] In retrospect, the appointment of Pelloux as premier in late June 1898 appeared a reactionary move. Contemporaries, however, regarded him as a liberal. From 1882 to 1895 he had represented Livorno in the chamber, first as a 'military specialist', and then, after his first and last political speech to his constituents in 1892, as a progressive. He collaborated closely with Giolitti in 1892 and 1893 and was recognised as one of Crispi's most vehement enemies. He was also an outspoken critic of Africanism, believing that Italian forces should be confined to the 'white continent' and not dispersed and frittered away on colonial adventures. Not offering himself as a candidate for the 1895 elections, he returned to parliament the following year, being created a senator just prior to his appointment as War Minister. His humane and unhysterical approach to the 1898 crisis from his command post at Bari simply reinforced the impression that he was a strong man, an able administrator and a loyal guardian of existing institutions and constitutional freedoms. As he lost no time in informing parliament, his programme was a simple one. *'Rétablir l'ordre et arriver à la pacification des esprits par une politique conservatrice et libérale en même temps: conservatrice pour sauvegarder l'ordre et les institutions, libérale dans tout le reste.'*[23] He declared his intention of ending the state of siege and dismantling the military tribunals as speedily as possible, believing that normal government, provided it were firm and vigilant, was a surer method of restoring order and freedom than recourse to extraordinary legislation. This won him the support of Giolittian moderates, the approbation of the *'uomini d'ordine'*, and even the tacit approval of the left.

Pelloux, however, had inherited from his predecessors several projects calculated to prevent a recurrence of the disorders of the spring. The chamber quickly approved a temporary law enabling the executive to proclaim the state of siege, to militarise the railwaymen and officials in the postal and telegraph service, and to 'confine dangerous persons' to house arrest. These powers were granted for one year only, but there were many deputies like Sonnino who pressed for a permanent law. Pelloux may not have been a skilled politician but he saw that the introduction of such a permanent law at that moment would have a divisive effect in the chamber, and for the ensuing six months he prevaricated. It was only in February 1899 that he felt that these *'provvedimenti politici'*, which were less harsh than Rudini's could safely be introduced. The country was tranquil, the harvest had been excellent, and the number of unemployed was dropping, so Pelloux did not introduce them as a panic measure. He hoped, in consultation with moderates like Giolitti, to strengthen the hands of the government so that in another crisis it would not have to resort to improvised legislation. At this point, Pelloux seemed to be poised between accepting the advice and support of two men, Giolitti and Sonnino.[24] It was perhaps unfortunate and certainly ironical that Pelloux's choice – Sonnino – was largely determined by events in China.

In March 1899, Pelloux allowed himself to be pushed by the King and his maladroit Foreign Minister Canevaro into demanding the naval base of San Mun. Russians, British and Germans had already begun the apparent partition of China and the Italian government wished to participate. The Chinese bluntly refused to make any concessions despite the appearance of three Italian warships off the coast. Britain refused to sanction the use of force, and the result was a distressing diplomatic fiasco. Rather than face the chamber, Pelloux resigned and constructed a second ministry, replacing six representatives of the left by six from the right; 'Sonnino, though not a minister, was acknowledged as its *éminence grise*.'[25] Pelloux had failed to secure San Mun and one of the most important consequences of this was that Giolitti failed to secure his liberal amendments to the coercive legislation the government was introducing; it was, in fact, made more repressive. Giolitti broke with Pelloux, ostensibly over the Chinese issue, and the extreme left led by the socialist Enrico Ferri began a campaign of obstructionism. Sonnino's reply to this was to induce the government to change the rules of procedure by introducing a closure system. When this too was obstructed, Pelloux issued his repressive legislation as a royal decree. This, in turn, prompted men outside the ranks of the left to brand the move as unconstitutional, a view which the Court of Cassation upheld the following year. Throughout June Pelloux allowed the parliamentary crisis to escalate until it culminated in the tumultuous scene of 30 June when radical deputies overturned the ballot boxes to prevent the president of the chamber from enforcing the closure. The Giolittians had refrained from any participation in obstructionism but began to regard reaction as a greater threat to parliamentary government than the tactics of the left. During the summer, while parliament was adjourned, more and more moderates were won over to this interpretation. Pelloux's liberal gestures in the autumn when the deputies reassembled were too little and too late. The debate raged on into the spring of 1900. The new closure procedure was approved in April after 160 deputies had walked out but when the president of the chamber refused to apply it Pelloux decided to hold new elections. This was his last mistake as an active politician and a mistake, incidentally, which suggests that Pelloux was never a convinced reactionary, prepared to act against the chamber and summon the troops. In the elections the government's opponents gained ground and Pelloux decided to resign on 18 June 1900. Just over a month later, King Humbert was assassinated by an anarchist who sought vengeance against the man who had praised General Bava-Beccaris for his efficiency in May 1898. Italy held its breath, wondering whether the wheel had turned full circle. The socialist newspaper *Avanti!* described Bresci, the assassin, as a criminal lunatic.[26] Republicans, radicals and many clericals followed suit. After three years of conflict there was unity under the Statuto. It was then remembered that 1898 was not only the fiftieth anniversary of the 1848 revolutions, but also of the granting of the Piedmontese constitution by Charles Albert. Crispi's megalomania, Rudini's panic, and Pelloux's mistaken reliance on Sonnino, had endangered the parliamentary system and made a royalist or militarist *coup* appear imminent. But, as in Dreyfusard France, parliamentary institutions had survived. In both countries, the socialists had defended the constitution they had previously attacked, many stranded politicians had been refloated as a result of crisis, and there had been a searching analysis of fundamental beliefs. It is also important to remember that in both countries the military establishment had shown itself unwilling to become the tool of any faction or to subvert existing institutions. At most, the generals had sought to maintain what was left of their autonomy in purely military matters. At times their defensive manoeuvres gave the appearance of aggression, of a militaristic desire to usurp the functions of the civilian element. That this view, however erroneous, was widely held is implicit in Pelloux's explanation of why he decided to resign in June: *'J'étais convaincu que le plus grand obstacle pour revenir à une situation tranquille c'était moi: c'était la présence d'un Lieutenant Général, en activité de service et Sénateur à la tête du Gouvernement.'*[27] Pelloux certainly never saw himself as a militarist. But after 1900 nearly everyone else did. He was blamed for the state of siege and the military tribunals which had in fact been the responsibility of Rudini and Zanardelli before he became premier. He was accused of conspiring against the constitution when, at most, he was guilty only of gross political ineptitude and undue subservience to authoritarian advisers. In 'Giolittian Italy' he did gradually come to resemble the caricature figure of a reactionary Savoyard general drawn by his opponents. He warmly approved of the new nationalism, deplored Giolitti's attempts to collaborate with socialists and radicals, and supported the Libyan War, criticising the government for making a premature peace. In May 1915, when the interventionists swept Giolitti aside, Pelloux was exultant. His old friends and associates, Salandra and Sonnino, had fulfilled one of the old senator's dearest wishes. He had never felt at home in Giolitti's Italy under a young King who preferred driving a motor car to riding a horse. He was disturbed by the prospect of war with Germany but had for some time regarded war with Austria as inevitable, and if war with Vienna implied war with Berlin this was regrettable but unavoidable. His wartime elation disappeared in the postwar period and in 1920 he discussed the miserable political situation with General Bava-Beccaris.[28] By the time Fascism was triumphing in Italy, Pelloux had become something of a public monument – and it was indeed the Minister of Public Works who represented the government at his funeral in 1924 – but Mussolini was basically uninterested in claiming the general as a precursor. One reason, undoubtedly, was the bad press Pelloux had received since 1900, and Mussolini was still an astute editor, but another reason may have been the realisation that this angular general would simply not fit into the Fascist mould.[29]

Notes

1. Seton-Watson, p.179.
2. Crispi, *Memoirs*. III, p.161.
3. Ibid., III, p.129.
4. Seton-Watson, p.171.
5. S. Romano, *Storia dei fasci siciliani* (Bari, 1959), p.516.
6. Baratieri to Crispi, 27 Dec. 1887, *DDI*, second series, XXI, p.383, f.1.
7. Battaglia, *La prima guerra d'Africa* (Turin, 1959), pp.339-45.
8. Stato Maggiore, pp.121-7.
9. Pelloux, p.159.
10. Seton-Watson, p.179.
11. Pelloux, pp.166-7.
12. Seton-Watson, p.181; Battaglia, pp.716-20.
13. Stato Maggiore, p.126.
14. For at least three months, Arimondi and Baratieri had been in disagreement and only Crispi had prevented the former from resigning his command. After this involvement in the defeat at Amba Alagi, Arimondi yearned for another victory like Agordat.
15. Apart from arms interests, shipping and steel, most northern industrialists had become opposed to Crispi's policies.
16. Seton-Watson, p.184, f.2.
17. Pelloux, p.XXXIII.
18. Ibid., p.XXIV.
19. Ibid., p.167.
20. Ibid., p.XL.
21. Ibid., p.XLIII.
22. Ibid., p.LIX.
23. Ibid., p.180.
24. Senator Roux to Giolitti, 9 April 1899, *Quarant'anni di politica italiana*, vol.1, ed. P. D'Angliolini (Milan, 1962), p.356.
25. Seton-Watson, p.193.
26. Ibid., p.196.
27. Pelloux, p.207.
28. Ibid., p.XCV.
29. Ibid., p.XCVI.

10 THE ARMY IN GIOLITTIAN ITALY

General Pelloux was an angry old man relentlessly pursuing his personal vendetta against Giolitti. He was far from alone, however, in condemning virtually everything attempted by this irittatingly phlegmatic Piedmontese. From Gaetano Salvemini on the left, with his commentaries on the *'ministro della mala vita',* to Salandra on the right, Giolitti was accused of corrupting the life of the nation. Then there were also the angry young men; socialists who deplored the conciliatory attitudes of leaders like Turati and Bissolati and who denounced any abandonment of the concepts of revolutionary violence or the class war, and the new nationalists who derided Giolitti's pragmatism and pacifism and exalted the virtues of irrationality and an imperialist war which would weld the nation together and restore the lost virility. Many Catholics and anti-clericals were suspicious of Giolitti's *rapprochement* with the church while others attacked him for continuing the policies of the *'Risorgimento scomunicato'.* Free traders opposed his high tariffs while protectionists opposed state intervention in industrial affairs. Southerners complained that he favoured the north and northerners that he pampered the south. It is quite clear that Giolitti possessed the capacity to arouse antagonism, but it is equally clear that he became premier on no less than five occasions, that he was the dominant politician between 1901 and 1915, and that even Mussolini felt constrained to admit that he was the finest statesman produced by Italy since Cavour.[1] It would have been amazing if this controversial man's relationship with the armed forces had not become the object of close and critical scrutiny.

Antonio Salandra, the premier who took Italy into the First World War, did indeed make some devastating remarks on this score even if they were not based on a particularly close or critical scrutiny. Giolitti, he argued, had so weakened Italy that she was the most unprepared of all the powers for waging war, and the 'years of compromises and expedients' had destroyed the morale of the army. So glaring were the deficiencies of the armed forces that the government had to postpone Italian intervention until the spring of 1915. Luigi Cadorna, appointed chief of staff in July 1914, agreed with this assessment, asserting that if Austria had attacked in 1914 Italy would have been virtually defenceless. Moreover, Giolitti had left the country 'morally unprepared for such a great enterprise' as entering the European war.[2] These are such sweeping statements by men who were respectively the civilian and military heads of Italy on the outbreak of war that the examination of army/state relations in the crucial Giolittian period becomes imperative.

On one occasion, while speaking in the chamber, Giolitti explained very succinctly some of his basic policies.

> We are in a period of formation, we have great problems to resolve that appertain strictly to the economic, social, and political life of the country; we must provide for the redemption of the South, we must provide for the improvement of the working classes, which in Italy have not yet attained the grade of well-being it is our duty to procure for them. We must also provide for public instruction, we have the obligation to promote tax reform and all this is impossible if we do not follow a policy of peace.[3]

As the fiftieth anniversary of the creation of Italy approached, he hoped to forge a prosperous and united nation. He sought to bring in from the political wilderness all those, like the socialists and the Catholics, who had been excluded or who had voluntarily excluded themselves from full participation in the activities of the state. Revolutionary socialists, Catholics and nationalists who strove to divide the nation endangered Giolitti's eminently sensible policies, but even the most intransingent he tended to confront more in sorrow than in anger. The army would, he hoped, promote his integrationist programme. He disliked anti-militarism as much as militarism, and while he regretted burdening the budget with the cost of 'unproductive armaments', he saw the necessity of providing for an efficient, modern army. In an increasingly warlike Europe, he remained loyal to the Triple Alliance because he believed that it helped not only to ensure Italian security but because it also helped to keep the peace in Europe.

I

When the Giolittian era began, the army was showing signs of a deep-seated malaise. As in most continental countries, the transition from the 'pre-industrial' army – and some would say 'feudal' – to the modern, 'industrial' army was often as painful as it was expensive. In addition, the necessity for a mass army implied universal conscription and the democratic implications of this could prove embarrassing.[4]

The increasing tempo of technological change meant that an army could quickly become obsolescent if it failed to re-equip at frequent intervals or if its officer corps failed to adapt itself to changing circumstances. Armies began to require the services of 'industrial managers' as well as of 'heroic leaders'. One of M. Janowitz's models of political-military élites, the 'aristocratic', can be used to describe the old regime in Piedmont before unification. Civilian and military élites are socially and functionally integrated, and the narrow base of recruitment for both, together with a relatively monolithic power structure, enables the civilians to exercise 'subjective control' over the military. 'The low specialisation of the military profession makes it possible for the political élite to supply the bulk of the necessary leadership for the military establishment.' Common social origins and educational patterns ensure that there is a common ideology. 'Political control is civilian control only because there is an identity of interest between aristocratic and military groups. The military is responsible because it is a part of the government.'[5] In his second model, the 'democratic', Janowitz describes the situation where civilian and military élites are sharply differentiated where the former exercise 'objective control' over the latter through a formal set of rules and where being a professional soldier is incompatible with playing any other social or political role. 'The military leaders obey the government because it is their duty and their profession to fight.' He adds that the soldiers are supposed to be committed broadly to the national and political goals of a democracy and that 'professional ethics as well as democratic parliamentary institutions guarantee civilian political supremacy', although this may represent more an objective than a reality.[6] After the granting of the Statuto, the Piedmontese and then the Italian army began to approximate towards the democratic model, but, like other armies, without losing its 'aristocratic' elements. The other models of Janowitz, the 'totalitarian' and the 'garrison state' do not seem applicable to the Italian army in the period under survey.[7] The Italian army is thus a combination of the aristocratic and the democratic, with the latter becoming gradually more conspicuous but never predominant, at least in practice.

Another sociologist, D.C. Rapoport, describes three 'military types', the 'praetorian state', the 'civilian-and-military state', and the 'nation in arms'.[8] He confesses that he has never studied the Italian situation, but the Italian army is readily identifiable as a combination of the military-and-civilian and the nation in arms, although the latter was largely a rhetorical flourish.

Perhaps mercifully unaware of these sociological implications, generals and politicians in Giolittian Italy attempted to define and, on occasions, to cure the malaise which afflicted their army. It showed a variety of symptoms, some of which were common to all armies in an industrialising state, some peculiar to the Italian army, and some which seem to be inherent in the profession of arms. When a state began to industrialise the need arose to recruit and train officers capable of handling the increasingly sophisticated weapons and techniques which emerged as a result of 'the military revolution' of the 1860s and 1870s. From the general staff downwards, some technological expertise – including reading railway timetables – became *de rigueur.* As the implications of modern warfare began to affect virtually the entire nation, military problems had to be seen in a wider context. Economic considerations – and not just the raising of taxation – questions of medical hygiene, public relations and a host of other factors, once the preserve of a few eccentrics, were now included in courses at the *Scuola di Guerra* and the military academies.[9] The old themes of 'the school of the nation', emphasising the educational aspects of military life, and the civilising role of the officer, had to be taken more seriously.

In March 1891 a young French officer contributed an article to the *Revue des Deux Mondes* which so impressed his superiors that they despatched him to Indo-China hoping that he and his thesis would be quickly forgotten.[10] The young officer was Captain Hubert Lyautey and his article was entitled: *'Du role social de l'officier dans le service militaire universel.'* In an army where *'frêquente l'êlêment civil'* was still the most damning comment on anyone's dossier, the very title was scandalous. Lyautey repeated much of what enlightened officers like Pagêzy de Bourdêliac or Durand had said many decades earlier.[11] In a period of prolonged peace when promotion prospects were slight and the eternal round of garrison duties sapped morale, it was necessary to re-examine the role of the officer, to emphasise his educative role in peacetime. Lyautey was aware of the steady growth of anti-militarism; indeed, since the publication of Abel Hermant's novel *Cavalier Miserey* in 1887 anti-military writings had become a popular literary genre. The French educational system, with its emphasis on individuality and the critical questioning of all authority, together with the rise of socialism, had given the movement new dimensions. As opposition to compulsory conscription was its most obvious manifestation, Lyautey urged the military establishment to adapt itself to the modern world, to try to understand and communicate with the young recruits.[12] His message was ignored at the time but after the storms of the Dreyfus Affair, many of his suggestions became the official policy of Rue Saint-Dominique.

In Italy, when the youthful De Amicis had first taken up his pen to defend the sword, similar suggestions had been made but in 'the golden years' of the eighties few officers had responded. An amusing, perhaps not very typical autobiographical account exists for this period, General De Rossi's *La Vita di un ufficiale italiano sino alla guerra.* It is worth pausing over because it underlines so many of the reasons for discontent among the military in the early years of Giolitti's dominance. He begins by explaining that his father, a captain, was married in Ancona in 1862, that he was born the following year in Brescia, and that the family then moved down south to Catanzaro. It is hardly surprising that the constant moving about from one garrison to the next – and the authorities insisted on a new posting at least once every four years – was a constant grievance. It was personally expensive and it often broke up the family if the officer married. Because of this system, De Rossi was educated in Turin, Capua, Elba, Bari, the military college at Naples and finally the military school at Modena, although the last two moves were the result of his decision to enter his father's profession. At Modena, he disliked the unhygienic accommodation, the poor lectures and the almost total neglect of any moral instruction. He was commissioned in 1881 and was appalled by the number of brutish, alcoholic fellow officers. A weapons course at Parma which he later attended he dismisses as a farce, and when he returned to his regiment at Turin, he found himself under the command of a paranoic captain who tended to barricade himself in his room equipped with a revolver! His superiors consistently rejected his requests to sit for the *Scuola di Guerra,* and were swift to pounce on him when they found him reading something like Räe's book on contemporary socialism. 'Whoever concerns himself with things outside his profession', he was told, 'is a bad officer.' He asked permission to give a course on 'the necessity of social studies for the officer', but this was predictably vetoed. After more than three years he finally succeeded in entering the *Scuola di Guerra* where he was impressed by the knowledge of his teachers but not by their technique. 'The *Scuola di Guerra',* he concluded, 'was not however a school for character.' Later, he went to Rome to attend a course with the general staff where, he claimed, he learnt more about gossip and intrigue than anything else. Returning to Turin in 1892 as a captain, he worked hard to raise educational standards, and, despite anonymous letters accusing him of subversion, he succeeded in establishing a small library and other amenities.[13] Even his posting to the Ufficio Storico of the general staff in Rome towards the end of 1900 had elements of farce about it. He found Colonel Fabris, the officer in charge of the historical section, a highly intelligent man, but his main occupation appeared to be writing and rewriting the history of the 1848-9 campaigns. De Rossi was employed by General Saletta, chief of staff from 1896 to 1908, to compile maps of Eritrea, and when Fabris died, to continue his uncompleted history of 1848-9. For light relief, he was often despatched on fact-finding missions, on one of which he discovered that certain secret gun emplacements constructed by the French in Corsica were in fact sheep folds. He was now a major, and acutely aware that 'very slow promotion and poor pay had produced noticeable discontent among the officers'.[14] But he was forced to spend much of his time on intelligence missions in various parts of Europe until in 1909 he was appointed to lecture at the Scuola di Guerra. He left in 1913 to become a colonel in the Bersaglieri and even in this period of nationalist agitation and increasing militarism he noted that the nobility and the middle classes were contemptuous of the underpaid officer corps.[15] After such a pilgrimage in peacetime, it was tragic that De Rossi was wounded and paralysed in one of the first actions of the war in June 1915. The King arrived to award him the first medal for valour. An award for satirical observation would also have been appropriate.

The poor pay, unsatisfactory quarters and slow promotion which De Rossi bemoans were important factors contributing to what General Bava-Beccaris described as a 'crisis' among the armed forces in the years 1898-1908. The officer corps of the 1900s, and particularly the junior officers, were in an invidious position. The rapid promotion in the fat years of the eighties had been exhilarating while it lasted, but those who had been promoted were still there presenting an insurmountable barrier to those entering the service later.[16] The officers, members of *'Italia legale'* and the NCOs and men, members of *'Italia reale'*, were not reticent about voicing their grievances. The King, the many soldiers who sat as deputies or senators, the military journals, provided a ready-made network of useful contracts and proselytising media for those who sought to promote army reforms. Unfortunately, between 1898 and 1908 there were no fewer than ten War Ministers, and as the War Minister was the indispensable link between the military and the civilians, there was scant possibility of any large-scale army reform. When Spingardi and Pollio were appointed in 1908, forming an effective team as War Minister and chief of staff respectively, prospects improved. Between 1900 and 1907 military expenditure, the navy excluded, remained close to the 250 million lire mark and only began to rise appreciably afterwards, reaching 340 million lire by 1909/10.[17] Nevertheless, some improvements took place. Increases in pay were granted, the prospects of promotion for lieutenants were improved by a law of 1902, and NCOs, the backbone of any army, had their grievances partially removed by a series of laws between 1902 and 1908.

But pay and conditions were only part of the problem. The results of the striking economic progress made by Italy between 1896 and 1914 were not entirely beneficial as far as the army was concerned. Economic growth and a rapid increase in wealth did not follow a uniform pattern throughout the peninsula. The new industrial centres in Lombardy and Piedmont forged ahead thereby accentuating the differences between an affluent and progressive north and a poverty-stricken and backward south. As opportunities for well-paid posts increased as business expanded, fewer northerners felt attracted towards an underpaid career in the army. In the very areas where a modern army might hope to recruit its best officers, the technologically aware cities of the north, there was a noticeable reluctance to serve. Apart from the financial inducements of a civilian career, improved educational and cultural facilities had an adverse effect on officer recruitment. As in France during this same period, an increasingly high proportion of the privileged classes rejected the army on moral and intellectual grounds. Richer bourgeois families, who had begun sending their sons into the officer corps after 1870, also developed reservations. The system whereby on the payment of 2,000 lire it was possible to serve as a volunteer for one year instead of being conscripted for the full term, was extensively used by the middle classes, making nonsense of claims that universal military conscription was egalitarian. An additional advantage of being a volunteer was that it was possible to serve in or near one's native town. It was hoped that this system, which had been borrowed from the Prussians, would produce a large reserve of capable officers and that the volunteers would be tempted to make the army their career. In fact, as it was reported in the chamber in 1910, out of over 19,000 volunteers who had served in the past ten years, only 622 had taken up commissions.[18] In view of the recurrent laments over the shortage of officers, this was a serious situation. Although it has been estimated that 50 per cent of the officer corps in 1914 was bourgeois,[19] the majority of them seem to have come from the lower middle class or from the smaller provincial towns, particularly in the south. Because, whereas industrial development in the north had a deleterious effect on officer recruitment, the slower development or even stagnation in other areas acted as a stimulus. Particularly in rural areas, hard hit by agricultural depression, there was more incentive to joint the army. Rent rolls were falling, profits declining, educational opportunities were limited and civilian posts were scarce. This is why Irishmen, Pomeranian Junkers, Provencal gentry and southern Italians entered their respective armies in such large numbers just prior to the First World War, providing a steady supply of potential *grognards.* Many of them, of course, were excellent fighting officers, but they had a tendency to resist new ideas.

So, until the eleventh hour, the Italian army, like so many other armies, was denied the services of some of the most talented and progressive elements in society. There was a steady drop in the number of infantry officers, even irrespective of quality, for while there were over 8,000 on the active list in 1895, there were only 6,632 in 1906.[20] It is true that the 'military dynasties' continued to supply their quota through that system of virtual self-recruitment which seemed to operate in every army, but the number of students in the military schools and academies declined alarmingly until 1909. The number of resignations, although never as serious as in France between 1898 and 1910, was equally disquieting.

In a book, which is in its own way as informative as De Rossi's, General De Bono points to certain tensions within the officer corps. Describing De Rossi as 'undoubtedly one of the best of our officers', he not unreasonably adds that his rather pessimistic outlook made him appear a 'malcontent'. De Bono attempts to redress the balance by showing how it was possible to come to love the army and what it represented, without ignoring its darker side.[21] Whereas the earlier regional differences within the army had been largely eradicated, there were still, he argued, serious divisions among the various branches of the officer corps. There was the gulf which seemed to separate the officers of the general staff from the rest of the army. *'Bel, biond e bestia',* and with well-developed bureaucratic tendencies, they lived a life of Olympian detachment which infuriated the lesser mortals in the hierarchy.[22] Then there was the mutual hostility between officers who had risen from the ranks, who could not expect to be promoted above captain, and officers who had passed out of the academies. Again, there was the superior attitude of the cavalry towards all other arms, the intellectual contempt of the officers of artillery and engineering for their less learned brothers, and the low regard of all three for the despicable infantry, except for the two grenadier regiments – and jealous officers dismissed even them as 'tall infantrymen' – the

Bersaglieri and the Alpini. Officers in any of the above regiments who had misbehaved in any way dreaded being sentenced to a line regiment. There were also the officers in the medical corps, struggling for recognition from their fellows while the veterinary surgeons, responsible for horses instead of mere men, were accepted with open arms. Officers responsible for administration and pay were wise enough not to seek recognition.[23]

These rivalries are encountered in all armies and in most professions, and are serious only if carried to excess. Far more important was the general attitude of officers towards their men and towards civilians. The overwhelming majority of conscripts were obviously lower class, so the relationship of officers to men was in the nature of a class confrontation. Since the Sicilian fasci, and particularly after the events of 1898, the relationship had become increasingly tense. The troops were constantly called out to repress disturbances in the towns and countryside. The progress of industrialisation fostered the growth of socialism and revolutionary syndicalism. The number of strikes, often violent, increased as the urban proletariat grew larger and as peasant communities in areas like the Romagna reacted against unwelcome economic developments. Officers and men alike detested their police duties, doing 'P.S' *(Publica Sicurezza)* as they called it. It was bad for morale, and although there were few examples of open mutiny, the troops resented being summoned to shoot down their fellow workers, and to guard the factories and farms of the propertied classes. This was the sort of atmosphere in which both militarism and anti-militarism could be expected to thrive, and it made the public relations role of the officer corps even more vital.

Reading De Bono one has the uneasy feeling that he rather than De Rossi represents the mood of the officer corps. He scoffed at the idealists in the Via XX Settembre,[24] who sent round circulars urging officers to raise their intellectual standards and to concern themselves with the moral welfare of their men. He recalls one typical instance when the regiment was ordered to economise and he suggested that they ceased purchasing all newspapers and periodicals for the reading room with the exception of the *Rivista Militare.* This met with general agreement but a small group of the more intellectual officers objected, arguing that it would be shameful for them to stop taking the *Nuova Antologia* or *Minerva.* But De Bono won the argument, clinching it by arranging for four Bersaglieri to come staggering into the room with the past copies of the *Nuova Antologia* and *Minerva,* all in mint condition with the pages still uncut. It was De Bono's opinion that officers read very little and that most of them were uninterested in politics, except perhaps those stationed in Rome who followed the sessions of the chamber and the senate very closely because they had to provide a guard whenever parliament was sitting. De Bono confessed that it was only by chance that he came to hear the name of current prime ministers. In such circumstances it is inconsistent of him to complain that Guglielmo Ferrero's work on militarism was never effectively answered by the army establishment. Relying on the force of example and discipline, that 'vague sense of unease when an inferior finds himself in the presence of a superior', De Bono had little patience with psychological or sociological theories which is perhaps a pity because he would have found in Mosca and Pareto abundant material for buttressing his own arguments. A self-confessed *menefreghista,* many of his postwar comments must be seen as an expression of that hearty bluster which was supposed to be the prerogative of the 'real soldier'.[25]

Until the Electoral Reform Bill became law after 1911, the vast majority of conscripts had no vote. Even if they were literate and therefore, under the terms of the 1882 law, entitled to exercise their political rights, this was forbidden as long as they remained under the colours. Officers, on the other hand, were acknowledged if poorly recompensed members of *'Italia legale',* and provided they were not of De Bono's persuasion, fully entitled to indulge in politics. Indeed, most of the names mentioned in this study became deputies or senators, diplomats, or, on three occasions, premiers. They were, it is true, a small minority of the entire officer corps, but they continued the old tradition whereby members of the military élite freely participated in government side by side with members of the political élite. This could have led to close civilian-military relations, but in the Giolittian era this decidedly failed to materialise, except perhaps on a purely personal level. The mutual incomprehension of each other's task was responsible for most of the tension and hostility which existed in the prewar period.

Just as De Bono's regimental colleagues were politically apathetic, so the majority of politicians and indeed of civilians in general showed a marked indifference towards the military establishment and its problems. Except in times of crisis like those of 1866, 1896 or 1898, both militarism and anti-militarism were minority movements, and there was nothing to match the sustained intensity of the military debates in Prussia during the 1860s or in France during the late 1890s. In the decade before the First World War, Italian nationalists and socialists were surprised to find how difficult it was to rally mass support either for or against military institutions. This indifference is remarkable when it is realised that the Italian state between 1862 and 1913 spent more on the armed services than on administration, diplomacy, justice, education and public works all added together.[26] Fear of France and distrust of her Austrian ally induced Italy to maintain a large fleet as well as a large army, and, in general, public opinion accepted this without enquiring too deeply into the intricacies of national defence. Even treasury officials, cutting military expenditure to balance the budget, were preoccupied by columns of figures rather than columns of men.

There were military debates in the chamber, but as Giorgio Rochat has pointed out:

> From 1900 to 1914 these debates all followed the same pattern; powerful opposition from the extreme left, opposed to the expenditure for political and economic reasons, and a generally small number of government supporters who express love for and faith in the army without considering any of its problems; to these can be added some speeches of a technical, military, or economic variety, always confined to the less important details; it seems almost as if military problems discussed in parliament come under the heading of either opposition speeches, rhetoric or merely technical explanation.[27]

Disclaiming any specialist knowledge, the majority of deputies and senators regarded their vote in favour of military expenditure as a patriotic gesture, an indication of their implicit faith in the army rather than the government. As a result of this uncritical attitude on the part of the majority, military laws were rarely challenged or modified. Between 1900 and 1914 only nine out of fifty laws were altered in any way, and five of these concerned minor points or questions of finance.[28] Occasionally someone like Colonel Marazzi would criticise the over-bureaucratisation of the army, justifiably complaining that it was the *'imponente e complicata macchina amministrativa'* rather than the soldiers under arms which was so expensive.[29] Few deputies or officers were prepared to support such moves, however, as they seemed to threaten all office holders in a state machine which often seemed to be constructed in order to institutionalise concealed underemployment. De Bono, De Rossi and virtually every serving officer complained about the excessive red tape, the interminable delays and the gross inefficiency of the military establishment, but very few were prepared, like Marazzi, to do anything about it.

More officers and civilians were, however, prepared to attack the pale-faced bureaucrats of the general staff. Fabio Ranzi, in a book which he wrote on the eve of the nationalist congress at Florence in 1910, listed a whole series of such attacks, from the *'grido di dolore della fanteria'* of 1884 to an article in the *Rivista Militare Italiana* of 16 July 1910. In nearly every case the method of selecting officers for the general staff is severely criticised. Ranzi recounted the bitter comments made in the chamber on 18 June 1904, including the statement by Compans that a former War Minister – and the deputies quickly realised he meant Ricotti – had regretted not having abolished the general staff.[30] There was a general feeling that staff officers rapidly lost all contact with the reality of military life, that they were promoted too quickly and that their all-pervasive influence was detrimental to the true interests of the army. The fact that a general staff had to remain aloof and closely guard its secrets, inevitably led to hostility and suspicion. That a chief of staff like Saletta or Pollio might be a sphinx without a secret was a theory which discontented officers and civilians could not easily resist. But, whatever the motive, these attacks came to nothing and there was no purge of the military élite.

Between 1900 and 1907 there were seven Ministers of War, but between 1907 and March 1914 there were only two, Senator Casana from December 1907 to April 1909 and General Spingardi from April 1909 to March 1914. The year 1907 is something of a watershed in the Giolittian era. Before 1907 military expenditure remained stable, but afterwards it began to rise very steeply. There were several very good reasons for this. In 1906, General Conrad von Hötzendorff became chief of staff of the Habsburg army, and his venomous hatred of the Italians was a thinly veiled secret. In fact, two years later, at the time of the Bosnian annexation, he was firmly convinced that Austrian interests demanded 'the overthrow of Italy so as to rid ourselves in time of a probable enemy'.[31] Although Giolitti and most of the ruling élite, civilian and military, remained loyal to the Triple Alliance, it became more difficult to ignore the warnings of those who emphasised the threat to Italy's north-east frontiers. Defensive fortifications in this area began to be undertaken seriously and this was a most expensive operation, especially as the defences against France could not be abandoned despite the growing *rapprochement* with the Third Republic. It was also cripplingly expensive to replace obsolete weapons, and in the 1890s and 1900s new models were being produced at bewildering speed. Genuine confusion over which Krupp gun, if any, to adopt, led to the Rogier-Mangiagalli affair in 1907 when a commission of enquiry severely censured the Ministry of War for mismanaging the re-equipment of the field artillery. To the disgust of Pelloux, who saw Giolittismo as the explanation for these expensive mistakes, two generals were ignominiously punished *pour encourager les autres.*[32]

An additional reason for increased military expenditure lay in the increasingly warlike international situation. The Boer War, the Russo-Japanese War, the Anglo-French Entente, the Tangier Incident and the Anglo-Russian Entente provided incontrovertible evidence of this. The closer relationship between Britain and the Franco-Russian alliance, combined with the intensification of Anglo-German naval rivalry, placed Italy in a highly embarrassing situation. The Triple Alliance had been renewed again in 1902, and Bülow had refused to become alarmed by Italy's flirtation with France, but after President Loubet's visit to Rome in 1904 and Visconti Venosta's unhelpful attitude at Algeciras in 1906, the German attitude hardened. 'The Bible says', wrote William II angrily, 'no man can serve two masters, much less three! France, England and the Triplice!' A few days later he added: 'Italy will remain with us only as long as we are friends with England. If that does not return, she will leave the Triplice.'[33] The Kaiser was also reported to have said that if Italy showed hostility towards Austria he would enthusiastically 'turn loose upon her his whole military strength'.[34] Italy was therefore in danger of finding herself at odds with her allies before she had made alternative security arrangements with France or Britain.

This heightening of international tension, moreover, had not resulted in the formation of any *union sacrée* within the states involved. It was rather the reverse, as socialists, revolutionary syndicalists and nationalists seemed to go from strength to strength. In Italy, there had been the general strike of 1904, but in 1907 the number of strikers in both agricultural and industrial sectors had more than doubled.[35] Propertied classes continued to make demands for protection from Giolittian governments which were reluctant to resume the repressive role of the 1890s. It was difficult to convince people that these strikes and disturbances were a manifestation of economic and political vitality.

It was in this atmosphere of crisis, and under pressure from many quarters, political and military, nationalist and diplomatic, that Giolitti reluctantly consented to allow a massive increase in military expenditure. Realising that this would anger many of his supporters as well as the traditionally anti-militarist groups like the socialists and the radicals,[36] he appointed Italy's first civilian Minister of War and established a commission of enquiry to examine the conduct of the army. Giolitti was determined to demonstrate that there was no military juggernaut in Italy and that the civilians were firmly in control. He was unquestionably correct in his assessment of civilian-military relations, but his methods of proving this were unconvincing and largely counterproductive. If Giolitti had really wanted to reconcile the army with civilian government and ensure their close collaboration under the new War Minister, it was puzzling to see why he had chosen the unknown Senator Casana for this key post. Again, if the commission of enquiry had been established to make a thorough examination of the sorry state of affairs revealed by the artillery scandal, why did he allow the King so to influence the selection of commissioners that only unimportant civilians and ex-officers took part?[37] Enrico Ferri was not alone in thinking that the answers to these questions were quite simple. Giolitti was erecting a facade. A civilian War Minister and a commission of enquiry would convince the deputies and the country that everything was under control and that they were being allowed to participate in a process which would secure their own and the nation's interests. In reality, Giolitti intended to use the commission as a *'lubrificante per i nuovi crediti militari'* and Casana had been appointed as an interim minister for the sole purpose of steering a vote of 210 million lire through the chamber.[38] The commission was indeed soon happily proposing expensive military reforms and, after producing two scapegoats, defining everything which it found reprehensible as the result of 'technical errors'. And as for Casana, as soon as the additional military expenditure had received legislative approval, he was replaced by General Spingardi. It was ironical that Casana felt constrained to resign when the treasury opposed his requests for more expenditure on the army, requests which were swiftly granted to his successor, Spingardi.[39]

The wizard of Dronero had shown his skill as an illusionist and to this extent the criticisms and assumptions of his critics were correct. But he had remained in control throughout, and his manoeuvres did not mask an increase in military influence on the government. What is undoubtedly certain is that Giolitti had secured a sufficient increase in military expenditure to enable Spingardi and Pollio to reorganise the army. Even larger grants were soon, of course, required, but Giolitti had established a precedent – unless Crispi could claim that honour – for his big spending, and what made this more bearable to Giolitti and his supporters was the continued growth of the Italian economy, so that although the amounts spent on the armed forces increased sharply, the percentage this represented of the overall expenditure remained stable at around 22 per cent.[40]

The appointment of General Pollio as chief of staff in 1908 can be seen as another triumph for Giolitti and as a defeat for any aspiring militarists. Interestingly enough, the King, or rather his indispensable aide-de-camp General Brusati, was of great assistance on this occasion. The King was, according to the constitution, the supreme head of the army, but in peacetime it was the Minister of War who had in fact come to assume responsibility for the military establishment. In time of war, however, it was the chief of staff, a circumstance which was to cause many problems in 1914-15 when Italy remained uneasily neutral. It was understandable that many officers disliked being subject to a 'politician' except in wartime and argued that a system of dual control was a dangerous division of powers. Casana's appointment had a powerful impact on this controversy, but even before this there had been a growing tendency to separate administrative from technical functions, the former in the hands of the War Minister and the latter devolving upon the chief of staff. Luigi Cadorna, promoted to lieutenant general in 1907, had very definite ideas on this subject. As a young student at the military academy between 1865 and 1868, he remembered the difficulties which had confronted his father in the campaign of 1866 as a result of divided leadership. He demanded that the chief of staff be granted full authority and that the disciplinary regulations which enforced the obedience of all soldiers to the Minister of War be amended.[41] When General Saletta retired as chief of staff in 1908, Cadorna confidently expected to replace him but in reply to General Brusati's careful enquiries he made it clear that if appointed he would insist upon being granted full authority over the armed forces in peacetime as well as in war. Cadorna asserted that he would allow the King his 'formal responsibility' but reserved for himself the right to appoint and dismiss officers of all ranks.[42] Brusati and the King, obviously offended by this attitude, allowed Cadorna to learn from the newspapers that Pollio had secured the coveted post. This brief episode gave a preliminary warning of what was likely to happen in the event of Cadorna being made chief of staff as he was in 1914 following the death of Pollio.

General Alberto Pollio was born at Caserta in 1852, studied at the military academies of Naples and Turin and also at the *Scuola di Guerra*. Commissioned in 1872 as a lieutenant in the artillery, by 1878 he had risen to the rank of captain in the general staff. After a period in the infantry he was appointed military attaché in Vienna. On his return, he became chief of staff to the divisional command in Palermo and in

1893 was promoted to colonel in the general staff. In 1900, at the age of 48, he was a major-general and a lieutenant-general six years later. His rapid rise, his close connections with the general staff, and his intellect made him the sort of officer which De Bono and his colleagues tended to detest. He had even written books, a study of Napoleon published in 1901 and his *Custozza 1866* in 1903.

His close study of the campaign of Custozza must have made him as aware as Cadorna of the dangers of divided leadership and an uncertain chain of command, but as he passed the scrutiny of General Brusati he had obviously not pressed the point in 1908. Again, his studies had introduced him to the social and economic problems associated with the maintenance of a large army, but he regarded an increase in military spending as absolutely essential. This was a time when the army establishment was being threatened by the naval programme being promoted by Admiral Mirabello who had the great advantage of being Navy Minister for six consecutive years from 1903 to 1909.[43] But despite this competition for funds – and public opinion seemed more prepared to spend lavishly on dreadnoughts than on infantry divisions[44] – Pollio succeeded in launching a vast programme of his own. He was assisted by the war scare of 1908-9 after Austria-Hungary's brusque annexation of Bosnia and the appointment of Spingardi as War Minister on 4 April 1909, gave him the warm support of Via XX Settembre. Working together as a team, they retained their posts in the successive ministries of Giolitti, Sonnino and Luzzati, that is until the spring of 1914.

Apart from anti-militarism or parsimonious Treasury Ministers, one of the greatest hazards facing any massive rearmament programme is the outbreak of a premature war, and for conscientious generals all wars tend to be premature. Without the Libyan War of 1911, the solid achievements of Pollio and Spingardi would have been much more apparent by the time Italy entered the First World War. As a result of this colonial venture, much more prolonged and costly than Pollio had originally envisaged, the earlier plans and calculations of 1908-9 were seriously disrupted.

Among the most important reforms of this period was the adoption of two year conscription for all branches of the army, except for the carabinieri, while the annual intake was raised by more than 30,000. Thus the army in 1910 comprised 1,393,000 men of whom 600,000 were front line troops. There were 14,000 officers on the active list and 16,000 more who could be summoned in time of war, 17,000 NCOs and 25,000 carabinieri.[45] Pay, rations and barracks were all improved, this alone costing 301 million lire just for the year 1908-9.[46] Pollio also pressed on with the fortification of the northeastern frontier along the line of the Tagliamento and the construction of strategic railways. Machine guns were introduced into infantry and cavalry units and a start was made on the motorisation of the army and the utilisation of aircraft.[47]

It naturally took time for all military establishments to realise most of the implications of the internal combustion engine and the development of aircraft, and despite the rapid proliferation of machine guns, orthodox military doctrine everywhere continued to ignore the tremendous fire power they gave to defensive positions. The 1907 commission of enquiry had called for the delivery of 500 lorries for use by the army, five for each infantry division and two for the cavalry. In 1910 the first school of aviation was established and the first substantial grant, 10 million lire, was allocated for aircraft construction.[48] From 1908 the army constantly demanded more and better guns and increasingly large quantities of ammunition for them. All this entailed huge imports of foreign equipment together with increased production by the Italian armaments industry, and this in turn necessitated massive imports of vital raw materials like coal and iron.

Even without the interruption of the Libyan War, the Pollio-Spingardi programme of modernisation would still have been incomplete by 1914-15 for the simple reason that Italian industry was unable to cope with this avalanche of orders, and foreign imports were always subject to unavoidable delays and rising costs. The Ministry of War had, indeed, created a small industrial empire. It had two large arsenals in Turin and Naples, arms factories at Brescia, Terni, Turin and Torre Annunziata capable of producing over 600 rifles per day, and three ordnance factories at Genoa, at Bologna, Capua, Fossano and Fontana Liri.[49] In 1911, after a decade of hesitation and the scandal of 1907, it was finally decided to equip the artillery with French guns and a consortium of 27 firms under the direction of Vickers-Terni was established.[50] Fiat, which had begun automobile production in 1899, had 66 factories in operation by 1906 with a total output of 18,000 vehicles.[51] But state and private industry combined failed to keep pace with demand. Under the stimulus of the Libyan War and the outbreak of the First World War, the labour force was increased and heroic efforts were made to double or treble the output, but there were still grave deficiencies in the army when Italy entered the war in 1915. To give an example, Cadorna requested at least 2,000 rounds per rifle in 1914 instead of the 700 available, but a year later his army took the field with only 900 rounds per rifle.[52] With limited national resources, material and financial, close co-operation between the army, the politicians and the arms manufacturers was essential. This required a degree of mutual understanding which simply did not exist, a fatal legacy of the unwillingness of both soldiers and civilians to comprehend each other's tasks and difficulties. In peacetime few countries, Germany included, have been willing to gear their economy to war production, and in 1914 only a handful of visionaries accurately predicted the nature of modern warfare. Even so, there was a disastrous failure of both businessmen and military to anticipate each other's needs. In the placing of mammoth orders, for instance, the army establishment was being totally unrealistic when it expected prompt delivery, particularly when there had been no preparatory discussions. But, in the last analysis, this failure stemmed from lack of foresight on the part of the government and the ruling classes.

Giolittismo was responsible for this only if it is defined as the political response of *'Italia legale'* rather than the diabolical invention of one politician. But Giolitti himself was, of course, the keystone of this system, and no Italian was as acutely aware as he of Italy's unpreparedness for large-scale warfare. Bitterly opposed to Italy's entry into the war in 1915, he pointed to economic weaknesses, diplomatic uncertainties, and, above all, to peasant antagonism, in order to justify his attitude. The rural population, he asserted, was neither primitive enough to fight like the Russians nor yet sufficiently assimilated into the state to fulfil their patriotic duties like the British, French, or Germans.[53] He was also contemptuous of the military élite, of army corps commanders like Brusati and Frugoni who were unfit to lead even a regiment. Salandra and Cadorna argued that Giolitti himself was responsible for this state of affairs. This was a gross overstatement, but equally untenable was the argument of Giolitti's supporters who emphasised the fact that he was out of office from March 1914 and fought strenuously to keep Italy out of the war. It is important to understand why Giolitti failed to return to power or prevent the declaration of war. One fundamental reason was that the ruling élite, loosely organised around the old liberal party, had become hopelessly divided over the question of war and peace, and on several other issues as well. As the supreme parliamentary tactician of his age, Giolitti was not only aware of the dangers of this development but by his manoeuvres in 1911-12 had greatly contributed to it. During the Libyan War and the debate over the extension of the suffrage, the divisions of 1915 were foreshadowed.

Notes

1. F. Coppa, 'Economic and ethical liberalism in conflict', *Journal of Modern History,* vol.42 (June), p.191.
2. A. Salandra, *La neutralità italiana* (Milan, 1928), pp.193, 30, 66-7, 244, 268, 292; L. Cadorna, *La guerra alla fronte italiana* (Milan, 1921), p.3.
3. Quoted in Coppa, p.213.
4. Universal suffrage was an obvious corollary. In 1911, when Giolitti granted a wide increase in the franchise, almost universal suffrage, he claimed that 'it was no longer admissible that a state born out of revolution and formed by plebiscites after fifty years of unification still continued to exclude from active political life the most numerous class in society, *a class which gave its sons for the defence of the nation,* and under the form of indirect taxes contributed in large measure to support the expenses of the state.' (G. Giolitti, *Memoria della mia vita* (Milan, 1922), vol.II, pp.306-8).
5. M. Janowitz, *The military in the development of new nations* (Chicago, 1964), p.111.
6. Ibid., p.112.
7. Some observers believed, erroneously, that Pelloux's objective was the 'garrison state'.
8. D.C. Rapoport, 'A comparative theory of military and political types', *Changing patterns of military politics,* ed. S. Huntington (New York, 1962).
9. *Archivio Centrale dello Stato,* Ministero della Guerra, Scuole Militari, V, p.16.
10. He promptly wrote about the *'rôle colonial'* of the officer.
11. Girardet, pp.148-53.
12. Ibid., pp.279-82.
13. E. De Rossi, *La Vita di un ufficiale italiano sino alla guerra* (Milan, 1927), pp.15, 25-6, 51-2, 66, 71, 72, 92.
14. De Rossi, p.181.
15. Ibid., p.253.
16. Bava-Baccaris, p.72.
17. De Rosa, p.214.
18. G. Rochat, 'L'Esercito italiano nell'estate 1914', *Nuova Rivista Storica,* 45 (L961), p.303, f.3.
19. M. Janowitz, *The professional soldier* (New York, 1964), p.94. In Britain the figure was 60 per cent and (in 1911) in Germany 67 per cent.
20. Ministero della Guerra, *L'Esercito italiano nella Grande Guerra,* vol.1 (Rome, 1927), pp.23-5.
21. E. De Bono, *Nell'Esercito nostro prima della guerra* (Milan, 1931), pp.13-15.
22. De Bono, p.24.
23. Ibid., pp.27, 31, 32.
24. Ministry of War, Rome.
25. De Bono, pp.188-9, 190-1, 312, 381.
26. Of the 45.5 per cent state revenue left after interest and debt commitments, 23.7 per cent was absorbed by the army and navy, leaving 22.8 per cent for all the other ministries (Rochat, p.297).
27. Ibid., p.304.
28. Ibid., p.305, f.3.
29. Ibid., p.301, f.2
30. F. Ranzi, *Nazionalismo e il problema militare italiano* (Rome, 1910), pp.111-13.
31. Albertini, I, p.194.
32. Pelloux, p.289.
33. Albertini, I, p.175.

34. Pribram, II, p.138, f.324.
35. A Salomone, *Italian democracy in the making* (Philadelphia, 1945), p.96, f.57.
36. Nitti and the radicals comprised a group of 34 deputies in 1900, 70 in 1913, and were, in general, anti-militaristic (ibid., p.32).
37. Rochat, p.307, f.1.
38. Ibid, p.307.
39. Casana to Giolitti, 10 May, *Quarant'anni,* III, p.447-8.
40. De Rosa, pp.216-17.
41. P. Pieri, 'Les relations entre gouvernement et commandement en Italie en 1917', *Revue d'histoire moderne et contemporaine,* XV (1968), p.133.
42. Rochat, p.308, f.1. Information from the private archives of the Cadorna family.
43. Italy's first dreadnought, the *Dante Alighieri,* was laid down in 1909. By 1915, Italy had built six to Austria's four, but to do this she had spent twice as much as Austria.
44. Although citizens of seaports might disagree, an infantry or cavalry regiment was seen as a greater threat to liberty than a battleship or cruiser.
45. Bava-Beccaris, p.83.
46. This figure rose to 320 million lire for 1909-10, and 434 million lire for 1910 but this latter figure apparently includes 145 million for improvements to the artillery (ibid., pp.90-3).
47. Stato Maggiore, p.195.
48. Ministero della Guerra, pp.31-4.
49. De Rosa, pp.199-200.
50. Ministero della Guerra, p.39.
51. W. Gottlieb, *Studies in secret diplomacy* (London, 1957), p.142.
52. Ministero della Guerra, p.121.
53. O. Malagodi, *Conversazioni della guerra 1914-1919,* vol. I (Milan, 1960), p.58.

11 THE LIBYAN WAR

What has been called 'Italy's war for a desert',[1] was an uncharacteristic stroke of *Katastrophenpolitik* on the part of Giolitti. Like later ventures in 1935 and 1940 it had far wider repercussions, national and international, than its instigators ever invisaged. The Libyan War helped to unleash forces in Italy and in Europe which Giolitti had been attempting to restrain or manipulate in order to construct a peaceful society with 'freedom for all within the bounds of the law'. If he regarded this colonial war as merely 'a brief parenthesis between the law for the state monopoly of life insurance (June, 1911) and the law for electoral reform (June, 1912)', he had grossly miscalculated.[2] Intended to unify the nation on its fiftieth anniversary, the war in fact created deeper divisions in Italian society. Catholics, socialists, republicans, radicals and even the ruling liberal party itself, were all affected during the course of the war. The pro-war attitude of moderate socialists, for instance, prompted the growth of revolutionism and anti-militarism within the party, helped the left to wrest control, and paved the way for the dramatic events of 'Red Week' in June 1914.[3] Nationalists, Futurists and other imperialist factions were momentarily intoxicated by the outbreak of 'their war', but rapidly became disillusioned and vented their frustration on Giolitti. The war, therefore, increased political polarisation, but it also played into the hands of the theorists of violence. The great earthquake which shattered Messina and Reggio in 1908 heralded a new era of instability. Young Turks took over the Ottoman Empire and Austria-Hungary annexed Bosnia in the same year. Sorel's *Reflexions on Violence* gained currency and in the bitterly contested strike in the area around Parma, the syndicalists tested their new theories, assisted by the dislocations afflicting Italian industry after 1907. In the following year, when Europe seemed close to war, the Futurist Manifesto glorified violence and war was seen as 'the hygiene of the world'. These views were echoed by the nationalist writers in the Florentine periodicals and D'Annunzio became a cult figure in many intellectual circles.[4] Hoping to satisfy this appetite for violence and adventure, Giolitti gave them the Libyan War but soon found that their appetite grew with eating.

Although all the great powers had recognised Italy's claim to Libya,

Giolitti's ultimatum to the Turks at the end of September 1911 was still a dangerous gamble. The Agadir Crisis over Morocco had threatened war between France and Germany since early July and was not finally resolved until 4 November, five days after Italy had gone to war. There was a danger that an Italian war in the Mediterranean, perhaps spreading as far as the Aegean, might rekindle Franco-German hostility and provoke a European war. At the very least, an Italo-Turkish war would exasperate the Germans, who had been wooing Constantinople for two decades, and alarm the Austrians, who were deeply concerned in any move which might have repercussions in the Balkans. Giolitti, always a staunch supporter of the Triple Alliance, threatened its very existence by going to war, and he was unlikely to be warmly welcomed by the British and French who were full of reservations about an Italian colony firmly implanted between Tunis and Egypt. Another dangerous possibility was that Conrad, the Austrian chief of staff who had been thwarted in 1908, might gain approval for a strike against Italy while her attention was fixed elsewhere. In his memoirs, Giolitti emphasises the diplomatic rather than the domestic reasons for the war of 1911.[5] He believed that if Italy had waited until the French had consolidated their hold upon Morocco, Paris may have refused to honour the agreements of 1900-2. Despite Giolitti's protestations to the contrary, Albertini was convinced that he decided upon war only 'at the last moment under the pressure of public opinion'.[6] The decision to send an unacceptable ultimatum to the Turks must have been taken only in the latter part of September because on 3 September the conscript class of 1889 was allowed home, leaving Italy temporarily with only one class under arms. Until 15 September big naval manoeuvres were being held and would seem to preclude any decision having been taken by that date.[7] It was on 23 September that a protest was sent to Constantinople, followed by an ultimatum four days later. More than pedantry is involved in trying to determine when the decision for war was taken because the Libyan War was the first major war which Italy had fought since 1866 and it is important to analyse the role of the army in the events of 1911-12. If the army had only a few days' notice of the imminence of war, for instance, some of the weaknesses revealed in the ensuing campaign become readily understandable.

Unlike the Banco di Roma and Admiral Bettòlo, General Pollio and the army establishment do not appear to have pressed for war in 1911.[8] It was the naval general staff which had warned San Giuliano, the Foreign Minister, that if an expedition were contemplated it must sail before the middle of October because of the unpredictability of weather conditions in the late autumn.[9] In his memoirs, Giolitti claims that Pollio was informed of the projected expedition in August.

> It therefore became necessary to calculate the effectives required for a given operation, and to put the machinery already prepared into motion. In the month of August I had even sent for our Chief of Headquarters Staff, Major-General Pollio, and I had instructed him to examine the question of an occupation of Libya and told him to decide on the number of troops that would be required to effect it.[10]

The passage conveys the impression that Giolitti was going through a rather unnecessary formality in informing Pollio at all, an attitude prevalent among civilians on the eve of 1914. Most of them assumed that a brief message to the general staff could almost instantaneously be transmuted into any specified military operation. For some, even outside Catholic Italy, the age of miracles had not yet passed. Pollio's estimate of 20,000 troops was ridiculed by Giolitti who ordered him to double the number. Being presented with such a vague brief, the chief of staff could hardly have been expected to calculate the size of the expedition in any scientific fashion but it is surprising that he did not adopt the traditional method of asking for twice as much as he could possibly need. Pollio probably envisaged 'the occupation of Libya' as the capture of a few key points on the coast like Tripoli and Tobruk, operations in which the navy and the marines would play a substantial role. Intelligence estimated that there were only a few thousand Turks in the area and that the Arabs would welcome the Italian invaders. The very existence of an expeditionary force would, it was hoped, compel the Porte to submit. Giolitti's shrewd farsightedness after the event is not very convincing.

Seton-Watson's assumption that 'only on the 24th was the final decision taken' seems well founded.[11] Although the army had contingency plans, the order to implement them in a matter of days cannot have been greeted with enthusiasm by Pollio or by General Caneva, who had been designated commander of the expedition. There is no evidence that the army had been secretly concentrating troops and supplies near Naples or Catania, nor do the naval manoeuvres earlier in the month appear to have been part of an elaborate scheme to prepare the armed forces for a dramatic *coup* even though San Giuliano had become convinced that a swift *fait accompli* was diplomatically essential.[12] He was so afraid that Berlin and Vienna would attempt to mediate that he only informed his Triple Alliance partners of Italy's exact intentions on the eve of the expedition's departure.

Pollio's task was made more difficult by his need to preserve intact the basic structure of the army in Italy in case Austrian intervention compelled him to order full mobilisation. This involved the creation of an expeditionary force of 35,000 men out of contingents drawn from all corps. Equipment and supplies were assembled in similar fashion, the object being to avoid depleting any single corps or region of its war potential. Unlike the other colonial powers, Italy's high command drew primarily on conscripts to fight in Africa, so that in a difficult military situation the troops might sometimes fail to show that steadiness under fire which was the hallmark of long-service regulars. Not surprisingly, the expedition was still unready when war broke out on 29 September. The navy and the marines simply sailed off without the troops, seizing Tripoli on 5 October and Tobruk, Derna, Benghazi and Homs by 21 October. Cagni's 1,600 marines, 'the Garibaldini of the sea', held Tripoli for six days until the first contingents of Caneva's troops began arriving on 11 October. This precipitate action by the navy, although in the best D'Annunzian tradition, prevented Caneva from implementing his plan to trap the Turks inside the city, cutting them off from the interior. What had been virtually a naval and military promenade came to an abrupt end with the bloody battle of Sciara-Sciat on 23 October.[13] After the so-called revolt of Tripoli, the Italians found themselves at war with a hostile population which steadfastly refused to greet Caneva's forces as liberators. The unexpected reverses at the end of October prompted Giolitti to proclaim the annexation of Libya on 5 November. Unable to secure a decisive military verdict the Italian government resorted to a diplomatic *fait accompli.* By December, the 35,000 troops had swollen to 72,000, and in the following spring was just short of 100,000.[14] Indeed, however well prepared the army may have been in September for a short colonial war, by early 1912 improvisation had become the order of the day, as Caneva struggled to make headway against a recalcitrant and elusive adversary. All machine gun detachments were sent to Africa, new units were formed, the magazines and depots in Italy were emptied, and even Eritrean troops were sent into Libya. By early 1913 Pollio asked Spingardi for immediate measures to be taken to augment the army where company strength had fallen to 15 and battalions were down to 50.[15] The seriousness of the situation is revealed by the fact that Pollio, an ardent supporter of the Triple Alliance, had to inform Germany in November 1912 that Italy could no longer send troops to the Rhine if war broke out with France. Although peace was signed with the Turks in October 1912, over 50,000 Italian troops were still stationed in Libya when the First World War began. After 1915, Italian authority in the area was restricted to a few coastal towns. The 'official war' which ended with the Treaty of Ouchy on 18 October 1912, cost the Italians around 3,000 dead and 1,300 million lire.[16] In return she had acquired an enormous colony in North Africa and, provided she could hold it, a potentially valuable asset in the Mediterranean. In addition, Italian efforts to put pressure on the Turks by naval operations in the Aegean had resulted in the occupation of the Dodecanese Islands. This was no mean reward, but the nationalists who had hailed the war so rapturously in late 1911 launched venomous attacks on the government in the course of 1912 and dismissed the Treaty of Ouchy as a 'mutilated peace'. *Italia* had failed to emerge and the despised *Italietta* of Giolitti continued to hobble along. Although the Libyan War had seen the first systematic use of armoured cars in warfare and bombs had been dropped from aeroplanes, it was the political rather than the military implications of the war which were to have the greatest impact.

In the Second Reich during the late 1890s men like Tirpitz, Bülow and Miquel had attempted to solve Germany's problems by pursuing a *Sammlungspolitik,* rallying patriotic opinion around a great battle fleet.[17] Giolitti had no such ambitious scheme in mind when he launched the Libyan War in 1911 even though his political system was in the process of disintegration. Basically, he saw the war as the logical outcome of the diplomatic agreements of the preceding decades and of Italy's quest for great power status. As a politician, he realised that any repetition of Corti's 'empty hands' policy would be suicidal, and he undoubtedly hoped that a colonial war would help to reconcile his nationalist critics, but he steadfastly refused to become emotionally involved and infuriated the zealots by his detached and prosaic attitude. It was clear then that Giolitti had no 'grand design', but his opponents had one. Their aim was to capture the imagination of the Italian people, to transform their nationalist rhetoric into reality, and revive the slumbering heroism of the Risorgimento.

Since their first congress in Florence in 1910, the nationalists, as distinct from old fashioned patriots, had become something more than a colourful group of literati attached to a remarkable series of periodicals which had sprung up in the early 1900s. Their membership ranging from reactionary monarchists to revolutionary syndicalists, the nationalists formed a political party. Although it remained small, it played a crucial role in Italian politics for the next thirteen years. From the beginning, militarism had been an integral part of their rather confused programme, and it was most appropriate that nationalism became a political movement during the Libyan War because it was 'Africanism' which provided an essential link between the nationalism of the Risorgimento and, via Crispi, its later manifestations in the prewar period. The fallen heroes of Dogali and Adua, including the martyred Crispi, had striven to make Italy powerful and respected and they had failed, not because they had suffered defeat at the hands of the Ethiopians, but because they had been disowned by petty-minded politicians who were so preoccupied with their own squalid bargaining within the system of *trasformismo* that they totally ignored national interests. This was the theme of Oriani's *Fino a Dogali,* published in 1889, and it still informed his last major work the *Rivolta ideale* of 1906. Largely ignored for most of his lifetime, his idealisation of war and bloodshed, together with his scathing attacks on parliamentary democracy, began to attract the attention of the new nationalists of the Giolittian era. In his rather contorted style Oriani had written: 'Italy's future consists entirely of a war which, while restoring her natural boundaries, may cement within her, by the tragedy of mortal dangers, the Unity of national sentiment.'[18] War, not only to attain national greatness but also to weld together the disparate classes and interests, war as the only alternative to revolution, had a powerful appeal. Enrico Corradini, converted to his nationalist views by 'the shame of Adua', reached the same conclusions and founded *Il Regno* in 1903 to convert others. He lashed out against 'the cowardice of the present hour' which seemed personified in Giolitti. Together with Papini and Prezzolini 'all those. . .who are for an intense and heroic life against a narrow and vulgar life' were invited to join their ranks.

> When lives have to be sacrificed we are not saddened if before our minds shines the magnificent harvest of a superior life that will rise from those deaths. And while the lowly democrats cry out against war as a barbaric residue of ferocious ages, we believe it to be the greatest awakener of the weak, a quick and heroic instrument of power and wealth.[19]

Corradini also developed the concept of Italy as 'the proletarian nation' fighting against the plutocratic powers of the world, an argument used in 1911 and again in 1935.

> Just as socialism taught the proletariat the value of class war, so we must teach Italy the value of international conflict. But international conflict means war? Then let there be war! And nationalism in Italy will arouse the will to victory.[20]

Unlike many nationalists Corradini was not content merely to shore up a decadent ruling class by forcing them to read relevant passages from Pareto or Mosca. His attitude was offensive not defensive. In his novel *Patria lontana,* published in 1910, his two major characters, a nationalist and syndicalist, begin to learn from one another to produce a kind of synthesis based on a common contempt for humanitarian bourgeois liberalism, and a joint appreciation of the value of violent struggle which verges on a belief in violence for violence's sake, or war for war's sake. Later events proved that Corradini had shown prophetic insight.[21]

More pervasive were the ideas, or rather the attitudes, of Gabriele D'Annunzio. As Prezzolini wrote:

> The Italian loves D'Annunzio, whom he feels closer to his own weaknesses, but he is shrewd enough to let himself be guided rather by Giolitti. In the former he enjoys the pleasures of poetry while in the latter he feels the solidity and satisfaction of prose.[22]

It has been persuasively argued that whereas one section of the Italian middle class aspired to become *superuomini dannunziani* the other turned to a constructive realism, political and economic.[23] The Libyan War revealed the dangers of this dualism, because in a period of heightened tension, international or domestic, the strident tones of D'Annunzian rhetoric tended to drown the sober but less exciting arguments of the realists. As a child, D'Annunzio had written in honour of King Humbert's visit to his school in Prato: 'New days are breaking for our Italy, days which once again will see the triumphant armies marching the streets of Rome, and a laurel-crowned conqueror riding in a chariot along the Via Sacra.'[24] After arriving in Rome, 'this city strewn with the mighty monuments of the past', this youthful *romanità* became more pronounced and was reinforced by his reading of Carducci. The provincial from the Abruzzi soon became a successful gossip columnist, causing a sensation by his marriage to the daughter of the 'black' Duke of Gallese, but it was his novels, from the decadent *Romanzi della rosa,* which gave him a national reputation. His blood-soaked metaphors and preoccupation with death and destruction began to make an impact, particularly on Italian youth. Marxism, which had spread like a bushfire among the intellectuals of the 1890s was burning itself out, or, as Giolitti expressed it in his more prosaic fashion, Marx was relegated to the attic. The danger was that the other floors might become tenanted by Corradini, D'Annunzio or Sorel, as nationalist doctrines and other activist theories exerted a growing fascination.

When it came to worship of modern weapons and other gleaming products of the new technology, even D'Annunzio was eclipsed by Filippo Marinetti. With his Futurist colleagues, he was probably more effective also in shocking Italians out of their pacifist torpor.

> In fact, although it is undeniable that our Futurist campaign in favour of militarism and war, the only hygiene of the world, and against pacifist and utilitarian cowardice, has served to prepare the great warlike atmosphere which inflames Italy today, I must also admit that our propaganda has not yet extirpated from the Italian soul those other vices from the past which are called: sentimentality, morbid compassion, love of cripples. . .
>
> If thanks to our tremendous efforts the students of Italy finally possess an ideal of daily heroism and a warm passion for all forms of danger, if our artillery is now sensibly improved, if our military aviators and our bersaglieri love to play lightly with death, it is no less true, unfortunately, that we are still afflicted with a tenderness of heart and an almost feminine sensitivity which are absolutely Italian.

In this passage from Marinetti's *La Battaglia di Tripoli* and scattered throughout the writings of other exalted nationalists there is a kind of hysteria born of frustration.[25] In a Darwinian world where war would determine who were the fittest to survive, how could Italy hope to compete successfully when her people seemed to be such reluctant warriors?

By creating the *Associazione Nazionalista Italiana,* the nationalist congress at Florence hoped to answer this question. Italians were to be shaken out of their apathy by a political and literary *blitzkrieg.* Their campaign seemed to gather an irresistible momentum after the outbreak of the Libyan War. Corradini wrote his *Ora di Tripoli,*

D'Annunzio wrote of the 'paradise that lies in the shadow of the sword' in his *Canzoni delle geste d'oltremare* and Marinetti's contribution was *La Battaglia di Tripoli.* That these were not generally regarded as the freakish outpourings of warped minds is a tribute to the growing success of nationalist propaganda. Significantly contributing to Italy's psychological preparedness for war, they obviously answered a spiritual need which the Giolittian system could not fulfil. It was fortunate for their cause that the war and the Treaty of Ouchy were not above criticism. For Giolitti to have emerged triumphantly would have been most damaging for them. Hostility to the *ministro della mala vita* who was incapable of any heroic action was one of the most powerful centripetal forces keeping together the disparate cohorts of nationalism. His failure to steal their thunder or to assuage the militaristic elements in society encouraged the nationalists to redouble their efforts. Unfortunately for Giolitti, the Libyan War not only whetted the appetite of the nationalists, it also intensified the activities of the anti-militarists.

At the Milan congress of 1910, the reformist socialists appeared to be in full control of the party. When Benito Mussolini attacked 'this old cliché of the fatherland in danger, the old cliché of all bourgeois democracies with which for the past thirty years the blood has been pumped from the poverty-stricken proletariat', there was 'some applause', but the congress was determined not to go beyond the pious hope of demanding that the military budget be frozen.[26] When, at the outbreak of war, the King expressed fears that the socialists might try sabotage, Giolitti reassured him.[27] On 25 September, an attempted general strike against the war had been a fiasco. Leaders like Bissolati and Bonomi actively supported the war and were prepared to collaborate with Giolitti although they declined to become ministers. But for the rank and file, as opposed to the leadership, and for the workers in the northern cities or for the peasants in the south and in the Romagna, Mussolini's invective was perhaps a more accurate reflection of socialist sentiments towards the army and the war. For them, the army was the praetorian guard of the propertied classes, prepared to indulge in 'proletarian massacres'. Except in years like 1898 and 1904, when cavalry and artillery came out on to the streets, the military presence was more subtly deployed in the north than in the south. It was more subtle because of the links which began to develop between the army establishment and the industrialists. The work force as well as management in the armament factories and in the textile mills, the shipyards, Fiat and Pirelli, had a vested interest in government orders for the armed forces. To strike against an inflated military budget or even against war meant the threat of unemployment in a lucrative industry. Profit and power went together and an armed peace or a war could be economically rewarding. Some southerners began arguing that Naples, Taranto and other cities in the area should become bigger military and naval bases to safeguard the inhabitants from recession rather than foreign aggression.[28]

Despite these tendencies and the attitude of some of the leaders, anti-militarism was an integral part of socialism. Sorel had argued that war was capable of destroying socialism and Pareto that it would retard the movement for at least fifty years.[29] Corradini's characters had expressed similar sentiments in *La patria lontana.* All three writers were amazed that the ruling élite failed to see this clearly and continued to pursue liberal, humanitarian policies. Italian nationalists were quick to see this, pointing out that *Giolittismo* nurtured the growth of socialism. In his *Discorsi militari,* published in May 1914 under the auspices of *La Voce,* Giovanni Boine stressed the political and social implications of nationalism. A great admirer of De Maistre and Gobineau, he presented a straightforward programme of 'God, king and country'. Liberty consisted in knowing how to obey and the army was the great *'generatore dell'ordine'* without which anarchy would reign. Italy, corroded by civil strife, relied upon the army to maintain order but war was the essential antidote to this internal conflict. The code of conduct prevalent in the army must be extended to the rest of the nation, a process which war would facilitate.[30] The anti-militarist left were thereby spared the necessity of drawing their own caricature of the ardent nationalist. The extravagant gestures of the anti-socialist right during the Libyan War undoubtedly helped the revolutionary faction to capture the socialist party at the congress at Reggio Emilia in July 1912. On both extremes, advocates of the slogan *'vivre ce n'est pas calculer c'est agir'* planned violent remedies which would make nonsense of the caution and compromise which lay at the heart of the Giolittian system.[31] 'After a year of foreign war', Mussolini asserted at the end of 1912, 'We now have a year of internal war.' The shooting incident at Roccagorga on 7 January 1913 was, according to the newly appointed editor of *Avanti!* the opening salvo of that war. 'With the cry of "Savoy!" the troops fired 300 rounds against unarmed women and children,' announced Mussolini's headlines.[32] Moderates like Turati still within the socialist party, and the increasingly apprehensive *'ascari di Giolitti'* had to avoid the crossfire which continued through the elections of 1913 to the congress of Ancona, and on to the bitter battles of Red Week in June 1914.

For the first time since the Risorgimento, Catholics also found themselves heavily involved in the fighting. Before 1910, conservatives in Italy could rely upon the support of the army but not on that of the church. Pius IX's refusal to acknowledge the existence of the Kingdom of Italy or to allow Catholics to participate in its political life had prevented any union between throne and altar, or between sword and mitre. Only in 1904 were Catholics allowed to vote in constituencies where a socialist seemed likely to win, and only in 1911 did Catholics openly support the army and its mission in Libya. Until then, Catholics, like socialists, had tended to criticise the barracks as the breeding ground of every conceivable vice and of some which even defied the imagination of the pure. On 3 October 1911, the prefect of Perugia reported to Giolitti that a celebrated Capuchin had told a Catholic audience that Italian missionaries in Tripoli awaited 'the high honour of being the first to embrace our brave soldiers'. This was followed by cries of *'Viva l'Italia, viva l'esercito!'*[33] The rhetoric of the *Croce e dell'Aquila* had begun. For the Jesuits at least, it was not the crescent flag of Islam which monopolised their attention but the red flag of subversion. *Civiltà cattolica* ceased referring to Italian troops as depraved oppressors of the church who deserved the thrashings they received at the hands of Ethiopians, and spoke of 'two institutions which still stoutly resist the raging tempest. . . These two institutions are the religious orders and the armies.'[34] This was welcome news for the nationalists, who could greet a new ally, and for the anti-militarist socialists, who could attack an old adversary in the manner of the French Dreyfusards. In vain the pope attempted to stand aloof, disavowing the pro-war pronouncements the *Civiltà cattolica.* The majority of the Catholic laity and a large number of the clergy felt unable to adhere to the cautious neutrality being advocated by the Vatican. Left-wing Catholics like Giuseppe Donati and Giuseppe Miglioli, the trade union leader, condemned imperialism with as much vigour as the left-wing socialists.[35] Catholic involvement in war was summed up by a cartoon in *Asino* where Giolitti and Pius X show each other newly designed uniforms for their respective armed forces, the papal guard wearing the white-red-green of the Italian tricolor, the Bersaglieri the yellow-red-blue of the Swiss at the Vatican. Filippo Meda, a Christian democrat who specialised in embarrassing his more reticent co-religionists, wrote that Catholics found irresistible 'the nationalist wind blowing from the coasts of Africa'.[36] For the first time since unification, the Italian army was accompanied by chaplains who were not defying the orders of their superiors, and for the first time, in March 1912, *Te Deums* were sung in the churches of Rome to celebrate the failure of D'Alba's assassination attempt on the King. When Humbert had been killed in 1900 only the American church and the Methodists had tolled their bells.[37]

Like the Libyan War, the granting of universal manhood suffrage proved irresistible to most Catholics. *Il Fermo Proposito* had given formal sanction to the selective abandonment of the *non expedit* and the lure of a largely rural electorate of eight million made the formation of a Catholic political party merely a matter of time. The Gentiloni Pact during the 1913 elections was a large step in this direction even if the new deputies did style themselves *'cattolici deputati ma non deputati cattolici'.* In agreeing to this manoeuvre, Giolitti gained a short-term advantage but he effectively ruined his own concept of *'parallelismo'.* Crossing the Tiber from both directions threatened to introduce too much religion into politics and too much politics into religion. The Libyan War had helped to destroy yet another rampart of *Giolittismo.*

Notes

1. The title of a book by F. McCullagh published in 1912. The background to the war is well presented in W. Askew, *Europe and Italy's acquisition of Libya* (Durham, N.C., 1942).
2. Salomone, p.103.
3. The best recent account is L. Lotti, *La settimana rossa* (Florence, 1972).
4. A wide selection of articles from these reviews is to be found in *La cultura del '900 attraverso le riviste* (Turin, 1960-). For a profile of Marinetti, see J. Joll, *Intellectuals in politics* (London, 1960).
5. Giblitti, p.249.
6. Albertini, I, p.343.
7. Ibid., p.344.
8. A parliamentary enquiry in 1906 had largely substantiated a claim made by Enrico Ferri that Bettolo, a former Navy Minister, had used his position to establish dubious links with the Terni steelworks (Seton-Watson, pp.265, 358), and in 1911 he does not seem to have been averse to intervening in diplomacy. The Banco di Roma, with interests in Tripoli, was prepared to use blackmail to ensure an Italian occupation (San Giuliano to Giolitti, 9 Aug.1911, *Quarant'anni,* III, p.57).
9. San Giuliano to Giolitti, 2 Sept. 1911, ibid., p.59.
10. Giolitti, p.270.
11. Seton-Watson, p.367.
12. Memorandum of San Giuliano, 28 July 1911, *Quarant'anni,* III, pp.52-6. Also F. Malgeri, *La guerra libica 1911-1912* (Rome, 1970), pp.131-2.
13. Stato Maggiore, p.145.

14. Rochat, p.312.
15. Ibid., p.313.
16. Askew, p.249.
17. V. Berghahn, *Germany and the approach of war in 1914* (London, 1973), p.24.
18. Thayer, p.137.
19. Salomone, p.91.
20. F. Gaeta, *Nazionalismo italiano* (Naples, 1965), p.85.
21. M. Isnenghi, *Il mito della grande guerra* (Bari, 1970), pp.10-18.
22. Salomone, p.89, f.15.
23. G. Carocci, *Giolitti e l'età giolittiana* (Turin, 1961), p.26.
24. A. Rhodes, *The poet as superman* (London, 1959), p.21.
25. Isnenghi, pp.30-1.
26. Salomone, pp.70-1.
27. Giolitti to the King, 25 Sept. 1911, *Quarant'anni,* III, p.61.
28. Francesco Nitti stated this case (De Rosa, pp.208-9).
29. Isnenghi, p.8.
30. Ibid., pp.71-4.
31. R. De Felice, *Mussolini il rivoluzionario* (Turin, 1965), p.65.
32. Ibid., pp.145-6.
33. G. Spadolini, *Giolitti e i cattolici* (Florence, 1970), pp.232-3.
34. Ibid., p.236, f.1.
35. Candeloro, VII, p.320.
36. G. De Rosa, *Storia del movimento cattolico in Italia,* I (Bari, 1966), pp.541-2.
37. Spadolini, pp.263-4.

12 NON-INTERVENTION

After the ending of the official war in North Africa in the autumn of 1912, army leaders had an opportunity to take stock of the situation. The outburst of patriotism and the increased respect for the army had been very gratifying. Equally satisfactory had been the tendency to blame Giolitti and his ministers for any military shortcomings revealed by the war. The fact that intransigent anti-militarists had been exposed and isolated and that sullen Catholic recruits could no longer justify their apathy or mass evasion of the call-up by claiming allegiance to a higher authority, further strengthened their position. But the Minister of War Spingardi and Pollio, the chief of staff, had also to confront the more tangible but less pleasing repercussions of the Libyan War. Like the foreign military attachés who had accepted their invitation to go on a 1,500 francs, one month's excursion trip to North Africa, they initially expected to witness a *coup de thêatre.*[1] When it became obvious that this latest attempt at gunboat diplomacy had miscarried, they had to reconcile themselves to the steady drain of men and materials which severely disrupted their original rearmament programme. It was not that casualties had been exceptionally heavy. Indeed, D'Annunzio and Marinetti must have been depressed by the official lists: 1,432 killed in action, 4,250 wounded and 1,948 contracting fatal illnesses.[2] What did appall everyone was the financial cost of the war. Only in the spring of 1914 was the figure of 1,300 million lire publicly admitted. This revelation was the signal for Giolitti to retire from office, temporarily he hoped. By early 1912 Spingardi and Pollio had become alarmed by escalating costs and by the desperate need to replace equipment which had been sent to North Africa.[3] In November of that year, although peace had been signed with the Turks, Pollio decided to send Colonel Zupelli to Berlin to inform Moltke that Italy would be unable to fulfil her military obligations on the Rhine if a general war broke out. He did this reluctantly as he was a convinced supporter of the Triple Alliance, which was in fact renewed again on 5 December 1912. As proof of Italian loyalty Pollio pledged immediate mobilisation should the *casus foederis* arise, and also proposed a naval convention, a suggestion which led to the signing of the Triple Alliance Naval Convention in June 1913.[4] The Germans were not unduly alarmed by Zupelli's news. Indeed, both Schlieffen and Moltke had previously expressed doubts about any Italian contribution to a war against France.[5] On 21 December 1912 the German chief of staff wrote to the Chancellor:

> It is almost certainly to be expected that we shall not be able to count on a resolute entry of Italy into the war with all the strength of her military potential. She will operate in a dilatory and cautious way and will await the development of events on the other side of the Alps, so as to be able to withdraw without serious losses if the other two allies were to suffer a check.[6]

During this exchange, it is interesting to note that Pollio, who had written about Italian action if the *casus foederis* arose, was unaware of the terms of the Triple Alliance. When he did ask about them he was told that the treaty contained no military clauses which he needed to know about.[7] Apparently, a military convention was the business of the military but the treaty to which it was attached was not, a curious division of labour between soldiers and civilians which was not confined to Italy.

General Pollio himself was not suspected of trying to weaken the alliance. The German ambassador at Rome affirmed that the Libyan War and the shortage of officers explained the Italian move,[8] and General Waldersee, who was sent to assess the true situation, agreed with him. Even Conrad, the Austrian chief of staff who hated everything Italian, was convinced of Pollio's loyalty. This opinion of him was reinforced when he attended the German manoeuvres in September 1913 and announced his willingness to send two cavalry divisions and eventually three to five infantry divisions into south Germany via the Tyrol.[9] It was appropriate for the author of a book on Custoza, which had stressed the need for unity of command, to insist that in wartime the Triple Alliance 'should act as a single state', and in February 1914 Pollio delighted his allies by informing them that the recovery of Italy now made it possible for him to send the Third Army to the Rhine as agreed originally. Moltke replied: 'The naval convention and the renewal of our old treaties are your work, and if it is God's will that Germany and Italy, fighting shoulder to shoulder, shall one day win the victory, your name will be honourably linked with it.'[10] According to Kleist, the German military attaché, Pollio even spoke of launching a preventive war 'quite in the spirit of your great King Frederick when in 1756 he broke through the iron ring of his adversaries'.[11] Kleist 'nearly fell off his chair' when Pollio also offered Italian troops for the Austrian front to prevent a Russian breakthrough. Crispi, it seemed, had not lived in vain, but as in the 1880s the Austrian suspected a diabolical plot.

Pollio, however, died of a heart attack on 1 July 1914, just two days after the assassinations at Sarajevo. His successor, General Luigi Cadorna, took up his duties on 27 July, one day before the Austro-Serbian war broke out and less than a week before the Schlieffen Plan was set in motion. The Germans and Austrians came to regard Pollio's death as a severe blow to the Triple Alliance. In reality it made very little difference because it was the civilian leadership which decided upon war or peace and the military who, willingly or reluctantly, obeyed their orders.

It was not only the chief of staff who had to assume new responsibilities in such inauspicious circumstances. In March 1914, Antonio Salandra replaced Giolitti as premier and General Grandi moved into Spingardi's office in Via XX Settembre. Salandra was a proud and independent southerner who detested Giolitti's system, but its rapid disintegration during the Libyan War, combined with a deteriorating economic situation, confronted him with severe domestic problems. In addition, the increasing tension in international affairs required constant attention and the re-equipment of the Italian army. General Porro, Salandra's first choice as War Minister, had to be passed over as his financial demands proved unacceptable to the treasury. General Grandi was less exacting and received the appointment but it was clear that the funds to be allocated were insufficient if the armed forces were called upon to play an active role in the immediate future.[12] With the Balkans in ferment and the two armed camps eyeing one another suspiciously, this was not a remote possibility. Nor, unfortunately, was the army's involvement in civil strife, perhaps even civil war.

Salandra, who remained premier until June 1916, began his crucial ministry bitterly resentful of his dependence upon the Giolittian majority elected in 1913. Like Sonnino, who had just refused to form a government,[13] he was an authoritarian and secretive figure who disliked politics and politicians although he had been a deputy since 1886.[14] Determined to handle the internal crisis resolutely, he himself took over the Ministry of the Interior. As a professor of administrative law at Rome he presumably felt well qualified. Since the Roccagorga incident, Mussolinian socialists, the Confederazione Generale del Lavoro (C.G.L.), and various anarchist and anti-militarist groups had been waiting for a pretext to take on the authorities. Scenting trouble, Errico Malatesta had returned to Italy in the summer of 1913 to reactivate Italian anarchism.[15] Failing to take advantage of the railway strike which Salandra resolved successfully, the activists had high hopes of the socialist congress at Ancona in April 1914, but Mussolini and his supporters had been too preoccupied with their anti-masonic purge.

The opportunity finally presented itself on 7 June, constitution day, when military parades were held throughout Italy. Malatesta had been astute enough to realise that anti-militarism was a more effective rallying cry among subversive elements of the left than either anti-clericalism or republicanism. For some time a campaign had been waged on behalf of two conscripts, Augusto Masetti, who had wounded a colonel in 1911 and been declared insane to avoid unwanted publicity, and Antonio Moroni, who had accused the army of consigning known militants to punishment battalions.[16] To ventilate these and other grievances, protest demonstrations were planned for 7 June. The intention was to goad the authorities into perpetrating another 'proletarian massacre', and, in Ancona, this tactic worked perfectly thanks to the incompetent handling of the situation by police and public security officers.[17] The news of three deaths in a clash between carabinieri and demonstrators spread rapidly and led to the declaration of a general strike. There were violent scenes in many cities but only in Emilia and the Marches did the government forces lose control. The C.G.L. called off the strike after two days despite Mussolini's yearning to become 'the poet of the general strike', but for a whole week Emilia was in rebel hands. Salandra sent in over 10,000 troops to restore order and the number of troops involved in this and other operations began to alarm War Minister Grandi, as the cohesion and discipline of the entire army was being threatened.[18] Red Week provided yet another shock for the tottering Giolittian system and hastened the polarisation which had been developing during the Libyan War. Extremism of the left produced a nationalist, militaristic backlash with the founding of vigilante groups to help the police and the army to track down subversives. To Salandra's relief, the crisis subsided quickly before these paramilitary activities became so widespread that they too could challenge the authority of the state. But no sooner had the Salandra cabinet surmounted the June crisis than it found itself confronting the implications for Italy of the July crisis in international relations. On 28 June Franz Ferdinand had been assassinated and on 28 July, with full German support but without any prior consultations with Italy, Austria declared war on Serbia.

Within the next few days all the great powers, with the exception of Italy, were also at war.

It was at a cabinet meeting on 31 July that Salandra and his colleagues decided that Italy must remain neutral. San Giuliano, the Foreign Minister, explained that there was 'nothing in the spirit or the letter of the Treaty of the Triple Alliance compelling us to join Germany or Austria over this issue'.[19] Austria was clearly the aggressor and the alliance was meant to be defensive; moreover, Rome had not been consulted or offered compensations as stipulated in the treaty. In addition, public opinion was hostile to waging war alongside the central powers, especially as Britain was expected to go to the aid of France. This decision was made public on 2 August and formally published the following day. It was a decision which won the almost unanimous approval of the Italian people. Giolittians, socialists, Catholics, factory workers and peasants all welcomed the news, Mussolini even threatening revolution if the government chose war. Sonnino was unhappy and so were several of the nationalists. Cadorna, who had just completed his first week in the post of chief of staff, was dumbfounded.

Cadorna had confidently expected Italy to fulfil her obligations to the central powers. On 29 July he had asked the War Minister to initiate various measures. These included the return of all troops in Libya whose presence there was not absolutely essential, the recall of all officers, the declaration of a state of readiness *('in preallarme')* for all units destined for the French frontier or the Rhine, and the making good of all material deficiencies.[20] On 31 July he sent a memorandum to the King asking for authorisation to send to the Rhine all those troops not needed in Italy or the colonies.[21] Like Pollio he believed that the decisive battles would be fought on the Franco-German frontiers and that they could be expected to take place in a matter of weeks rather than months. The government's decision to remain neutral took him by surprise and reinforced his contempt for politicians who meddled in military matters. Indeed, it was this attitude of hostility to the prevailing civil-military power structure which prevented his appointment as chief of staff in 1908. According to the constitution, the King was supreme commander of the army; in practice and written into paragraph 16 of army regulations, it was the War Minister who held this position in peacetime. On the outbreak of war, however, the chief of staff assumed command. Because War Ministers were appointed by politicians and were accountable to parliament, Cadorna believed that the army was at the mercy of political manoeuvring and party squabbles. In a period of political instability, for instance, War Ministers would remain only a short time in office, and this lack of continuity of leadership was dangerous for the army.[22] Cadorna's criticisms of divided control were justified, but the way he presented his case only increased civilian suspicions. Indeed, the military and the civilians showed a remarkable ignorance of each others' techniques and difficulties. Military debates in parliament were poorly attended with only a handful of intransigent socialists or 'military experts' prepared to debate the issues. On the other hand, there were many officers who never read daily newspapers or even knew the name of the current prime minister.[23] This was not, of course, a peculiarly Italian phenomenon, but this mutual incomprehension of each others' sphere of activities is astonishing. Political, technical and organisational developments had, by 1914, dictated that a major war required total mobilisation involving close collaboration between military and civilians. Salandra and Cadorna, the two men in charge of their respective hierarchies, were by temperament and background unlikely to achieve any close liaison. Also open to question was their ability to inspire trust and confidence within their own specific areas of competence.

Italian neutrality did not prevent Cadorna from pressing for immediate mobilisation, a view which was shared by Sonnino and others. With all the major powers locked in combat, an unprepared Italy seemed very vulnerable to a sudden attack. Salandra, however, rejected this proposal after a high level conference which included the chiefs of staff. In reality, both men faced a very similar task. Salandra and his Foreign Minister began to realise that they must cautiously effect a reversal of alliances, and Cadorna and his staff had to scrap the old war plans and devise new ones. These were very delicate manoeuvres and there was an understandable reluctance to say too much in case foreign governments or the Italian public heard about them, but it was surely carrying secrecy to unnecessary lengths for Salandra to refuse to keep Cadorna informed or to seek his advice on military matters. It was true that the chief of staff was a difficult, aloof man – when Mussolini kept him waiting on one occasion in 1927, Cadorna stalked out muttering that he never even kept his horses waiting for more than five minutes – but if Salandra distrusted him or found him unbearable he should have either dismissed him or humoured him.[24]

It was only in September that tension between Salandra and Cadorna began to subside. The battle of the Marne was fought in the second week of September, and from that moment it became apparent to both men that if Italy did intervene in the war, it would be on the side of the Entente. Throughout this period, as the published diplomatic documents show, the government was uneasily aware that their decision to veto Cadorna's plan to mobilise may have been incorrect.[25] Some progress was made, however, and from 9 August mountain guns and alpine troops had begun to flow eastwards after the build-up on the French frontier had been countermanded.[26] Salandra also agreed to call up two additional classes for conscripts 'for political rather than technical reasons', to give Italy the appearance of being prepared for everything.[27] The Foreign Minister wrote that 'Italy must not break with Austria and Germany if she cannot be certain of victory. This is unheroic but it is wise and patriotic.'[28] The government wanted the army to play a secondary role, assisting in its political and diplomatic initiatives. The rewards of *'sacro egoismo'* were to be reaped either without fighting at all or by intervening when the central powers were at their last gasp. Salandra's concept of an essentially limited war, to round off the wars of the Risorgimento by the acquisition of the *terra irredenta,* had important implications. Such a war would not require the total mobilisation of the country, economically, politically or psychologically. A *piccola guerra* would not strain her limited resources or, equally importantly for a conservative southerner, transform the existing *status quo.* Sonnino, soon to be appointed Foreign Minister, agreed with the Prime Minister, but from the beginning he had tended to stress Italian claims to the eastern shores of the Adriatic.[29] Cadorna, on the other hand, did not regard the army's role as secondary and believed that only a full-blooded intervention by Italy could break the European stalemate, and that only after total victory could diplomats and politicians hope to achieve anything. It was this fundamental difference in emphasis which helps to explain why civil-military relations were so bad at this time. Grandi, the War Minister, who could have acted as an intermediary, appeared to be too neutralist for either Salandra or Cadorna. The often opposed views of Grandi and Cadorna merely confirmed Salandra's distrust of the military mind and perhaps made him even more disinclined to take them into his confidence.

Many interventionist groups began to form in the autumn of 1914. Much attention has been focused on Mussolini's dramatic conversion and the founding of *Il Popolo d'Italia,* or D'Annunzio's dazzling performance in the following spring,[30] but the most effective of all these groups was a most exclusive and secretive coterie comprising

Salandra, Sonnino, the King and one or two trusted colleagues. This high level conspiracy which eventually produced 'Salandra's war' in May 1915, began activities after the German defeat on the Marne.[31] Their extreme caution was dictated not only by fear of Austrian or German reprisals, but by the certain knowledge that the majority of Italians, including the powerful Giolittian bloc in the chamber of deputies, were hostile to war. Giolitti's followers, the bulk of the socialist party, and most of the Catholics remained steadfastly neutralist, and Salandra's intention was not to convert them but to trick them into war by presenting them with a *fait accompli.* The noisy and often clownish antics of interventionists led by men like Marinetti, Mussolini and D'Annunzio were treated with alarmed disdain. Eventually, they played their part in the scenario of Radiant May and helped to dig the grave of democratic Italy, but in the meantime they were a dangerous nuisance. So was Cadorna, if he continued to advocate provocative military measures.

In later years, Salandra unjustly blamed the unpreparedness of the army and its leadership for Italy's late entry into the war.[32] Initially, Cadorna had been prepared to fight alongside the Triple Alliance but Italian neutrality had prevented this, clear proof that the military were subordinate to the civilians. Cadorna had then advocated mobilisation, but this had been rejected. It was only in the autumn that Salandra found Cadorna unwilling to contemplate immediate action and that was because the season was too late. As early as 13 August, Cadorna had explained that towards the end of October the Austrian frontier became unsuitable for military operations, and that as mobilisation would take a month, any decision to go to war must be taken at the beginning of September.[33] He was justifiably apprehensive about a winter campaign, as the army was ill-equipped for it. He had asked Grandi to implement a plan drawn up by Pollio in 1912 for the provision of winter equipment but one of the difficulties was that this plan envisaged a defensive war against France not an offensive war against Austria. Cadorna wanted to break through the eastern Alps into Slovenia and drive straight at the heart of Austrian power, a vastly different project from the 1912 plan or the more limited objectives of the exponents of the *piccola guerra.* Grandi, when pressed to speed up supplies, became evasive and asked for detailed estimates of the cost. Cadorna produced a figure of 46 million lire on 10 September, adding that anything lower than that would necessitate postponement of operations until the spring. Cadorna again emphasised this in a letter to Grandi on 25 September, and it is this letter which

Salandra used to justify his decision to delay intervention until the late spring of 1915. The army leadership had vetoed Italy's entry into the war throughout the latter half of 1914!

By October 1914, civil-military relations began to improve. When it became clear that both Salandra and Cadorna no longer contemplated an attack prior to the following spring, it became possible to plan ahead more calmly and rationally. The army now had six months to send officers through a crash course and convince the government of the need to launch a lavish rearmament programme. The removal of Grandi and the appointment of Zupelli, a personal friend of Cadorna, also helped to ease the tension. Between October, when he became War Minister, and November Zupelli secured 600 million lire, and a further 340 million lire between January and May 1915.[34] Like Pollio and Spingardi, Cadorna and Zupelli worked together as a team, but as yet there was no one in charge of co-ordinating military demands and economic resources. This defect was remedied by the emergence of General Dallolio as Under-Secretary of State for Arms in the summer of 1915. Fortunately, he proved equal to this formidable task and won unanimous approval for his efforts to ensure that the armed forces and industrial interests collaborated harmoniously.[35]

Salandra and Sonnino, who became Foreign Minister in November 1914, did not concern themselves with such developments. They concentrated almost exclusively on the diplomatic and political preparations for intervention on the side of the Entente. On 4 September, the Entente powers had signed a treaty committing themselves to common action until they won the war, so any secret negotiations with Italy would need the approval of London, Paris and Petrograd.[36] This complicated proceedings, but what made this a particularly dangerous game was the prolonged German diplomatic offensive spearheaded by Prince Bülow after his arrival in Rome as ambassador extraordinary at the end of 1914.[37] Bülow's mission was to keep Italy neutral as the Germans were realistic enough to drop their demands for her active support. In these negotiations among the Triple Alliance partners, everything turned on German ability to act as honest broker between Austria and Italy. Article VII of the alliance had promised compensations for Italy if Austria altered the *status quo* in the Balkans and Rome had made it plain that this entailed the cession of the Trentino and Trieste. Italian forces occupi[ed] Valona on Christmas day 1914, but Sonnino had no intention of allowing Albania to become a substitute for *Italia irredenta.*[38] Austrian reluctance to surrender territory enabled the Italians to spin out their negotiations with the central powers while they came to terms with the Entente. This double game reached its climax in early March. On 3 March 1915 Salandra instructed Imperiali, his ambassador in London, to present the Italian proposals which had been kept in readiness for over six months.[39] On 9 March the Austrians, pressed by Berlin, agreed to consider compensations. Rome had reached the parting of the ways, and the talks in London were speeded up, culminating in the signing of the Treaty of London on 26 April. On 4 May Italy denounced the Triple Alliance, mobilisation was ordered on 22 May and two days later she was at war with Austria.

Equally exciting and tortuous was the progress of the political conspiracy inside Italy which began, suitably enough, with a secret conversation between Salandra and Martini in a Frascati *albergo* on 17 September. They trusted the pianist Sgambati who lived in the adjacent room, said Martini, *'tuttavia parliamo a bassa voce'.*[40] So, in whispers, they plotted war with Austria and resolved to continue as they had begun – in the strictest secrecy. Salandra was inclined to seek the advice of Giolitti but eventually decided against this. Sonnino, the King and one or two others were brought in, but whereas at least two journalists – Malagodi of *Tribuna* and Albertini of the *Corriere della sera* – seemed reasonably well informed of what was happening, Cadorna and the general staff were unaware of these developments. It was to Malagodi on 12 December 1914 that Sonnino admitted that he fully realised that the majority of Italians inside and outside parliament were opposed to war, but that if the government decided on intervention it was its duty to ride roughshod over all those who stood in the way.[41] Even more explicit was a letter from Salandra to Sonnino on 16 March 1915, just two weeks after negotiations with the Entente had begun in earnest. He realised that a final break with the central powers was imminent and he noted down the major difficulties they faced. They had not yet won the explicit consent of the King, they could not count on the support of the country or the chamber, the army would not be ready until the end of April and they had no formal pledge on the part of the Entente. Undismayed, Salandra wrote that if the army were ready and a pact signed, or on the point of being signed, they had nothing to fear from King or country.[42] On 12 April Salandra sounded out public opinion by sending circulars to all prefects, asking them to report on 'the real feelings of the various classes of citizens' in their respective provinces.[43] It was true that various interventionist groups had made some headway by April 1915, but Salandra viewed them with as much distaste as Cadorna observed the exploits of the Garibaldian volunteers.[44] He can hardly have expected massive endorsement for a war policy, even though he and the other interventionists had been immeasurably helped by the publication of Giolitti's famous *'parecchio'* letter in February. Giolitti had remarked that Italy could gain 'quite a lot' without resorting to war. Seton-Watson has summarised the importance of this: 'The *Parecchio* letter had been a turning point. By publishing it, Giolitti unintentionally assumed the leadership of all the neutralist forces and turned the campaign for intervention into an anti-Giolitti crusade.'[45] Fighting Giolitti had a far wider appeal than fighting the central powers. Salandra, however, was disturbed by the growing momentum of the interventionism of the piazza which could well ruin Sonnino's delicate diplomacy and his own political manoeuvres, and he may have been relieved to hear from his prefects that neutralism was still predominant. He called off the survey on 21 April as he then had sufficient evidence to realise that the majority of Italians were still neutralist but, and this was the crucial finding, they were hopelessly divided and politically apathetic. This *indifferentismo* would pose few problems for a resolute government. The same could not be said for the Giolittian majority in the chamber. As the Treaty of London, commiting King and country to war, had been signed on 26 April, there were two alternatives to this problem, either the Giolittian deputies had to be swept away by recourse to a *coup d'état* or they had to be coerced into abandoning their policy. Radiant May, when D'Annunzio and the other interventionists took to the streets to create the illusion that Italians were irresistibly bent on war, enabled Salandra to opt for the second alternative and avoid calling in the army. Giolitti's return to Rome on 9 May and depressing news from the fighting fronts gave the neutralists a last chance to fight back. Salandra's cabinet resigned on 13 May and for three days there was a frightening power vacuum. Giolitti declined the King's invitation to form a ministry and returned to Piedmont, a clear indication to his 300 or so followers in the chamber that they were leaderless. Salandra was asked to resume the reins of government and when parliament reassembled on 20 May it granted full powers to him. Four days later Italy was at war.

Notes

1. J.C. Allain, 'Les débuts du conflit Italo-Turc: Oct. 1911 – Jan. 1912', *Revue d'histoire moderne et contemporaine,* XVIII (1971), p.109, f.2.
2. Askew, p.249.
3. *Archivio centrale dello stato,* Archivio Ugo Brusati, scat.10, no.1.

4. Halpern, pp.220-52.
5. Albertini, I, p.556.
6. Ibid., p.557.
7. San Giuliano to Giolitti, 7 Dec. 1912 and San Giuliano to Spingardi, 10 Dec. 1912, quoted in Halpern, p.223.
8. Ibid., p.229
9. For earlier plans to send them through neutral Switzerland, see M. Mazzetti, 'L'Italia e le convenzioni militari segrete della Triplice Alleanza', *Storia contemporanea,* I (June, 1970) and for a planned assault on Provence see Halpern, p.268.
10. Albertini, I, p.560. Also A. Alberti, *L'azione militare italiana nelle guerra mondiale* (Rome, 1924), p.24.
11. Albertini, I, p.561.
12. G. Rochat, 'L'esercito italiano nell'estate 1914', *Nuova rivista storica.* 45, pp.314-15.
13. S. Sonnino, *Diario 1914-16,* vol. II, ed. P. Pastorelli (Bari, 1972), p.4.
14. F. Martini, *Il diario 1914-18,* ed. G. De Rosa (Milan, 1966), p.534.
15. Lotti, p.3.
16. Ibid., pp.54-60.
17. Ibid., pp.61-9.
18. B. Vigezzi, *L'Italia neutrale* (Milan, 1966), p.707.
19. Martini, p.7.
20. Rochat, p.324, f.2.
21. L. Cadorna, *Altre pagine sulla grande guerra* (Milan, 1924), pp.15-23.
22. P. Pieri, 'Les relations entre gouvernement et commandement en Italie en 1917', *Revue d'histoire moderne et contemporaine,* 15, pp.133-4.
23. 'Whoever concerns himself with things outside his profession', a young officer was told by a superior who learnt he was reading a book on socialism, 'is a bad officer' (General De Rossi, p.66). General De Bono admitted that officers in the Rome garrison knew about politics. They had to provide guards whenever parliament was sitting! (De Bono, pp.190-1).
24. L. Cadorna, *Lettere famigliari* (Milan, 1967), p.20.
25. *Documenti diplomatici italiani,* 5th series, I (Rome, 1954).
26. Rochat, p.329, f.2.
27. A. Salandra, *La neutralità italiana* (Milan, 1928), pp.261-2
28. San Giuliano to Salandra, 16 Aug. 1914, *DDI*, 5th series, I, p.160.
29. Sonnino, *Diario,* II, p.9.
30. See the sources in W. Renzi, 'Mussolini's sources of financial support. 1914-15', *History,* vol.56 (June, 1971), De Felice, pp.276-7 and B. Vigezzi, 'Le Radiose Giornate del maggio 1915 nei rapporti dei prefetti', *Nuova rivista storica,* vol. 43 (1959) and vol.44 (1960).
31. W. Renzi, 'Italy's neutrality and intervention into the great war: a re-examination', *American historical review,* vol.LXXIII (June, 1968), and the excellent article by A. Monticone, 'Sonnino e Salandra verso la decisione dell'intervento', *Gli italiani in uniforme* (Bari, 1972) pp.57-87. This and other aspects dealt with in this chapter can be found in J. Whittam, 'War and Italian society 1914-16', *War and Society,* ed. B. Bond and I. Roy (London, 1975), pp.144-61.
32. Salandra, pp.30, 66-7, 193.
33. Rochat, p.330, f.1. Evidence from the Cadorna archives.
34. Ibid., p.347, f.2.
35. S. Clough, *The economic history of modern Italy* (New York, 1964), p.179.
36. C. Lowe, 'Britain and Italian intervention 1914-15', *The Historical Journal* XII, 3 (1969), pp.533-48.
37. Exhaustively treated in A. Monticone, *La Germania e la neutralità*

italiana 1914-15 (Bologna, 1971).
38. Sonnino, *Diario,* II, p.70.
39. A. Salandra, *L'Intervento (1915). Ricordi e pensieri* (Milan, 1930), p.149.
40. Martini, p.103.
41. O. Malagodi, *Conversazioni della guerra,* vol.I (Milan, 1960), p.32.
42. Monticone, *Gli italiani,* pp.63-4.
43. Ibid., p.67, The replies of the prefects are in B. Vigezzi, *Da Giolitti a Salandra* (Florence, 1969), pp.321-401.
44. R. Garibaldi, *I fratelli Garibaldi delle Argonne all'intervento* (Milan, 1933); R. De Felice, *Mussolini il rivoluzionario* (Turin, 1965), p.305.
45. C. Seton-Watson, *Italy from liberalism to fascism* (London, 1967), p.439.

13 WAR

The 1915-18 War was the greatest crisis which the Italian state and army had had to face since the creation of both in 1861. It had three phases. The first can loosely be called 'Salandra's war', from what he called the *idillio nazionale* of the summer of 1915 to the sour aftermath of the Austrian *Strafexpedition* in the summer of 1916. The leitmotiv of this first year of war was expressed in the King's proclamation to the troops: 'For the conquest of national independence your fathers have fought on three occasions: finally to achieve this will be your good fortune and your glory.' Written by Martini, it expressed the views of Salandra, Sonnino and the leading ministers.[1] Essentially, they wanted to fight a limited war to round off the campaigns of the Risorgimento, to avoid committing themselves to the *grande guerra* being waged by the other combatants, and thereby to obviate the necessity for the total mobilisation of resources. By delivering a swift *coup de grace* eliminating Austria, Italy would end the war for everyone. *'Sacro egoismo'* might be cynically translated as 'making war on the cheap', but if the Italian army achieved the vital breakthrough which had so far eluded all the belligerents, Salandra's realism would be excused. Unfortunately, these expectations proved illusory and as the war of attrition ground on, Salandra's views appeared increasingly anachronistic. This revived the old antagonism between him and Cadorna, because although the chief of staff shared Salandra's distaste for the political mobilisation of the nation, which would be a natural consequence of fighting a total war, he deplored the government's refusal to see Italy's contribution as an integral part of the European-wide conflict. A personal duel developed which Cadorna won. With the fall of Salandra in June 1916 and the formation of Boselli's ministry of all the talents, the second phase in the war began. Italy at last declared war on Germany and the period up to October 1917 marked a transitional stage in her conduct of the war. The first serious attempts were made to bridge the appalling gap between the home front and the war front, and to involve the nation in what was now quite clearly a *grande guerra.* The final phase began with the disaster of Caporetto, Orlando's appointment as premier, and the removal of Cadorna. As Italy fought for survival, the government felt impelled to make more and more extravagant promises to the troops, the industrial workers and the peasants. This led to a rapid, almost exotic growth of national consciousness. It helped Italy to convert defeat into victory but by the time the armistice was signed on 4 November 1918, wartime propaganda among both soldiers and civilians had promoted a mood of restless expectancy which peacetime Italy was going to find hard to accommodate.

Cadorna and the general staff did not force Italy into war. By rejecting unrealistic demands for a winter campaign and asserting that an offensive could not be launched before the end of April, he and Zupelli had indeed provided Salandra and Sonnino with a basic timetable. Cadorna had played no part in the negotiations leading up to the Treaty of London. Later, when he became aware of the terms, he supported the annexation of the Trentino and the Tirol up to the Brenner, the acquisition of the line of the Julian Alps and Istria, but he justifiably objected to demands for the central Dalmatian coastline which he regarded as militarily indefensible and – if the South Slavs inherited that portion of the Habsburg Monarchy – morally indefensible too. As in 1911, the navy lobby seemed more assertive and Sonnino, with his obsession about the Adriatic, was fully prepared to back their request for naval bases. It was primarily this aspect of the treaty which led Albertini to describe it as 'a serious obstacle to the success of our arms'.[2] Slavs, inside and outside the empire, began to regard Italy more as a threat than as an ally.

Likewise, Cadorna did not participate in Salandra's conspiratorial activities nor in the demonstrations of Radiant May. Members of the cabinet and the piazza mob took Italy into the war. Cadorna's task was to implement as quickly as possible the directives of the government. In his more sanguine moods, he does seem to have believed in the feasibility of an Italian *blitzkrieg.* In his first manuscript plan for an offensive against Austria, he had advocated a swift thrust across the Isonzo through the Ljubljana Gap, the main force aiming for Marburg and Zagreb while another army moved against Villach and Klagenfurt. The ultimate objective was the Vienna-Budapest line. This was no *Italia farà da sè* as the plan assumed that Russians and Serbs would be co-operating.[3] Again, in a room in the senate building at the beginning of April 1915, Cadorna had explained that within a month he could be in Trieste and menacing the heart of the Habsburg Empire.[4] In the summer and autumn of 1915 these ambitions proved to be totally unrealisable.

The nature of the Italo-Austrian frontiers helps to explain Cadorna's initial and subsequent failures to achieve a decisive breakthrough. For most of its 400 miles, it was hilly or mountainous and the Austrians controlled the crests. The Italians could attack the Trentino salient which pointed at the heart of the Lombard plain, and was a persistent threat to the armies operating to the north of the Gulf of Venice, but Cadorna decided to remain basically on the defensive in that sector as the strategic goals appeared unattractive.[5] That left the Isonzo front for the implementation of his plans, a series of swift river crossings followed by a drive through the rugged terrain on the opposite bank which included Monte Nero, the Bainsizza Plateau and the howling wilderness of the Carso in the south. A surprise offensive was ruled out by the French leaking information about the April pact prematurely. The Austrians, with 14 divisions against the Italians' 35, were outnumbered but already alerted and prepared to fall back before the initial onslaught to well-sited defensive positions. By inclination and through reports from the Western Front, Cadorna was cautious in his approach to the offensive, so he was unlikely to prove a dashing commander with a penchant for the lightning blow. There was another consideration, as he explained later, and that involved the fact that whereas the two Moltkes in 1870 and 1914 were the commanders of an ever victorious army, 'I was the leader of the army of Custoza and Adua'.[6] In addition to all these factors, there was also the depressing news from the other fighting fronts. It had been hoped that the Italian attack would coincide with the victorious advance of the Russians into the Hungarian plain, the declaration of war by Rumania, a vigorous assault by the Serbs, Entente successes along the Western Front and the capture of Constantinople. None of these expectations were fulfilled; indeed, if Italy had entered the war one month or ten months earlier she would have found the position of the Entente much stronger and that of Austria much weaker.

By the middle of June, when Italian mobilisation was finally completed, Cadorna's armies had crossed the frontiers and pushed the Austrians back to their main defences in many sectors. For a time, the morale of the 400,000 men involved was high. For them, and the half million men in the rear areas, this was *'il sacro entusiasmo del '15'.* Carried along by the élan of their officers and the interventionist volunteers, the troops fought with courage and determination even though most of them must have been ignorant of or indifferent to the basic aims of the war. Very quickly, however, trenches and barbed wire, artillery duels and mortars, brought about a stalemate war of attrition familiar on the Western Front since the Marne. Also familiar was the sudden realisation that artillery pieces and the ammunition for them were too scarce. In December 1914 and again in February, Cadorna had asked for an increased tempo in armaments production, including the utilisation of private industries like the automobile plants. The government began following this advice, but only after 26 June, and its appointment of General Dallolio as Under-Secretary for Arms on 9 July 1915 was one of the most crucial decisions of the war.[7] Cadorna had also requested a report on the number of aircraft available early in December 1914 but little had been done and Italy began the war with only 30 Blériots, 20 Neuports and 8 Farmans. Few individuals in any belligerent country had foreseen the importance of airpower, but more remarkable was the failure to perceive that the machine gun was the queen of the *'piccolissima guerra'* of the infantrymen. Italy began with only 618, two per regiment whereas the Austrians possessed two per battalion. Hand grenades were virtually unknown, howitzers were in short supply and most of them had been supplied by Krupp, and rifles of the 1891 model, being produced by Terni at the rate of only 2,500 per month, were so scarce that many troops were issued with 1870-87 Wetterlis. There were 3,000 motor vehicles and 216,000 horses.[8] Despite various expedients, Cadorna had not succeeded in providing the army with a sufficient number of officers and this was more serious than any material deficiencies. In 1915 the Italian army possessed 15,858 officers and in the deadly battles which raged along the frontiers, and particularly on the Isonzo, so many were killed or wounded that there were constant demands for replacements. In the opening battles between May and November 1915, over 62,000 officers and men had been killed and about 170,000 wounded. For civilians and soldiers anticipating a war of independence like those of the nineteenth century, this appalling wastage came as a tremendous shock. It was not at all like the glorious battles of the Risorgimento and thus *'moriva la guerra garibaldina'.*[9] Patriotism and conscription somehow managed to make good these losses, and by 1918 there were 21,926 career officers, together with no less than 153,000 reserve officers![10] In the interests of maintaining the efficiency and fighting quality of the officer corps, Cadorna was quite inflexible. In all he dismissed 807 officers, including 217 generals and 255 colonels. The commission of enquiry on Caporetto later accused him of ruthlessness and egocentricity, but he replied that all commanders had done the same and that his successor Diaz had seen fit to restore only 13 of the dismissed generals. During his much shorter period of command,

Diaz himself removed 176 officers.

Much more justified were criticisms of Cadorna's indifference to the question of morale. He believed that his huge army would remain an effective fighting force as long as strict discipline was enforced and everyone obeyed the orders of his superiors. The military code then in operation dated back, in its essentials, to July 1840. Its references to crimes 'in the presence of the enemy' or 'in the face of the enemy' may have been appropriate for a nineteenth-century army fighting limited engagements but in the context of 1915-18 they were ambiguous and anachronistic.[11] Desertions, self-mutilation, indiscipline and defeatism were crimes which Cadorna intended to punish through the military tribunals or by summary shootings. After some disorders among the Alpini, and again after the *Strafexpedition,* Cadorna even attempted to resort to decimation to reinforce discipline.[12] Like Salandra in the civilian sector, he believed that soldiers must obey the laws, fight hard and fulfil their tasks unquestioningly. It was not the duty of the army – or the state – to try to take them into partnership, to inform them of Italy's war aims or to institute welfare agencies.

For waging a short war with limited objectives, this unimaginative approach by the civilian and military leadership may have proved tolerable. After over six months of war and four battles of the Isonzo, exclusive reliance upon obedience and discipline began to create more problems than it solved. At first, the outbreak of war had united the nation, and the indifference which Salandra's prefects had noted among the rural masses could be largely discounted because it would all be over before they needed to be integrated in the war effort. Giolittians followed their leader's advice on 5 July and loyally supported King and government. The last great neutralist demonstration had taken place in Turin on 17-18 May, and socialists thereafter accepted the directive *'non aderire né sabotare'*. Most bishops were 'patriotic and moderate', urging all Catholics to obey the laws and co-operate with the secular power.[13] But this unity on the home front and the 'sacred enthusiasm' of the troops began to suffer erosion during the winter of 1915-16. Ironically, the first to be seriously disillusioned were the interventionist volunteers. As in earlier wars, such men were regarded with suspicion by the military hierarchy. Their attempts to propagandise the troops scandalised Cadorna and the career officers. Left-wing interventionists soon found themselves closely watched, barred from attending the military school at Modena or becoming officers.[14] The Garibaldi brothers on their return from

France and Cesare Battisti and his Trentino volunteers complained of the harsh treatment meted out to them.[15]

A more diffuse exasperation slowly spread among officers and men during the autumn of 1915 and assumed more serious proportions when many of them took their first leave in December. The desperate war of attrition had begun to sap the morale of the men and some of the officers. In the spring of 1915 Cadorna had written a book, *Attacco frontale e ammaestramento tattico,* and then had proceeded to implement his theses in the summer and autumn.[16] The result had been huge losses and negligible gains. For the ordinary infantryman, especially the uniformed peasants from central and southern Italy, the whole war was incomprehensible. '*La Patria* was a concept beyond their powers of understanding,' wrote Malaparte. Trieste and Trentino meant nothing to them. When their officers explained that they were fighting against the militarism of the central powers, they listened politely but they remained unenlightened. They fought, said Malaparte, because 'there were certain paragraphs in the Regulations which they knew by heart', a view which Cadorna fully endorsed.[17] Farmers and labourers looked at the inhospitable and infertile terrain of the battle zone and wondered why anyone would wish to conquer it. Either their masters were mad or the war was some kind of punishment for their sins. Padre Gemelli, commenting on the passive heroism of the peasant soldier, argued that they obeyed orders whatever the danger because they could not conceive of doing anything else.[18] Front line troops also fought, of course, because Austrians were trying to kill them and this situation could generate its own rationale of kill or be killed. But the explanation of Barbusse is probably the most comprehensive; conscripts everywhere fought 'for their mates'. They did their duty to preserve the lives of all those in their particular unit. When their sector was quiet and supplies came through, there were advantages. Many of them enjoyed a higher standard of living at the front, and for the first time consumed regularly exotic items like sugar, coffee, alcohol and meat.[19] The comradeship of the trenches which sometimes even extended to NCOs and reserve officers, also helped them to endure their long nightmare.

When they went home on leave at the end of 1915, they quickly became aware of the contrast between the battle zone and the home front. This soon produced the divisive controversy over the *imboscati,* the shirkers. For the infantryman in the trench nearest to the enemy and on an active front, all those behind him were *imboscati.* This included the artillery, the engineers, the cavalry, all rear units and all civilians.[20] Perhaps the most hated, apart from the general staff and patriotic politicians, were the munitions workers. Dallolio's armaments programme required the retention of skilled workers and, when they had been conscripted, their recall from the front. A large proportion of the urban population in the northern industrial cities were therefore exempted from service. In addition, munitions workers were well paid, well housed and usually socialists. This resulted in most active infantry units being composed primarily of southern peasants. Members of the urban proletariat who were conscripted tended to be posted to rear units of the artillery or the engineers where their literacy and 'intelligence' could best be utilised. It was the same in the officer corps. The career soldiers who survived and northern reserve officers were deemed too valuable to be thrown away by posting them to the front line. The officers commanding in the battle zone therefore tended to be from what Serpieri called the semi-rural and medium and petty bourgeoisie of central and southern Italy. The north-south division within the kingdom was thus perpetuated by these wartime developments. *'La guerra la fanno i contadini!'* The peasants in uniform, earning half a lire per day, were fighting for the northern war workers earning seven and a half lire per day, and the southern lower-middle-class officers were leading them into battle to make the world safe for industrialists and bankers, who all seemed to be doing very well out of the war. War profiteers, in particular, were plying a lucrative trade in defective equipment.[21]

There was an additional complication which soon alarmed Cadorna and the civilian authorities. Soldiers on leave – everywhere in Europe – had a tiresome habit of trying to explain to an incredulous public what was involved in a modern war of attrition. Their talk of mud, blood and muddle amidst the barbed wire and mortar shells, was liable to spread alarm and despondency. Censorship of letters from the front, the attempted exclusion of journalists and interfering politicians from the war zone, the silencing of loquacious officers, were all part of the general effort to ensure that official bulletins were a credible substitute for the truth. On 12 January 1916 Cadorna issued a circular in a vain attempt to stem what he called defeatism and neutralism.[22] In his personal letters, he was as alarmist as his troops.[23] From this period until Caporetto, Cadorna never quite knew whether to attribute the growing discontent to his soldiers, whose malaise infected the home front, or to subversive civilians, who deliberately poisoned the minds of the troops. It was two days after his circular that Cadorna wrote to Salandra suggesting 'decimation' as a possible solution. His daughter, Carla Cadorna, had a more humane suggestion, the establishment of *'case del soldato'* for the rest and recreation of the troops in the battle zone and in the rear areas. She secured financial help from Ansaldo, Fiat, Terni and Luigi Albertini, but the military and civilian authorities proved obstructive. It took Caporetto to break down their resistance.

Towards the end of June 1915 a French officer in Rome had written: 'Unlike us the Italians do not seem to feel that this is a crucial war *(guerre à fond)* for the independence and existence of the country. They perhaps think of it as a big Libyan campaign.'[24] It was a just observation at the time but it ceased to be true as 1916 wore on. In the towns, the industrial peace began to break down and in Florence and Mantua women came into the streets demonstrating against the endless war. In the countryside, indifference turned into a sullen anger as the economic boom which accompanied the outbreak of war evaporated and as more and more peasants were drafted, leaving the women and children to run the farms. Pensions, state relief and private charity seemed to operate, however ineptly, in most of the towns, but in the countryside the authorities were only interested in forced sales of livestock, the requisitioning of timber and more recruits for the Isonzo. It was the beginning of what Turati called 'the revolt of the countryside against the towns'.[25] Only in the last year of the war were attempts made to conciliate the rural sector, by granting exemptions and short leaves for agricultural labourers, and by promising – as a reward for their suffering – *la terra ai contadini',* the only recompense the peasants really appreciated. This growing antagonism between town and countryside and between home front and war front led to the great debate on the responsibility for the increase in defeatist sentiment. This, in turn, emphasised the rift between the civilians and the military, and even that between career officers and reserve officers. But, appropriately enough, it was General Conrad and the Austrian army who precipitated the first great crisis of the war and brought about the fall of Salandra and his concept of a *'piccola guerra'*.

It was at a cabinet meeting on 26 January 1916 that resentment at Cadorna's autocratic handling of the war began to surface. Disputes over Italian participation at Salonika, which Cadorna supported, and over reinforcements for Albania, which he opposed, were less significant than the government's gradual realisation that the war was too important to be left solely to Cadorna.[26] Ministers like Martini and Sonnino hoped that a defence council could be set up to determine strategy and clip Cadorna's wings. On 9 February 1916, Orlando, the

Minister of Justice, started a rumour that General Robilant was about to replace Cadorna at military headquarters in Udine.[27] But these plots and manoeuvres came to nothing, because Cadorna was in such a strong position. Although he had failed to break the Austrian front, he was still an undefeated commander. He was respected by the allies, and he had powerful friends inside and outside the army. That he was aware of these growing criticisms and did not regard himself as immune, is evidenced by the very uncharacteristic decision to allow Ugo Ojetti to act as his press agent with instructions to counterattack his enemies and put his case before the public![28] Critics from among the numerous officers he had dismissed for incompetence or worse could easily be routed, but the disquiet of serving officers like Generals Grazioli and Capello presented more difficult problems, and so did Salandra and his cabinet. His opposition to involvement in Albania had alienated War Minister Zupelli and Cadorna used this as a test case. Reverses in Albania disconcerted Zupelli and Sonnino, and Cadorna chose this moment, at the end of Feburary, to inform Salandra that he would resign if Zupelli kept his post. Salandra told him not to act in such an unconstitutional fashion, and the King was called in to mediate. Cadorna sent in his resignation, and so did Salandra, but both later withdrew them and on 9 March it was Zupelli who resigned, to be replaced by General Morrone, a Cadorna supporter.[29] There followed a two months truce which was abruptly broken by the *Strafexpedition* of 15 May. For a time it looked as if the Austrians would break out of the Trentino and into the Lombard plain. On 24 May – a sad first anniversary – a worried cabinet called for a meeting between leading generals and ministers. A defeated Cadorna was about to be ignominiously dismissed. He refused to attend this meeting, claiming he had more pressing business at the front. Morrone was sent to Cadorna to ask for information. He was given a small sheet of paper containing the basic facts together with a warning that it might become necessary to retreat to the Piave. This so shocked the cabinet that Sonnino spoke of betrayal and of 'either him or us', and Salandra went to see the King at Udine to secure Cadorna's dismissal. The King left the final decision to the government and Salandra wavered and eventually did nothing. Meanwhile, Cadorna stabilised the military situation and ambassador Barrère voiced the allies' disapproval of any attempt to change the commander.[30] Salandra now began to feel isolated. The Giolittians were unfriendly, the interventionists clamoured for war with Germany – and were supported by Cadorna – and there was a general dissatisfaction with Salandra's whole approach to the war. It was this, as much as his conflict with Cadorna, which led Salandra to resign in June 1916.

Boselli's government of national unity, 'the ministry of weakness simulating strength' as Nitti called it, appeared eminently satisfactory to Cadorna. The new premier would be easier to handle. Orlando and Sonnino remained in office, but Cadorna felt confident that he could again outflank them if necessary. He was, in fact, more apprehensive about the Minister without Portfolio, Leonida Bissolati. At the age of fifty-eight, this reformist socialist had volunteered and fought with the Alpini, being wounded and winning two silver medals, the last one in May 1916. Like Dallolio, Bissolati typifies that tiny minority who strove to unite the civilian and military sectors, the home front and the war front, in order to achieve the total mobilisation of the nation's resources, spiritual as well as material. Already, before the fall of Salandra, he had called for a parliamentary enquiry into the military events of May and June, and he lost no time in going to see Cadorna after his appointment as minister. He explained that an enquiry would combat the rumours – and Salandra's public criticism of the defensive positions adopted in the Trentino – which were being spread by dismissed officers concerning the incompetence of the supreme command.[31] With his distrust of any civilian interference in military matters, Cadorna remained icily aloof, and on 7 August he wrote to Boselli asking him to prevent anyone except for the Minister of War from acting as an intermediary. He also wanted all ministers to be excluded from the war zone unless they had a specific mission, and made it clear that the army command and the civilian government must remain separate. Boselli agreed to this and Cadorna circularised his commanders to this effect. Cadorna also strengthened his position by a military victory, the seizure of Gorizia on 9 August 1916. He was widely acclaimed by Italy's allies for this and for the declaration of war on Germany on 24 August.

In the face of growing demands for a programme of 're-education' for the troops and of intensive propaganda for civilians, Cadorna remained unmoved, claiming that all his best officers and men had been killed, and that with an army of untrained officers and raw recruits only stern discipline could keep Italy in the war.[32] Bissolati, of course, disagreed and seems to have played with the idea of replacing him with Luigi Capello. Opinions vary about Capello, but most observers agreed that he was an exceptional general. Conrad thought him the only Italian general of European stature, and Cadorna saw him as the best man for all great offensive operations.

Malagodi thought he was the most intelligent of the generals.[33] The son of a telegraphic official, his promotion had been slow, perhaps because of his origins and perhaps because of his lively intelligence. His attacks on the *'spirito di casta'* and promotion through seniority had not endeared him to his superiors. He became a mason – and this led to his arrest during the Zaniboni affair of 1925 – and was attracted by Bissolatian socialism. Even before Italy joined the war, Capello was one of the few generals who saw the importance of officers communicating with their men, keeping them informed of developments, and paying close attention to morale.[34] As commander of VI Corps in late 1915, he had annoyed Cadorna by referring to his men as 'pieces of walking mud', which was far too realistic to be acceptable.[35] Cadorna also objected to him as *'un generale politicante'* who turned his headquarters into a political rather than a military centre of operations.[36] Finally, he resented the fact that sections of the press had acclaimed Capello as the hero of Gorizia. If Bissolati and others were looking for an alternative commander in chief, Capello seemed the obvious choice. Cadorna survived this threat to his authority. In September, he removed Capello from the command of VI Corps and sent him to the Trentino front. It was only in the following spring that relations improved, and Cadorna ordered him back to the Isonzo and appointed him commander of the Second Army. Bissolati's position was also weakened at this time through his involvement in the 'Douhet affair'. In October 1916 Colonel Giulio Douhet wrote a memorandum hostile to Cadorna and gave it to Gaetano Mosca who promised to pass it on to Bissolati or Sonnino. It was lost or stolen during the railway journey to Rome and ended up on Cadorna's desk. Douhet was tried and imprisoned for a year. Cadorna and Bissolati subsequently became allies as both men supported the scheme for Anglo-French participation on the Isonzo front to knock Austria out of the war.

Between the ending of the Ninth Battle of the Isonzo on 4 November 1916 and the launching of the Tenth on 12 May 1917, there was relatively little fighting and Cadorna succeeded in putting sixteen new divisions in the field and restoring something of the old spirit of 1915. The army was given far greater fire power, medium artillery being doubled and heavy artillery quadrupled; there were over 8,000 machine guns and nearly 4,000 military aircraft. News of the February revolution in Russia and American entry into the war in April gave additional encouragement. Unfortunately, all these assets were largely squandered in the ferocious battles which raged from June until the the end of August. Between 20 and 26 May the 26th infantry regiment lost 74 per cent of its effectives and between 13 and 27 May 41 regiments lost over 50 per cent. In all, 127,000 were killed or wounded.[37] The advances made at such high cost were all nullified by a successful Austrian counterstroke at the end of the month. Incredibly, morale still remained high on the eve of the Eleventh Battle of the Isonzo fought on the Bainsizza Plateau from 19 August to 12 September. The basic reason for this was rather ominous; everyone expected this to be the last, decisive battle of the war. The army suffered 100,000 losses and the gains made left the Italian front line more vulnerable than before. Fifty-one divisions and 5,200 pieces of artillery had been thrown into this massive struggle but by the second week in September the end of the war seemed as far away as every. This bitter disillusionment on the Bainsizza was the prelude to Caporetto.

On 15 August 1917 there was a serious outbreak of mutiny in the Catanzaro brigade, which General Tettoni of VII Corps attributed to the activities of civilian subversives. The Duca D'Aosta, however, was convinced that purely military factors were involved, that the men had justifiable grievances concerning lack of leave and being kept on an active front much longer than other units.[38] On the home front too, disaffection spread leading to bread riots and culminating in the *Fatti di Agosto* in Turin.[39] Cadorna accused the octogenarian Boselli and Orlando of inability to govern and of failing to contain 'the internal enemy'. When the commander met the cabinet at the end of September, Orlando accused Cadorna of being unable to control defeatism within the army and failing to prevent it from infecting the civilian population.[40] On 12 July Treves had said in parliament: *'Il prossimo inverno non più in trincea!'* At the time, and during the inquest on Caporetto, this was seen as a sinister appeal to defeatist elements, but even Cadorna and his staff had made the same prophecy before Bainsizza! Certainly the pope's peace note in August which referred to the fact that *'ogni giorni di più apparisce inutile strage'* had even greater relevance after the slaughter on the plateau.[41] It was while Italy was in this mood, that the Austrians, supported by German divisions, launched their surprise attack on 24 October.

During the Rome meeting of January 1917, before Lloyd George had been seduced by Nivelle's plan, Cadorna had had reservations about Anglo-French troops being sent to the Isonzo. It was not only the opposition of Robertson and the French generals which perturbed him, but the fear that it might precipitate an Austro-German offensive in this sector.[42] This nightmare became a reality in the autumn of

1917. So much has been written about Caporetto that it has tended to distort one's view of Italian efforts during the First World War.[43] The temptation to add to this literature will be resisted. The central powers, despite rumours of an impending attack which circulated as early as September, achieved a complete strategic surprise, and this, combined with the new German tactics which succeeded at Riga, is the basic explanation for the Italian defeat, the loss of 300,000 taken prisoner, 3,136 guns, and most of the Veneto. Accurate shelling of Italian artillery and communications, gas attacks and infiltration tactics are the important factors, and not the state of morale of troops and civilians or Capello's obsession with counterattacks. By the time the Italians fell back on the Piave in the second week of November only 33 out of the original 65 divisions were militarily effective. Eleven Anglo-French divisions were sent from the Western Front to constitute a general reserve. The Austro-German thrust began to lose its momentum, the Italian divisions fought stubbornly, and the line of the Piave was held and Italy saved.

On 25 October, as the first reports of the defeat were coming through, the same combination of Giolittians and interventionists which had toppled Salandra after the *Strafexpedition* brought down Boselli. But unlike the events of June 1916, Cadorna did not survive the change of government. Orlando became premier on 28 October and on 7 November Cadorna was dismissed. This inaugurated the third and final stage of the war, from the retreat to the Piave to the victorious advance to Vittorio Veneto and the armistice of 4 November.

Caporetto did produce a kind of 'Dunkirk spirit', but only in the course of the following spring. As in 1866 or 1896, bitter recriminations broke out and it appeared at first that the Italians were determined to convert a military reverse into a stultifying political crisis. Cadorna's deplorable communiqué attacking the cowardice of the Second Army and attempts to place the responsibility for this 'military strike' on civilian defeatism, were hardly calculated to produce a spirit of unity in adversity.[44] In a parliamentary exchange Bissolati had threatened to shoot socialists in defence of his country, interventionists ridiculed the elevation of Orlando who had been such a weak Minister of the Interior, Sonnino sought the advice of Robertson and Foch rather than trying to rally his colleagues, and there was no possibility of the King rising to the situation.[45] No one in this unpromising situation looked remotely like a Clemenceau. Stories of troops voting for peace with their feet, the news of Lenin's *coup* on the day Cadorna was dismissed, and a demoralising barrage of propaganda from the Austrian lines, all required an immediate response from the government if it hoped for a *'natale eroico'*.

There were some advantages in the situation. The spectacular invasion of national territory elicited a patriotic defiance. The line of the Piave held distinct possibilities for any student of Clausewitz. The Anglo-French military presence and the moral and financial support of the US reminded Italians that they were not fighting alone. The defeat at Caporetto had solved the Cadorna problem and made it most unlikely that his successor would treat the war zone as his personal kingdom. In addition, the new ministerial team possessed in Bissolati and Nitti two men who were convinced that total mobilisation demanded the unification of the war and home fronts and a nation-wide programme of propaganda. The government and the reorganised high command had to convince civilians and soldiers that it was *their* war, and in order to do this effectively they had to prove that it was *their* Italy, that *'Italia legale'* and *'Italia reale'* were now synonymous and the Risorgimento completed.

There had been some progress in the nationalisation of the war effort in the months before Caporetto, but it was now necessary to consolidate these gains and push ahead vigorously with wartime programmes geared to the postwar situation. Italians had to capture something of the crusading fervour of Wilson and Lenin, Lloyd George and Clemenceau, and counteract the insinuations of the central powers. After the war had ended, Mussolini wrote that 'the defeat at Caporetto has also been the defeat of the old militarism. At Vittorio Veneto *la nazione armata* triumphed.'[46] This was not mere rhetoric. Dallolio and the central and regional mobilisation committees, empowered to designate industrial enterprises essential and therefore 'auxiliaries' under military jurisdiction, took over nearly 2,000 plants during the war.[47] This organisation of factories and manpower – and 200,000 women engaged in war production – helped to provide supplies for an army of around five million.[48] Transport, trade, shipping and agriculture came under state supervision with varying degrees of success. In the spring of 1917 a system of food rationing was introduced. All this required an enormous bureaucracy which often created more problems than it solved. During the final year of the war, under the spur of Caporetto, this centralisation proceeded ever more rapidly. So also did the persistent appeals and promises emanating from the civilian and military authorities.

Among the first to organise themselves to ensure that some of these promises were kept, were veterans and men still on active service. At the end of April 1917, for instance, the *Associazione Nazionale fra Mutilati e Invalidi di Guerra* (ANMIG) was founded. Both the government and high command gave it official blessing, but the authorities did begin to have misgivings when meetings were held to discuss political events and officers and politicians also participated. By the spring of the following year, both Orlando and Diaz became alarmed as more and more unauthorised groups sprang up, all claiming some mythical affiliation to ANMIG's central office in Milan. The War Minister was forced to issue a circular calling for more disciplined organisation and less political agitation.[49] A Bologna newspaper, *La Voce dei Reduci,* had already begun to see the veterans' association as the possible nucleus for a future political movement but it was Mussolini who realised the full potential of the situation and coined the term *'trincerocrazia'*, a word which must have given pleasure to Marinetti and his friends.[50] He was referring to the aristocracy of the trenches and to the millions of soldiers who would soon be returning home to demand, so he believed, the construction of a new, anti-Marxist socialist order in Italy. Before the war ended, revolutionaries of right and left were frantically bidding for the support of various ex-combatant associations and of soldiers still serving, particularly the truculent and activist *arditi,* but the history of *combattentismo,* D'Annunzio's legionaries, the *Associazione Nazionale Combattenti* and Mussolini's fasci, belongs essentially to the postwar period.[51]

For the first time since its creation, a significant proportion of the army was ceasing to be apolitical. Ironically, the civilian and military authorities were largely responsible for this. It was thought that Caporetto had proved that there was a basic lack of communication between officers and men. Officers were therefore instructed to discuss current affairs with their men, and to make them aware of the government's promises to grant *'la terra ai contadini'* and all the other benefits they could expect if they fought the war to a victorious conclusion. They were encouraged to support trench newspapers and explain the new insurance and pension schemes which were being implemented. Among officers at this stage of the war the ratio of career officers to reserve officers was about 1:7. Most of the 16,000 reserve officers were young men holding the rank of captain or lower, and most of them served in the infantry – the arm which accounted for 95 per cent of all casualties. The majority of them were lower middle class, from the smaller towns of central and southern Italy, with a tendency to resent the patronising attitudes of their social superiors, particularly after they had exercised command and perhaps learnt to relish the authority they wielded. This resentment was accompanied by a growing fear that the common soldiers whose qualities many of them came to admire might, after the war, resume the role of class enemy. The very democracy which they advocated, through conviction or by military directive, could so easily erode their bourgeois status and standard of living unless they could maintain their control after demobilisation. Offering 'land to the peasants', for instance, would cause complications for many of them when they returned to their landowning or lawyer fathers. The more adventurous, impatient of the traditional discipline and mores imposed by career officers, joined the *arditi* units being formed in the summer and autumn of 1917.[52] With their special insignia, their own training camps and privileged treatment, both officers and men developed unorthodox views about warfare and life in general. If properly organised, they could become the shock troops of peace as well as of war.

Meanwhile, the Orlando ministry, which had taken office in such tragic circumstances, developed into one of the strongest governments Italy had ever possessed. 'At last we are a government', said Bissolati in January 1918, 'because we have a prime minister, that is, a co-ordinator.'[53] Bissolati himself took over a new ministry of pensions and army welfare, while Nitti at the treasury supervised the economy. He alienated Dallolio, who resigned in May, and he established perhaps too close a working relationship with the Perrone brothers of Ansaldo, but Nitti's efforts were dramatically successful.[54] Orlando struck hard at defeatists and subversives, and Diaz struck hard at the Austrians when they attempted to cross the Piave in June. After three months of intensive preparations, Diaz ordered 57 divisions – including 5 Anglo-French – and nearly 8,000 guns, to launch the final offensive on 4 October. Throughout this period, Italy had been fully integrated into the allied war effort, and this final onslaught led not to the disillusion of the Bainsizza but the victory at Vittorio Veneto and the disintegration of the Habsburg state and army.

On 20 November 1918, a justifiably proud Orlando commented: 'This war is at the same time the greatest political and social revolution in history, surpassing even the French Revolution.' A very different Salandra from the man of 1914-16 said: 'The war is a revolution, yes, a very great revolution. Let no one think that after the storm it will be possible to make a peaceful return to the old order. Let no one think that the old habits of leisurely life can be resumed.'[55] It was like an echo of Carlo Bianco, Giuseppe Budini or of Mazzini who had cried at the end of August 1848: *'La guerra regia è finita; la guerra del paese incomincia!'*[56] In November 1918, the Kingdom of Italy with her massive army appeared stronger than ever before. The stubborn heroism on the Isonzo, in the Trentino and on the Piave had surely wiped away the memories of Custoza, Novara, Lissa, Adua and even Caporetto. The promises of a better future showered down upon civilians and soldiers alike would surely be kept. If *'Italia una e grande'* did not take up her rightful place, fulfilling all the pledges stretching back to the early Risorgimento, there were members of 'the fifth estate', the ex-combatants, who would demand an explanation even at the price of revolution or civil war.

Notes

1. Martini, p.427.
2. L. Albertini, *Venti anni di vita politica,* IV (Bologna, 1953), p.10. It is, unfortunately, too fanciful to assert that Italy's choice of allies depended on the requirements of the Italian fleet which burnt Welsh coal as Ruhr coal was unsuitable.
3. E. Faldella, *La grande guerra. Le battaglie dell'Izonzo 1915-17,* vol.I (Milan, 1965), pp.36-7.
4. F. Nitti, *Rivelazioni. Dramatis personae* (Naples, 1948), pp.183-4. Nitti also claims that he met Salandra in August 1915 and asked if winter equipment had been provided for the troops. Salandra expressed astonishment at this pessimism and wondered how anyone could imagine the war lasting as long as that!
5. For basic strategic considerations, see P. Pieri, 'Italian Front', *A concise history of World War I,* ed. V. Esposito (London, 1965), pp.161-2.
6. Faldella, I, p.50.
7. Ibid., pp.30-1; Clough, p.179.
8. Stato Maggiore, p.205.
9. On this theme see the magnificent A. Omodeo, *Momenti della vita di guerra* (Turin, 1968), p.18 and many other references.
10. G. Rochat, *L'esercito italiano da Vittorio Veneto a Mussolini* (Bari, 1967), pp.25-6. Of the 205,000 officers employed during the war, about 17,000 were killed. 50 per cent of officers (and 75 per cent of troops) were at the front where the ratio of officers to men was 1:26; the home front ratio was 1:7. See also G. Sabbatucci, *I combattenti nel primo dopuguerra* (Bari, 1974), p.31.
11. Monticone, *Gli italiani,* pp.185-308. Also in E. Forcella and A. Monticone, eds., *Plotone di esecuzione. I processi della prima guerra mondiale* (Bari, 1968).
12. Monticone, *Gli italiani,* pp.268, 272-3.
13. In 'I vescovi italiani e la guerra 1915-18', Minticone defines 'nationalist bishops' and 'neutralist bishops', both tiny minorities and 'patriotic and moderate bishops' (ibid., pp.145-84).
14. Martini, p.476.
15. C. Battisti, *Epistolario,* ed. R. Monteleone and P. Alatri, vol.II (Florence, 1966), pp.222, 308-9.
16. Faldella, pp.133-9.

17. Quoted in Malagodi, p.13.
18. A. Serpieri, *La guerra e le classi rurali italiane* (Bari, 1930), p.44.
19. Ibid., p.47.
20. Whereas only 6 per cent of artillerymen were killed and 7 per cent of engineers, 22 per cent of infantrymen died in combat (ibid., p.42).
21. Melograni, pp.121-3.
22. Ibid., p 107.
23. Cadorna, *Lettere famigliari* for 17 Jan. 1916: 'Chi avrebbe immaginate una catastrofe di questi genere e cosi lunga?'
24. H. Contamine, 'La guerre italienne vue par des officers français', *Annuario dell'Università di Padova* (1958-9), p.7.
25. Melograni, pp.333-4.
26. Martini, pp.620-1.
27. Ibid., p.632.
28. Melograni, pp.179-80.
29. Ibid., pp.182-4.
30. Martini, pp.714-15.
31. R. Colapietra, *Leonida Bissolati* (Milan, 1958), p.228.
32. L. Cadorna, *Pagine polemiche* (Milan, 1950), pp.82-3, 96.
33. L. Capello, *Caporetto, perchè?,* introduction R. De Felice (Turin, 1967), pp.xvi-xviii.
34. Ibid., p.xx. See also pp.27-8 and doc. no.5, 'Opera di propaganda presso le truppe della 2 Armata', pp.257-8.
35. Melograni, p.67.
36. Capello, p.xxi.
37. Melograni. p.287.
38. Ibid., pp.303-5.
39. Monticone, *Gli italiani,* pp.89-144.
40. Melograni, p.354.
41. Malagodi, I, p.159.
42. Faldella, pp.259-63.
43. The Commissione d'inchiesta su Caporetto which met in January 1918, published (in part) its findings the following year in two volumes entitled *Dall'Isonzo al Piave* (Rome, 1919). Generals Capello, Cadorna, Caviglia, Cavaciocchi, Giardino and others all wrote at least one book about it. R. Seth, *Caporetto* (London, 1965) and C. Falls, *Caporetto 1917* (London, 1966) and J. Edmonds, *Military operations, Italy 1915-19* (HMDO, 1949) are readily available versions in English. The official Italian version is *Ufficio storico dello stato maggiore dell'esercito, l'esercito italiano nella grande guerra 1915-18,* vol, IV (Rome, 1967). Extensive bibliographies can be found in P. Pieri and G. Rochat, *Badoglio* (Turin, 1974) pp.867-83, and in *Atti del primo convegno nazionale di storia militare* (Rome, 1969) pp.114-22. Perhaps the two best recent books are M. Silvestri, *Isonzo 1917* (Turin, 1965) and M. Isnenghi, *I vinti di Caporetto nella letterattura di guerra* (Padua, 1967). Reference to Austrian-German sources can be found in Pieri and Rochat, *Badoglio.*
44. Malagodi, I. pp.171-2; Martini, p.1023.
45. Colapietra, p.250; Sonnino, *Diario,* III, pp.204-5; Malagodi, I, p.195.
46. 9 February 1919, *Il Popolo d'Italia.*
47. Clough, p.181.
48. Silvestri, p.38.
49. Sabbatucci, pp.25-7.
50. R. De Felice, *Mussolini il rivoluzionario* (Turin, 1965), p.403.
51. This has been examined by Rochat and Sabbatucci, by F. Cordova,

Arditi e legionari dannunziani (Padua, 1969), and A. Lyttelton, *The seizure of power* (London, 1973).

52. For their early history see C. Baseggio, *La compagnia arditi Baseggio* (Milan, 1933) and P. Giuliani, *Gli arditi* (Milan, 1919).
53. Malagodi, II, p.261.
54. The authoritative work on this is A. Monticone, *Nitti e la grande guerra 1914-18* (Milan, 1961).
55. G. Salvemini, *The origins of Fascism in Italy* (New York, 1973), p.121.
56. F. Della Peruta, ed., *Scrittori politici dell'ottocento,* vol.I (Milan, 1969), p.582.

BIBLIOGRAPHY

Agrati, C., *Giuseppe Sirtori,* Bari 1940.

Alberti, A., *L'Opera di S.E. il generale Pollio e l'esercito,* Rome 1923.

Albertini, L., *Venti anni di vita politica,* 5 vols., Bologna 1950-53.

The origins of the war of 1914, 3 vols., Oxford 1952-7.

Archivio Centrale dello Stato: Ministero della guerra, Scuole militari; Ispettorato della Guardia Nazionale; Archivio Pellion di Persano; Tribunali militari di guerra per il brigantaggio; Archivio Generale Brusati.

Askew, W., *Europe and Italy's acquisition of Libya,* Durham (N.C.) 1942.

Atti del XLIII Congresso di Storia del Risorgimento italiano, Rome 1968.

Barnett, C., 'The education of military élites', *Journal of Contemporary History,* vol.II, 1967.

Battaglia, R., *La prima guerra d'Africa,* Turin 1959.

Battaglini, T., *Il crollo militare del Regno delle Due Sicilie,* 2 vols., Modena 1938.

Bava-Beccaris, F., *Esercito italiano,* Milan 1911.

Berselli, A., *La Destra storica dopo l'unità. Italia legale e Italia reale,* Bologna 1965.

Bush, J., *Venetia Redeemed,* New York 1967.

Cadorna, L., *La guerra alla fronte italiana,* 2 vols., Milan 1921.

Lettere famigliari, Milan 1967.

Altre pagine sulla grande guerra, Milan 1924.

Il Generale Raffaele Cadorna, Milan 1922.

Capello, L., *Caporetto perchè?,* Turin 1967.

Carandini, F., *Manfredo Fanti,* Verona 1872.

Carocci, G., *Giolitti e l'età giolittiana,* Turin 1961.

Cassese, L., *La spedizione di Sapri,* Bari 1969.

Chabod, F., *Storia della politica estera italiana dal 1870 al 1896,* vol.I *Le premesse,* Bari 1951.

Clough, S., *The economic history of modern Italy,* New York 1964.

Colapietra, R., *Leonida Bissolati,* Milan 1958.

Il '98, Milan 1959.

Cordova, F., *Arditi e legionari dannunziani,* Padua 1969.

Corsi, C., *Sommario di storia militare,* Turin 1884.

D'Azeglio, M., *Things I remember,* Oxford 1966

De Bono, E., *Nell'esercito nostro prima della guerra,* Milan 1931.
De Felice, R., *Mussolini il rivoluzionario,* Turin 1965.
De Jaco, A., *Il brigantaggio meridionale,* Rome 1969.
Della Rocca, M., *The autobiography of a veteran,* London 1899.
Della Peruta, ed., *Scrittori politici dell'ottocento,* vol. I, Milan 1969.
De Rosa, L., 'Incidenza delle spese militari sullo sviluppo economico italiano', *Atti del Primo Convegno Nazionale di Storia militare,* Rome 1969.
De Rossi, E., *La vita di un ufficiale italiano sino alla guerra,* Milan 1927.
Documenti diplomatici italiani, series I vols.I and XIII, series II vol. XXI, series V vol.I, Rome1952-.
Edmonds, J., *History of the Great War. Military operations: Italy 1915-19,* London 1949.
Faldella, E., *La grande guerra,* vol.I, Milan 1965.
Foreign Office (PRO), FO 43/86a; FO 64/512; FO 170/382; FO 170/387.
Gaeta, F., *Nazionalismo italiano,* Naples 1965.
Gigli, L., *De Amicis,* Turin 1962.
Giolitti, G., *Quarant'anni di politica italiana. Dalle carte di Giovanni Giolitti,* 3 vols., Milan 1962.
Memoria della mia vita, Milan 1922.
Girardet, R., *La société militaire dans la France contemporaine 1815-1939,* Paris 1953.
Grew, R., *A sterner plan for Italian unity,* Princeton 1963.
Guerzoni, G., *Garibaldi,* 2 vols., Florence 1882.
Halpern, P., *The Mediterranean naval situation 1908-14,* Harvard 1971.
Hibbert, C., *Garibaldi and his enemies,* London 1965.
Howard, M., *Soldiers and governments,* London 1957.
The theory and practice of war, London 1965.
Il Parlamento dell'Unità d'Italia 1859-61, 2 vols., Rome 1961.
Isnenghi, M., *Il mito della grande guerra,* Bari 1970.
I vinti di Caporetto nella letteratura di guerra, Padua 1967.
Janowitz, M., *The professional soldier,* London 1964.
The military in the development of new nations, Chicago 1964.
Joll, J., *Intellectuals in politics,* London 1960.
La cultura del '90 attraverso le riviste, Turin 1966-.
La Marmora, A., *Un po più di luce,* Florence 1873.
Lemmi, F., *La politica estera di Carlo Alberto nei suoi primi anni di regno,* Florence 1928.
Licata, G., *Notabili della Terza Italia,* Rome 1968.

Lotti, L., *La settimana rossa,* Florence 1972.
Lyttelton, A., *The seizure of power,* London 1973.
Malagodi, O., *Conversazioni della guerra 1914-19,* 2 vols., Milan 1960.
Malgeri, F., *La guerra libica 1911-12,* Rome 1970.
Martini, F., *Il diario 1914-18,* Milan 1966.
Massari, G., *Il Generale Alfonso La Marmora,* Florence 1880.
Il diario dalle cento voci, Bologna 1959.
Mazzetti, M., 'L'Italia e le convenzioni militari segrete della Triplice Alleanza', *Storia contemporanea,* vol.I, 1970.
Melograni, P., *Storia politica della grande guerra 1915-18,* Bari 1969.
Ministero della Guerra, *L'esercito italiano nella grande guerra,* vol.I, Rome 1927.
Molfese, F., *Storia del brigantaggio dopo l'unità,* Milan 1964.
'Lo scioglimento dell'esercito garibaldino', *Nuova rivista storica,* 1960.
Monticone, A., *Gli italiani in uniforme,* Bari 1972.
La Germania e la neutralità italiana 1914-15, Bologna 1971.
Nitti e la grande guerra 1914-18, Milan 1961.
Mori, R., *La questione romana,* Florence 1963.
Il tramonto del potere temporale, Rome 1967.
Nisco, N., *Il Generale Cialdini e i suoi tempi,* Naples 1893.
Omodeo, A., *La leggenda di Carlo Alberto nella recente storiografia,* Turin 1940.
Momenti della vita di guerra, Turin 1968.
Pelloux, L., *Quelques souvenirs de ma vie,* Rome 1967.
Pieri, P., 'Les relations entre gouvernement et commandement en Italie en 1917', *Revue d'histoire moderne et contemporaine,* 1968.
Storia militare del Risorgimento, Turin 1960.
Guerra e politica negli scrittori italiani, Milan 1955.
Le forze armate nella età della Destra, Milan 1962.
Pollio, A., *Custoza,* Turin 1903.
Pribram, A., *The secret treaties of Austria-Hungary,* 2 vols., Harvard 1920.
Ranzi, F., *Nazionalismo e il problema militare italiano,* Rome 1910.
Restifo, G., 'L'esercito italiano alla vigilia della grande guerra', *Studi storici,* XI, 1970.
Rhodes, A., *The poet as superman,* London 1959.
Ridley, J., *Garibaldi,* London 1975.
Rivista militare italiana, 1856-.
Rochat, G., *L'esercito italiano da Vittorio Veneto a Mussolini,* Bari 1967.
'L'esercito italiano nell'estate del 1914', *Nuova rivista storica,* 1961.

Romano, S., *Storia dei fasci siciliani,* Bari 1959.
Romeo, R., *Cavour e il suo tempo,* Bari 1969.
Rota, E., ed., *Questioni di storia del Risorgimento e dell'unita d'Italia,* Milan 1951.
Rubiola, C., *L'Armata Sarda in Crimea,* Pisa 1969.
Sabbatucci, G., *I combattenti nel primo dopoguerra,* Bari 1974
Salamone, A., *Italian democracy in the making,* Philadelphia 1945.
Salandra, A., *La neutralità italiana,* Milan 1928.
L'Intervento (1915). Ricordi e pensieri, Milan 1930.
Salvatorelli, L., *La Triplice Alleanza,* Milan 1939.
Sandonà, A., *L'Irredentismo nelle lotte politiche e nelle contese diplomatiche italo-austiache,* 3 vols., Bologna 1938.
Serpieri, A., *La guerra e le classi rurali italiane,* Bari 1930.
Seton-Watson, C., *Italy from liberalism to fascism 1870-1925,* London 1967.
Silvestri, M., *Isonzo 1917,* Turin 1965.
Smith, D. Mack, *Italy,* Michigan 1959.
The making of Italy 1796-1870, New York 1968.
Victor Emanuel, Cavour, and the Risorgimento, Oxford 1971.
Cavour and Garibaldi, 1860, Cambridge 1954.
Smyth, H., 'Piedmont and Prussia: the influence of the campaigns of 1848-9 on the constitutional development of Italy', *American Historical Review,* LV, 1950.
'The armistice of Novara: a legend of a liberal king', *Journal of Modern History,* 7, 1935.
Sonnino S., *Diario 1914-16,* 3 vols., Bari 1972.
Spadolini, G., *Giolitti e i cattolici,* Florence 1970.
Stato Maggiore dell'Esercito, *L'esercito italiano,* Rome 1962.
Thayer, J., *Italy and the great war,* Wisconsin 1964.
Toscano, M., *Il Patto di Londra,* Bologna 1934.
Ufficio Storico della Marina Militare, *La marina militare nel suo primo secolo di vita 1861-1961,* Rome 1961.
Vagts, A., *A history of militarism,* London 1959.
Valsecchi, F., *L'Alleanza di Crimea,* Florence 1968.
Vigezzi, B., 'Le "Radiose giornate" del maggio 1915 nei rapporti dei prefetti', *Nuova rivista storica,* XLIV, 1960.
L'Italia di fronte alla prima guerra mondiale, vol. I, *L'Italia neutrale,* Milan 1966.
Da Giolitti a Salandra, Florence 1969.
Volpe, G., *L'Italia nella Triplice Alleanza,* Milan 1941.
Whittam, J., 'War and Italian society 1914-16', *War and Society,* ed. B. Bond and I. Roy, London 1975.

INDEX

DATE DUE

AP 7'80			
24'88			

Whittam, J.

The politics of the Italian army, 1861-1918.